THE ENERGY MEDICINE SOLUTION

MIND BLOWING RESULTS FOR LIVING AN EXTRAORDINARY LIFE

JACQUELINE M. KANE

FEATURING: MANDY PULLEN BARR, KATHY BOYER, EDWARD CLEVELAND, MICHELLE CLIFTON, ELIZABETH WAUGH DUFORD, ERIKA DWORKIN, DR. EDWARD L. FREY, VERA HALINA, ALANA HEIM, REV. EVANGELINE HEMRICK, CONSTANCE KOCH, SUNSHINE LAYNE, SANDRA LEE, BETH MANNING, CAROLYN MCGEE, PAT MCGRATH, DR. MAKEBA MORGAN HILL, LORI PIEPER, THERESA PRIDE, LISA G ROCHE, DENISE M. SIMPSON, TRUDY M. ROUILLARD SOOLE, CHRISTINE BADALAMENTI SMITH, BRADFORD W. TILDEN

THE ENERGY MEDICINE SOLUTION

MIND BLOWING RESULTS FOR
LIVING AN EXTRAORDINARY LIFE

JACQUELINE M. KANE

FEATURING: MANDY PULLEN BARR, KATHY BOYER, EDWARD CLEVELAND,
MICHELLE CLIFTON, ELIZABETH WAUGH DUFORD, ERIKA DWORKIN,
DR. EDWARD L. FREY, VERA HALINA, ALANA HEIM,
REV. EVANGELINE HEMRICK, CONSTANCE KOCH, SUNSHINE LAYNE,
SANDRA LEE, BETH MANNING, CAROLYN MCGEE, PAT MCGRATH,
DR. MAKEBA MORGAN HILL, LORI PIEPER, THERESA PRIDE,
LISA G ROCHE, DENISE M. SIMPSON, TRUDY M. ROUILLARD SOOLE,
CHRISTINE BADALAMENTI SMITH, BRADFORD W. TILDEN

The Energy Medicine Solution

Mind Blowing Results for Living an Extraordinary Life

Jacqueline M. Kane

©Copyright 2022 Jacqueline M. Kane

Published by Brave Healer Productions

Paperback ISBN: 978-1-954047-84-6
eBook ISBN: 978-1-954047-83-9

DEDICATION

I dedicate this book to my loving husband, who's always had more confidence in me than I did in myself. I'm grateful for your constant love and support during our 30 years of marriage. Looking forward to having more fun and adventures! I love you with all my heart.

Also, to the two men who made me a mom—you both taught me how to parent you the way you needed to be parented. Through the challenging times of being a parent, you taught me there was a better, easier way. It wasn't always easy, but we made it through, and I'm so proud of both of you! I love you both!

I also dedicate this book to my amazing clients! Those of you who told me story after story of how you felt unheard by your doctor and felt that the medical system was failing you. I heard your frustration of being in pain for years or decades with little to no relief from medical treatments.

My favorite moments are when you share your excitement and amazement when you say, "You won't believe it! I had no pain for three days! I've had no back pain since that last session!"

You cried tears of joy as you told me, "It was the first time I was able to get on the ground and build sand castles at the beach with my two-year-old grandchild. All pain-free. It was the first time in decades that I was able to focus on having fun with my kids instead of the pain in my back. Jackie, you gave me my life back, thank you."

You may not have known it at the time, but you are the reason I kept going. When most people told me, "It's impossible to get out of pain!" You showed that it is possible!

Because of you, I believe it is possible to:

- Get out of physical pain, even when you've had it for years and decades.

– Release the anxiety that has plagued you for your entire life.

– Thrive after being diagnosed with cancer.

– Release the pain from autoimmune conditions.

– Thrive no matter what is going on in your life.

I dedicate this book to you—for being open to healing. You went above and beyond what I thought was possible!

In this book, you'll get to know 25 amazing healers and practitioners who are helping their clients live extraordinary lives. Reach out to those whose story resonates with you. It took courage to share their story and to do what they're doing.

You came here to have an awesome life experience, not a mediocre one. Let's see what's possible for your health, wealth, relationships, and most importantly, for your ability to stand in your power. I'm looking forward to hearing you say, "You will never believe what happened!"

DISCLAIMER

This book offers health and nutritional information and is designed for educational purposes only. You should not rely on this information as a substitute for, nor does it replace professional medical advice, diagnosis, or treatment. If you have any concerns or questions about your health, you should always consult with a physician or other healthcare professional. Do not disregard, avoid, or delay obtaining medical or health related advice from your healthcare professional because of something you may have read here. The use of any information provided in this book is solely at your own risk.

Developments in medical research may impact the health, fitness, and nutritional advice that appears here. No assurances can be given that the information contained in this book will always include the most relevant findings or developments with respect to the particular material.

Having said all that, know that the experts here have shared their tools, practices, and knowledge with you with a sincere and generous intent to assist you on your health and wellness journey. Please contact them with any questions you may have about the techniques or information they provided. They will be happy to assist you further!

TABLE OF CONTENTS

INTRODUCTION

You know that thing you've been telling yourself about how nothing will work to stop the pain in your low back, or that excuse about how your pain is physical, so no energy work is going to help you, or that story about how you've had this condition since birth so there's nothing that will change it?

Does that all sound familiar?

Well, get ready because I have a book full of powerful, effective, long-lasting healing modalities which will get rid of those excuses forever!

As I drive down East Main Street in Torrington, Connecticut, I'm amazed that there are now as many urgent care centers as there are Dunkin' Doughnut shops. When my husband, my two-year-old son, and I (who was nine months pregnant with my second son) moved from Waterbury to New Hartford, there were only a few stores and restaurants on East Main Street. I remember saying to my husband, "We need a Chinese restaurant closer to home." Along with getting a few Chinese restaurants, we're now inundated with walk-in centers and coffee shops.

Are we getting sicker as time goes by or healthier? It seems like every day there's a new rare disease being discovered and more health problems cropping up.

As a woman who has lived with physical and emotional pain, I know the frustration that can come with not feeling good.

I've seen our health care system fail when my mother asked for pain meds before her hip surgery only to be told, "We don't give out pain meds anymore for patients." Her doctor's recommendation was to take over-the-counter Tylenol for what I could imagine was excruciating hip pain. As I scratched my head and asked again, "She's in severe pain. Can you give her a few of the stronger pain meds? She's 80 years old, in pain, and I promise you she won't get addicted to them." My mother was the tough Italian kind, who, even if she did have Percocet, took them sparingly and saved them for when the pain was really bad. Again he said, "No, just take the over-the-counter medication."

It's not the first time I've seen a doctor fail their patient. My clients share many stories of how they've been failed by the system and left to live with daily physical pain and exhaustion day after day. That's the reason behind the creation of this book.

It's because of these failed attempts that I went in search of finding natural ways to heal. Many of these methods came to me by accident. For example, when a massage therapist friend of mine asked me, "Hey, there's this class on Bowen therapy; would you like to take it with me?" Even though I had no idea what it was about, I felt this inner excitement inside of me that I had never felt before—as if I was about to learn something really special.

This therapy helped me release the repetitive strain pain I felt in my thumbs after becoming a massage therapist. The pain in my thumbs became a daily problem. No matter how much I iced or massaged them, nothing helped to relieve the pain. It wasn't until four to six months after learning Bowen therapy that I realized my thumbs no longer hurt. The healing was so subtle I couldn't tell you the exact time the pain disappeared. All I know is it hit me one day as I came out of doing a massage. OMG, my thumbs don't hurt! It was unheard of to hear that pain went away on its own without medication or surgery!

You can imagine my excitement as I started using this new therapy on my children, husband, and clients. The results were amazing! We were all getting out of pain, and I'm talking about pain that people lived with for years and decades! My clients were coming in saying, "Let's do Bowen today instead of massage because I played hard with my grandkids, and I know Bowen will take the pain away." We all felt more energy, were sleeping better, recovering from surgery faster, and healing from fibromyalgia and all kinds of other illnesses. It was wild! My excitement for what was possible didn't stop there.

Even though Bowen helped a lot of people get out of pain, there were still some who only had short-term relief or no relief at all. That kept me going to find the root causes of pain. Soon I was learning EFT (Emotional Freedom Technique), then ancestral energy clearing, voice dialogue, and how to heal our inner saboteur. I could then say that everyone was getting relief from pain and illness.

Clients were coming in saying, "This is mind-blowing! The back pain that I had for 50 years is gone!" With results like that, it just fueled my passion to keep sharing and letting people know that it is possible to get out of pain and stay out of pain.

This book is filled with stories of people experiencing pain relief using powerful tools and techniques that your doctor isn't telling you about. This book will put the healing ability back in your hands. You are that powerful! You have the ability to heal yourself, and it's time you take back control of your health and what's possible for your life.

The healers in this book are all experts in their fields, helping people to heal from all kinds of illnesses. They're helping their clients go from surviving to thriving. What would your life be like if you didn't have that low back pain? What would your life be like if you were living pain-free and energized? What if you achieved the goals you created every January? How much fun could you have on a daily basis if you're living a life filled with ease, flow, and abundance? That's what we have in store for you here!

CHAPTER 1

INHERITED ENERGY

HOW TO CLEAR A PATH TO ABUNDANCE AND EASE IN LIFE

Jacqueline M. Kane, Master Energy Healer, R.T., LMT, EFT

MY STORY

"My pain is physical, so what you do won't help me."

"I was born with this condition, and nothing so far has helped to relieve the symptoms."

"I had a great childhood! There was no trauma."

I hear these statements often from clients when they first start working with me. It's normal to think that if you have physical pain, you have to do something to the physical body to heal that pain. That is just not true.

Working with hundreds of clients in pain, I've learned that the mind-body pain connection is complicated. If you're living with chronic physical pain and illness, it's important to look at the energy you're carrying in order to heal the root cause for permanent long lasting vibrant health.

My love and excitement for all of this started back in 2016 when I experienced my first ancestral energy clearing. It blew me away!

This story began when I was at the Old Corner Bar on Thanksgiving of 2015 with my husband Don, his parents, his brother, and his wife, Pam. It was cold outside—inside, the air was noisy with my favorite singer, Mark James, playing Irish tunes. We were trying to cheer Pam up from her father's illness and subsequent recent death. Even though he was 80 years old, it was still tough after the sudden death of her sister earlier that year.

A part of me is always looking to make people feel comfortable. Some people call it the "team player" part of the psyche. I knew my sister-in-law was very close to her family and that the holidays would be tough.

My solution was to plan a family trip for 13 of us. Over frosty glasses of Guinness, I said, "Let's go to Ireland for Christmas." The more we talked as the beer slid down our throats, the more excitement bubbled up for some of us.

Since my mother-in-law was born in Ireland, I thought they would enjoy a family trip to her hometown. The grandkids were at a great age to travel. I thought it would be the perfect time to show them where their grandmother grew up and also introduce them to their Irish cousins and family. What some remarked on was where to find a house to accommodate 13 of us, with a big kitchen for communal cooking and a table to gather at for card games. We also needed enough personal space to accommodate six teenagers and their hormonal mood swings.

It came as a great surprise when I heard my in-laws say, "We don't want to go back to Ireland, especially at Christmas time. It's too cold to go there to visit. It'll be too hard to get the family together, and will we all get along?"

I was so disappointed hearing this great idea and excitement fizzle out. So many times in my life I had ideas, then experienced rejection, then disappointment. Because I've been doing so much personal development work, I recognize this as a deep-seated belief: *No one ever wants to do what I want to do.*

Wow, Really? I thought. So many questions flooded my mind. *Why not?* After some discussion, the subject was dropped, and we moved on. My husband and I decided that if we really wanted to go, we'd take our two teenage sons and go on the trip.

Christmas came and went with little discussion about vacationing in Ireland.

In January of 2016, I had the pleasure of going to visit my mentor and friend Alan Davidson in Houston, Texas. He was hosting a three-day retreat, and I was excited to spend the weekend with friends to experience Alan's mystic meditation processes.

On the second day of the retreat, he took us through his Ancestral Karma Energy clearing. I don't remember feeling or noticing anything during the process. It was immediately after the process when I became aware that something amazing had just happened.

As I was leaving the event hall, my phone started buzzing. It was my son texting to say that he'd found a house to rent in Ireland, perfect for all 13 of us to stay in. It had enough bedrooms, bathrooms, and space so we could join for activities, but not so close that we'd want to kill each other.

My first thought: *That's nice, but we aren't going.* Then, I was shocked to read the next text from my husband saying that the family had reconsidered. Everyone, including my in-laws, agreed to go on vacation together—all 13 of us!

I shook my head, walked up to Alan, and asked, "Okay, what just happened? What on Earth did we just do to create this kind of shift?"

Alan replied, "No mistakes," as he nodded with quiet satisfaction.

I know there are no coincidences in life. Something inside of me said, "Pay attention, Jacque."

From the moment I received the text from my son, everything became easy planning for our upcoming vacation. We found the perfect large house which had bedrooms to accommodate everyone's needs. It had a huge kitchen where we could cook together, and I envisioned playing card games and drinking wine while socializing with my Irish relatives. And that's how it turned out.

It's such a blessing to think that it all became real with one ancestral energy clearing. I learned I could turn my energetic pattern of disappointment into excitement to create unlimited possibilities. I believe it changed my energy enough that it helped change my family's minds from a "No" into a "Yes!" And I've now had the honor to provide ancestral energy clearings for my clients so that they release limiting patterns to create *their* unlimited possibilities. I love witnessing the "Yes!" in their lives.

This family vacation was eight years ago, and I continue to be blown away by the miracles that happen every day as I continue to use energy clearings to live a life with ease, flow, and abundance, which brings me to the intention of this book. What is energy? And if everyone has the potential to shift from an energetic state of disappointment and frustration to happiness, joy, and excitement, then why aren't more people using it?

One reason is that most people can't see energy, so it's hard to understand it. We may not see it, but we feel it when we walk into a crowd of people and sense that they're not friendly. We get that sick feeling in our stomach, letting us know something isn't right.

We sense the excitement when a woman first knows she's pregnant and shares that information with her loving partner.

The energy we're conceived from impacts our lives the most, and many people don't even realize it. For example, if we grow up in a very chaotic, energetic family, we're actually more comfortable when things are chaotic. On some level, our nervous system is actually looking for chaotic situations to feel comfortable. If there is no chaos, we will create more chaos to feel comfortable.

If we're raised in a family that has a lot of health issues, then we have an energy around us that feels more comfortable when we are sick and unhealthy. On a subconscious level, we'll create more unhealthy conditions to feel comfortable.

This may seem illogical because it seems unlikely that a person would want to create unhealthy conditions. I don't believe anyone wants to create an unhealthy life; they're doing it from an unconscious level of awareness.

"If you want to be successful, you have to take 100% responsibility for everything that you experience in your life. This includes the level of achievements, the results you produce, the quality of your relationships, the state of your health and physical fitness, your income, your debts, your feelings—everything! This is not easy."

~ Jack Canfield

It took me years to believe this quote. At first, I would think: *Do you mean I caused this car accident? Or I made myself fall down and break my foot?*

I thought that was crazy until I started healing on a deep level and really examined the energetic environment I created my thoughts and beliefs from. For example, for the last few years, I've been taking my mom to her doctor's appointments for her knee pain. Every drive to the doctor's, she would say, "He can't do anything to get rid of my pain. Nothing ever works." And guess what, nothing ever helps her knee pain, and there never seems to be a solution.

She has made up her mind that nothing is going to make it better, so nothing ever does. Even though I could help her, you know how it goes with parent relationships. They're not going to listen to their child, no matter how many success stories we have.

My mother was born in Sardinia, Italy, during World War II. She was the oldest of three children, and I heard stories from my nonni (Italian grandmother) about how my mom wasn't healthy as an infant. She had a lot of ear infections and was sick often.

While my grandmother was pregnant with my mother in 1942, there were German soldiers walking around her tiny village of Borutta, Sardinia. Her husband would be off fighting the war, which left her home alone to take care of her three children.

My grandmother didn't talk a lot about those days, and when she did, she talked about it without much feeling. I imagine she learned to suppress all that fear and worry in order to survive.

My mother was formed in that container of worry and fear. She couldn't run from it. All of her cells, DNA, and every inch of her was breathing and living in that energetic container of emotional stress.

That same fear and worry were then passed down to me, my siblings, and my children without my awareness.

I heard my mom's worry every time I wanted to try new things, like practicing meditation or experiencing a yoga retreat.

"Why do you want to do that? What will you do there? What do they do? How can you trust those people?"

"Who are you going out with? Bring your friends inside so I can find out who their parents are and also get to know them."

I saw the effects of worry and stress on her body when she was told her digestion problems were due to Crohn's disease.

She would say, "I've always had hearing problems, and nothing the doctors tried ever helped me to hear better."

After years of doctors not helping her to feel better, she created hard core beliefs that life is filled with disappointment and frustration. Life became one disappointment after another for all of us.

Little did I know that this life of disappointment was about to change after one ancestral clearing! My brain was on fire as I asked, "what else is possible?"

There seemed to be more ease and flow in my life after that session. My body felt lighter, my relationships felt easier and fun, and business was booming. Clients were calling and showing up everywhere. All of a sudden, every area of my life was better.

I started using this new healing method with my clients. They started coming in saying, "My low back pain has not come back since that session. No more headaches since that session! I feel amazing! How do we keep this good feeling going?"

Not only did clients begin to feel better, but many of them started noticing that we turned on the money flow. Clients began to say things like, "Boy, do I have a story for you; when I left your office, my mom called to say that she was giving me $3000 to buy a new car. I didn't even ask for it."

After her clearing, another client said, "I finally received $6000 that was owed to me by a friend."

My clients who owned their own businesses began saying that clients were showing up from known and unknown places, and business was booming.

It was as if the ability to create the lives they craved for so long was being spiritually up-leveled.

It was getting easier and easier to manifest everything we needed. One day while having breakfast with my friend Denise Simpson I was saying, "I'd like to do more interviews and give more talks on how people can get out of pain and stay out of pain."

At the same moment as that idea came through me, I received an email from the Boston Women's Facebook group asking me to give a talk to their group. Clearing energy was one way to quickly up-level my health and business.

It was becoming very clear that energy, beliefs, thoughts, and conditioning are always impacting what we manifest. It is possible to receive everything you desire when you align your energy to your desires.

That's when miracles happen!

Here's one tool I'd love to share with you to help you clear any residual energy that is holding you back from manifesting your heart's desire.

THE TOOL

FREE YOURSELF FROM ENERGY INHERITED AT BIRTH

Step 1: Set aside some quiet time, and grab a pen and your journal or writing device. Create a sacred space for self-discovery so that you can uncover the exact energy holding you back.

Step 2: Awareness is the first step. Take three deep breaths to become present and get grounded in your body. Allow your mind to paint you a picture of when you were five, six, or seven. Imagine what you would have looked like. Then allow your mind to paint you a picture going even further back to the time of your birth in this lifetime. Imagine your birth. What was that like? Was it chaotic? Was it difficult and long? Who was there for you?

Step 3: Become aware of what you may have felt at that time? What did that baby experience? Was she/he taken care of? Were you comforted and wrapped in a blanket immediately? Were the nurses and doctors disorganized? What was that little baby feeling? Were you happy or sad? If you could imagine what that little baby was feeling, what would it be? This is your energetic birth pattern. Is it one of frustration, or do you feel annoyed at times? What's the emotion that you notice you feel often?

Step 4: How has your energetic birth pattern played out in your life? Which area of your life is it impacting the most? For example, if your energetic birth pattern was frustration, do you feel frustrated with your health? Are you frustrated when you deal with your finances? Is there a common emotional theme that is playing out in many areas of your life?

Step 5: Time to release the old limiting pattern. Imagine you're holding that little baby (you) in your arms. Look into the eyes of that little baby. Imagine pouring unconditional love into that little baby. Tell her/him that they are safe. It's safe to release this old pattern. Imagine this energy of love filling up every cell of that little beautiful human being.

Step 6: Time to receive. Now switch places with the baby. Imagine that you are now the baby, and you're looking up into those loving eyes. Take in all of this love and compassion. What does it feel like to feel so loved and adored? Visualize this new energy filling up every cell of your being. Give yourself time to absorb this new way of being.

You can also go to my resource page at https://jacquelinemkane.com/resources/ and listen to a video that I recorded for you to take you through this process.

This is a powerful process that can make a huge impact on your health and your life. The more you do it, the more you will trust the process and will notice your health and life are improving for the better. Basically, all areas of your life will improve.

I would love to know what you noticed during this process. Feel free to send me an email and let me know what you noticed or if you have any questions. Email me at jacqueline@jacquelinemkane.com

Jacqueline M. Kane is a master energetic healer who guides women to uncover their hidden energetic and karmic blocks that keep them in physical, emotional, and financial pain. By using her Uncover The Root Cause process, we unravel negative thoughts and clear limitations, including inner child and ancestral karma that has held them back for decades.

With over 20 years in private practice as a healer and over 35 years in health care, Jacqueline has merged her innate wisdom with a multitude of healing modalities, including Bowenwork, Emotional Freedom Technique, evolutionary meditation, soul clearing, and more to create unique, results-oriented methods for healing. Her clients are able to quickly and easily achieve major shifts to create a new level of health, wealth, and lifestyle they desire now.

Jacqueline's powerful programs, available to individuals, groups, and organizations, liberate clients from physical pain and financial struggle, so they can create a path to energy, health, ease with money, and personal fulfillment.

When Jacqueline is not working, she enjoys bike rides with her husband on their electric bikes, golfing with family and friends, and traveling to new exciting destinations.

Connect with Jacqueline:

Website: https://jacquelinemkane.com/

Free Soul Activation
Meditation: https://jacquelinemkane.com/qmb-meditation/

Facebook: https://www.facebook.com/jacqueline.kane.313/

Facebook Group:

https://www.facebook.com/groups/healingcirclebyjacquelinekane/

https://www.instagram.com/heal_with_jacque/

https://www.tiktok.com/@heal_with_jacque

LinkedIn: https://www.linkedin.com/in/jacquelinekane/

If, after reading this chapter and you become aware that you have ancestral energy that is impacting your ability to create better health, greater wealth and an extraordinary life, I invite you to click this link, and let's have a chat about what you could do to create your new extraordinary life:

https://JacquelineMKane.as.me/RealPainRelief

I would love to hear what you thought of this chapter. Feel free to email me at jacqueline@jacquelinemkane.com.

CHAPTER 2

INSTANT BLISS

SOUND HEALING WITH TIBETAN SINGING BOWLS

Michelle Clifton, Master Sound Healer, Teacher, LMT

MY STORY

With outstretched arms, I vividly remember feeling the hot ball of energy in the palm of my hands. My Reiki teacher said, "You are holding the energy of the universe in your hands." I was in awe. Afterward, I asked my instructor, "How long will I have this feeling in my hands?" She said, "For the rest of your life!"

I started studying energy healing in 1987 when my friend Julie Motz asked, "Do you want to study Reiki with me so we can do Reiki sessions on our 19-year-old friend with an astrocytoma brain tumor."

"Yes," I said.

Over the next 30 years, I learned a variety of energy medicine practices from all kinds of teachers. Once a month, a group of us Jin Shin Jyutsu practitioners met to work on each other and learn from each other. A fellow practitioner asked, "Does anyone want to study sound healing with me?"

"I do!" I announced, surprising myself.

I was initially skeptical when I first started studying sound healing. I didn't know anything about it. I thought, *"Why not?"* The Sage Center created a year-long class (their first class) for our group of eight. The first thing we learned was to clear and strengthen the auric field with the BioSonics "C" and "G" tuning forks. They are the sound of the nervous system. You can hold them up to the ears once you strike them on your knee's patella or the still point headrest for craniosacral therapy, and they will immediately balance the nervous system. Next came Koshi chimes, crystal singing bowls, Tibetan/Himalayan singing bowls, rattles, drums, and more. It was all new. I was drawn to the metal singing bowls but felt I could never afford them.

An energy medicine friend whispered to me at the end of class, "I'm studying Tibetan singing bowls with a man from India, Master Satya Brat. He's teaching in New York City next weekend. I think you'll like it." This is how I came to learn about the International Academy of Sound Healing and found myself in his weekend training.

I feel so nervous and insecure when the class first starts. I want so much to be able to memorize everything the teacher is doing and saying so I can dive right in with my first sound healing client booked for next week. Because I'm working so hard concentrating on every word Satya says, *Do you think I relax and just enjoy the meditation? Hell, no!*

As we go around the room, revealing our reactions, I exclaim: "I was not able to relax at all!" Satya reprimands me: "Next meditation forget about memorizing everything and just enjoy the experience." I feel my face flush with embarrassment. I feel total humiliation.

Everyone around me experienced deep relaxation moving into delta brain waves. My mind races. My heart hammers. My temples pulse at high speed. This has been my state of mind for most of my life. Relaxing has never come easy for me. What I know now is being the daughter of a suicidal mother, I was constantly in a hyper-vigilant beta state. When you worry your mother may not be alive to take care of you, you do everything you can to make sure she stays alive. When my mother made her serious attempt at suicide, I was away at college—the University of Illinois in Urbana-Champaign. My mom was in a coma for four days—her body completely black and blue. She took a huge number of sleeping pills. No one ever told me!

My two younger sisters, Annette and Cecile, found my mother passed out on her bedroom floor. They called my dad, and he and Annette's boyfriend carried my mom to the car and drove her straight to the hospital. When I came home for Thanksgiving, I no longer felt part of the family. I felt so isolated and alone. I couldn't understand why. My dad told my sisters, "Don't tell anyone what happened, not even your sister, Michelle." My sisters were sworn to secrecy. Evidently, everyone felt the reason my mom tried to kill herself was because I had gone off to college and because she missed me so much.

This secret cut me off from everyone in my family. I felt I no longer wanted to go home for the holidays. Instead, I'd get a job over the break, catch up with my homework, do several oil paintings in my art class studio and stay in my boyfriend's apartment. I felt that this was my new home. Tears well up in my eyes as I remember the loneliness and sense of isolation I felt for at least six years. Then in a phone conversation, my mom blurts, "You know when I tried to kill myself."

"What are you talking about?" I say.

"Didn't you know?" my mom says.

"No! No one ever told me."

"I took an overdose of sleeping pills. I was very depressed."

My mom was often depressed. We walked on eggshells when around her. My dad always said, "Don't do anything to upset your mom." Much of the time, she would isolate herself in her bedroom, reading a book. "Don't disturb your mother," was my dad's mantra.

Every so often, she'd emerge from her bedroom in a rage and go into the kitchen, pull every plate, cup, and bowl out of the kitchen cupboard and throw them on the floor. Thousands of pieces of broken multi-colored dishware covered the terrazzo floor. As she finished her rampage and returned to her bedroom den, my father would sheepishly come out of his home psychiatrist's office and start cleaning up the mess. During these events, I'd go into my bedroom; I wanted to be as far away as I could from her outrage.

"Who wants to come up and lie down as I demonstrate treating knee pain with the singing bowls?" I was the first person to thrust my right hand up into the air. "I do."

After my initial humiliation during Satya's first singing bowl meditation, I'm determined to let go and experience the bowls.

Satya looks right at me: "Come up and lie down on your back." "*Oh! My God! He chose me. I've got goosebumps!*" What I learned later about Satya: He always calls on the first person who wants to participate and never calls on anyone who does not respond. I love this about him.

Satya places the #2 New Age singing bowl (for all joint protocols) between my knees to be sure there's enough space before he starts the session. I'm excited and nervous all at once. Satya instructs me: "Close your eyes!" I feel the slightest weight of a bean bag eye pillow being placed over my eyes. I'm in total darkness.

"You are in a very comfortable position. Relax. . .Relax. . .Relax. . ." He continues in a heavy Indian accent. My body melts into the yoga mat atop a soft Indian rug. I feel like a bird safe in its nest.

My right knee hurts, reminding me of my past injury. When I was 16 years old, on a ski trip to Colorado, I dislocated my right knee doing the limbo. Instead of allowing it to rest and heal, I skied with my injured knee every day we were in Colorado and damaged it even more. Ever since, it has been my Achilles heel. Intermittent jabs of pain strike my right knee. I no longer jog the way I did years ago. *Will the singing bowls relieve my pain? I'm skeptical.* I feel the #2 singing bowl positioned on my right knee. My body jumps with the first strike of the bowl. With each subsequent strike, I'm aware of waves of vibration throughout my body. Once the entire treatment is complete, all pain in my knee is gone—my skepticism with it.

It was the last day of training, and our teacher, Satya Brat, was instructing us on how to play a Tibetan singing bowl on our chest. The hard wooden floor beneath me begins to melt away as I start to strike the bowl. My ears hear the most soothing sound. My body feels waves of vibration ripple across my chest and travel throughout my being. All at once, a sense of peace engulfs me. I'm no longer aware of the other sound-healing students. All that exists is the vibrating bowl on my chest and the sounds emanating from it. Pure magic!

As I placed this beautiful copper and tin Tibetan/Himalayan singing bowl on my chest and played it, I think it was the first time in my life I felt so calm, safe, peaceful, and in bliss. I was one with the universe, aligned with the heavenly stars.

I felt totally alive and part of the whole world family. What a blessing! This is why I play Tibetan singing bowls. I want to introduce whoever is ready to experience this incredible calm to try it. I know it has transformed my life. All I ask is that you try it once. If you are ready to relax, let go and activate the self-healing mechanisms within your body, sound healing is for you! Please go to my website: https://www.sonicbowls.com or email: clifton. michelle1@gmail.com to introduce you to the bowls—they are pure magic!

Now I'm going to teach you how to prepare yourself for the experience.

THE TOOL

Sound and its vibration are the most important part of sound healing. If you don't have a Tibetan/Himalayan singing bowl right now, don't fret. You can tune into the wonderful sounds of the natural world around you. As you walk or sit, you can engage with the world in a more positive and healing way by listening to the wind, the chirp of birds, the call of frogs, the wings of hummingbirds, and the waves of the ocean or the pitter-patter of rain drops. Become aware of the sounds that allow you to become one with the universe. I'm going to prepare you to relax and heighten your experience of the beautiful sounds around you, whether they are natural sounds or sounds of the Tibetan singing bowls. Once you are ready to receive the sounds of the singing bowls, you can access one of my Sound Baths or Sound Healing videos or mp3 recordings on my website: https://www.sonicbowls.com/resources—resources page. Or, if you have a Tibetan singing bowl, I will teach you to play it on your body. You will encounter the relaxing world of sound and vibration, both hearing it with your ears and feeling it with your body.

What you will need:

1. A quiet space.
2. A comfortable place to sit or lie down.

3. If lying down, have a scarf or an eye pillow nearby to place over your eyes to mimic a sense of darkness. This allows you to relax and go deeper within yourself.

4. Take whatever quiet time you have. Anywhere from three minutes to an hour.

5. Wear comfortable clothes.

6. A way to listen to my website recordings: computer, smartphone, iPad, etc.

7. If you have a singing bowl, you will need the following:
A Tibetan/Himalayan singing bowl, a soft felt mallet (for a warm sound), and/or a wooden striker wrapped in suede leather (for a higher sound).
You will also need one or two 4"x 4" sticky pads (A square piece cut from a roll of rubber shelving material.)

A. Sit or lie down in a comfortable position:

Place an eye pillow or scarf over your closed eyes if lying down.

B. Start with a Prayer:

Place your hands in a prayer position in front of your heart. As you open your hands out away from your heart, you say the following prayer:

"I open my heart.

To all of the blessings.

God has for me."

Allow yourself time to feel the words you have just spoken. Whenever ready, place your hands in a comfortable position.

C. Scan your body and begin to relax:

Allow your eyes to sink deep into your head.

Feel the muscles of your face soften.

Let your jaw softly open.

Ask the neck muscles to relax.

Allow any tension in the shoulders, arms, and hands to melt away.

Bring your attention to your torso. Ask each vertebra to settle into the mat or chair.

Feel the chest ebb and flow with each breath.

Feel the tummy soften.

The back of the legs rests and relaxes.

Every tiny muscle in your ankles and feet softens and relaxes.

Your entire body melts and feels held and comforted by the earth.

You feel relaxed from the crown of your head to the tips of your toes.

If any thoughts flash across your mind, acknowledge them and allow them to drift away.

D. Meditation:

Imagine there is a beautiful golden light that emanates from very deep within you.

Allow this light to grow and fill your entire body.

Once your entire body is glowing with this incredible light, allow the sounds of the Tibetan/Himalayan singing bowls to merge with the light as you go on a wonderful sound healing journey—enjoy your travels.

E. Recording:

Have the recording ready to begin.

Push the start button.

Enjoy the journey.

F. Experience with a Tibetan/Himalayan Singing Bowl:

If you have a metal (copper and tin—bronze) singing bowl, you can play it several ways. What I love most is placing the bowl on my body and playing it with a soft felt mallet. I'm going to teach you to play the metal singing bowl on your chest. Ideally, you want a bowl that has a harmonious sound and rings on for a relatively long time. My favorites are the Jambhati Bowls which are usually 8-14 inches in diameter. They have a beautiful, deep, rich, resounding tone that rings for a long time.

Here's how to play a bowl on your chest:

Lie down on a yoga mat, a bed, or on the ground outside, wherever you can be comfortable and safe to relax and let go.

Place a 4"x 4" sticky pad on your chest.

Place your singing bowl on top of the sticky pad, be sure it feels like the perfect place to put the bowl. Once you start playing the bowl, you can always move it if it isn't in the best spot.

Take the felt mallet into your dominant hand and strike the bowl at its upper edge.

Continue hitting the bowl until you find the most comfortable approach.

Once you are comfortable with your mallet, allow your arm and hand to find a restful position after each strike of the bowl.

Allow the bowl to ring out, and then strike it again.

Close your eyes and feel waves of vibrations wash over you.

With each strike of the bowl, allow yourself to relax and go deep within.

Once you are ready to come back into your everyday world, allow the bowl to slowly ring out.

Now carefully lift the bowl off your chest and place it next to you.

Take the sticky pad off your chest.

Enjoy the feeling of deep relaxation you have just experienced.

Notice how long you continue to have that wonderful feeling.

Please go to my website resources page (https://www.sonicbowls.com/resources) to see the video of me playing a bowl on my chest.

Have a great time. I am looking forward to connecting with you soon.

Master Sound Healer **Michelle Clifton, LMT**, is an expert energy healer with over 30 years of study who uses a powerful mix of modalities to help her clients experience healing and transformation. Michelle transitioned from a massage and bodywork practice to sound therapy.

Michelle's passion is placing bowls on participants' bodies and playing the bowls, creating an environment for deep healing and profound relaxation. She provides private and group sound meditation services to individuals of all ages. Her sound baths are transformational.

Michelle is a teacher/trainer for the Academy of Sound Healing (IASH). She teaches privately or in group workshops and certifies you in IASH's sound healing course. One of her students said, "Michelle is an amazing teacher with great passion and love."

Michelle's artwork has been exhibited in the Smithsonian and is in the permanent collection of the Museum of the City of New York. She designed the Sneaker Bed featured in Bloomingdale's Designer Rooms. As a filmmaker, Michelle co-founded the Emmy Award-Winning Hudson River Film and Video Company (hudsonriverfilm.org). She produced numerous films and was a sound recordist for her company and major television networks.

Michelle lives in the middle of the woods in the Hudson River Valley. She provides sound healing in-person in New York, New Jersey, Connecticut, and online.

Connect with Michelle:

Website: https://www.sonicbowls.com

Resources page: https://www.sonicbowls.com/resources

Facebook: https://www.facebook.com/michelle.clifton.397/

Email: clifton.michelle1@gmail.com

CHAPTER 3

MIDLIFE AND MENOPAUSE

MAPPING YOUR PATH TO EMPOWERMENT

Erika Dworkin, BCHN
Board Certified Holistic Nutritionist, Wellness Guide

Tears rolled down my cheeks and onto the sheets. *Damn it! Why didn't anyone ever warn me that menopause would be like this? How am I **ever** going to get through this? Dear God and my angels, please help me!*

My mother went through it. My father treated it. But I was called to figure out my own path through this painful phase of my life. Now I see that I had to walk alone through the fire of my journey to rise from the ashes stronger, more awake, and better equipped to guide others.

MY STORY

DISCOVERING MENOPAUSE

I was living in Washington, DC, when I called my father, heart pounding, sobbing, hair soaked with sweat, feeling dizzy, bloated, and ugly.

"Dad, *what* is happening to me? I'm sweating all the time, I can't sleep, I'm depressed and always exhausted, I can't focus on my work, and I'm *fat!* I've *never* weighed more than Mom!"

As I closed my eyes, I could see his smile and heard the understanding in his voice, "Don't worry, you're just starting menopause. I'll tell you what to do."

"*What?!* I'm only 45! Didn't Mom start much later? I thought it doesn't start til the 50s!"

"It can start earlier in some women and can last for ten years. And, yes, Mom started when she was older."

"So what should I do? I can't live like this! I don't even feel like myself."

"You have progesterone cream, right? If you've been using the wild yam cream one-quarter teaspoon twice per day for PMS, try doubling it to balance your estrogen. That's what Dr. John Lee recommends. You should also take Hot Flash. I'll mail it to you. Take one tablet three times a day, then we'll see how you feel."

MAPPING MY MENOPAUSAL MIDLIFE PATH

And that was about it. My father was a well-loved, highly respected, Connecticut licensed clinical nutritionist with a doctorate in pharmacy, but I was the proverbial cobbler's child without any shoes. Though he had helped many women with their menopausal symptoms over the course of twenty-plus years in his practice, I couldn't get the relief I needed from just the supplements he recommended.

From that first phone call until just recently, I've been on a self-guided healing quest without realizing it. With the almost crippling life changes I endured during the past thirteen years, I'm beyond grateful that I was still able to follow my intuition and Source. My growing connection to Source and my higher self, with my loving Earth Angels, eased the anxiety, fear, and self-doubt that had plagued me throughout my life. They led me through my midlife madness to wholeness, from student to teacher.

Somehow, I kept it together (well, just barely!) as each midlife episode unfolded. I had spent two years struggling with my menopause symptoms and severe food sensitivities when I had an a-ha moment. Just when I was worrying about what would happen to my father's nutrition center if he didn't have someone to mentor and take it over, it hit me that that "someone" was supposed to be me. I never had any plan to move back to Connecticut but could feel I was being called to a new assignment. I thought returning to my home state was just about keeping the business going and helping my parents retire. Boy, was I wrong!

My midlife, which started with losing my husband at thirty-nine, was to be *anything* but an ending. I co-created with Source a long period of growth and self-discovery. At the same time I moved to take over my family's business, my then 81-year-old father, my best friend, soulmate, and steadfast safety net, went in for hip surgery. From there, in just 12 fast years, I endured PTSD from my husband's death, and the deaths of two key employees, my fur-baby Sydney, my father (three weeks after Sydney died and after his one-year decline), and our family business (after pushing through the COVID-19 pandemic). With all that stress and outpouring of cortisol, it's no wonder my hormones were out of control and I had only one foot on the ground most of the time!

Thankfully, the many tools I gathered over those years enabled me to create another new beginning. I'm finally who I want to be and can see clearly where I'm going. I spent ten years in Al-Anon, three years in weekly private Kundalini Yoga classes, and over five years in The Avatar Course; I worked intensely with a medical intuitive and researched incessantly. I've done all the necessary hard work to create the rewarding personal and business lives I've been manifesting for so long. I now feel I'm a far better version of myself—healthier, happier, more relaxed, better connected to my higher self and Source, a more powerful manifester, aligned with my soul's mission, and, yes, thinner! I'm prepared to move forward on what is surely to be an exciting new journey. And, with Source, my angels, and my spirit guides, *nothing* can stop me!

My greatest desire is to empower you with this same clarity, confidence, and positivity. The five-step process below will start you on your way, and I invite you to go to www.vitathenawellness.com for more detailed guidance.

THE TOOL

Before we jump into mapping your path to empowerment beyond midlife and menopause, let's look at what it means to be in this phase of life in the first place.

WHAT EXACTLY **IS** MENOPAUSE?

Menopause is the point in time twelve months after you have your last period, when your ovaries stop releasing fertile eggs due to their reduced production of estrogen and progesterone. Estrogen levels drop 40-60% (the ovaries, adrenal glands, and body fat continue to make it), but progesterone levels can fall to near zero in some women, creating estrogen dominance. In most women, menopause occurs around age 51, but it can also set in as early as age 40.

Perimenopause, also known as the menopausal transition, is the label for the years preceding menopause when you begin to experience changes in your monthly cycle. During those four-to-seven years, or possibly even as many as twelve, you might experience a mix of the symptoms noted below. (Here, I will refer to perimenopause as menopause.)

Postmenopause begins after the twelve-month point of menopause. Most women's symptoms tend to subside, but they then become more vulnerable to heart and bone diseases, diabetes, obesity, cognitive decline, depression, and cancer.

The root cause of menopause is declining gland function. Like the ovaries, the hypothalamus, pituitary, adrenal, and thyroid glands begin to produce lower amounts of hormones, which negatively affects the nervous system. Genetics, age, diet, lifestyle, and environmental factors impact the time of onset. Surgical removal of the ovaries, or uterus and cervix (hysterectomy), chemotherapy, and drugs designed to shut down ovarian estrogen production, can induce menopause.

The physical aspects of menopause can be extremely challenging, but not all women experience the transition to the Age of Wisdom similarly. Some of your friends may barely have any symptoms, while you and others might feel like you are falling apart. You menopause warriors might experience more than you can handle on your own as your fat cells change, your bodies begin to use energy differently, and your shapes and physical functions take on burdensome, unrecognizable characteristics. You might suffer:

- Fatigue
- Insomnia
- Achy joints
- Hot flashes
- Night sweats
- Thyroid issues
- Memory lapses
- Breast tenderness
- Increased belly fat
- Digestive challenges
- Unwanted hair growth
- Urinary tract infections
- Cardiovascular challenges
- Hair, skin, and nail difficulties
- Reduced libido and painful sex
- Extreme or unpredictable irritability or depression
- Excess dryness that ages skin and interferes with intimacy
- Occasional incontinence (especially when sneezing or laughing, yikes!)

Well, I have some exciting news! The five essential steps below will make a real difference in the frequency and degree with which you experience menopausal symptoms and can empower you to celebrate those symptoms as portents to an exciting rebirth. You will transform into a menopause goddess as you reshape your consciousness, balance your hormones, achieve emotional equilibrium, and meet your future self. Though I have outlined the process as individual steps, you can take them however you feel they work for you, one at a time, a few at a time, or all together, in order, or out of order. I have **just one recommendation:** since Step 1 interweaves through and directly affects the success of Steps 2-5, it will be ideal to start there and continue to work on it as you move through the others. I'm providing Step 1 details here since it is most critical to launching your mapping journey. For guidance through the other four steps, go to www.vitathenawellness.com.

THE 5 ESSENTIAL STEPS TO MAPPING YOUR MIDLIFE EMPOWERMENT

Step 1: Create Positive Beliefs About Midlife and Menopause

Step 2: Learn to Cope Better with Your Other Life Stressors

Step 3: Change Your Diet and Make Other Lifestyle Changes

Step 4: Add Supportive, High-Quality Supplements and Essential Oils

Step 5: Explore Energy Medicine Options

Step 1: Create Positive Beliefs About Midlife and Menopause

Having grown up believing that scientific evidence must inform an individual's healing process, I'm excited that studies demonstrate a strong link between positive mindset and good health. On the other hand, my personal experiences with metaphysics and energy medicine have convinced me that there is so much more to wellness than what any experiment can prove.

MINDFULLY APPRECIATE AND EMBRACE CHANGE

There are many universal principles that our five senses alone can't easily explain. One of these is that your life does *not* just happen. Your thoughts and beliefs precede and ultimately become your reality. Though there are nuances of this idea, you can take my word for it that you are a powerful Source being, with Source energy within you, and therefore the powerful co-creator with Source of all that you experience, including your physical and emotional well-being. Mind-blowing, right?! Imagine what you can create in your life by deliberately shifting your energy, by changing your viewpoints and expectations! When you explore your deepest desires and focus on what you prefer, and remove all doubt and resistance, you will have the experiences you seek. Since resisting the experiences you have created is causing most of the misery you're experiencing (what you resist persists), appreciating and even embracing all aspects of your midlife transition is the first crucial element of this first step.

Uncovering your midlife and menopause beliefs through this exercise will enable you to begin to move forward. In fact, just determining your impeding beliefs could dissolve them.

YOUR PATH TO EMPOWERMENT
MAPPING STEP 1
MIDLIFE & MENOPAUSE BELIEF SURVEY

- Sit comfortably in a quiet, private place where you can reflect without interruption for at least 30 minutes.

- Take three, three-count deep belly breaths. Breathe into and expand your belly for three counts, hold for three, and exhale for three. This will help you move from your mind to your body so you can tap into your intuition and higher self.

- Contemplate the statements in this table and feel into what most resonates.

- Place a 1 in the column to the left of the belief that feels the most right.

- If you can't choose, then place a 1 in both columns. If you feel both statements are true, but one seems even a bit more applicable, then place a 2 in that column and a 1 in the other.

- On another piece of paper, write down any other Impeding and Supportive Beliefs that come to you.

- Tally the columns to see whether Impeding or Supportive beliefs are primarily creating your reality.

IMPEDING BELIEF		SUPPORTIVE BELIEF	
	Everything in my life is out of control and I'm powerless to change things.		It's time to take control of my life and I have the power to do that.
	I'm completely alone in this midlife battle and there's no hope.		I'm not alone. I'm optimistic about the future and know I can tap into Source and seek support from the army of angels and spirit guides that are awaiting my request for help.
	My life is now empty and without meaning because some valuable relationships have changed or dissolved, and other people I care about don't need me as much.		Because some valuable relationships have changed or dissolved, I now have the freedom to change, to map the life path that I want without having to take care of, or worry about, others.
	I have too much to do and don't have time for myself.		My life and I are important, so I will make time to focus on myself and reflect on what I want and need.
	All the physical, personal, and financial stressors in my life are part of a midlife crisis.		I am grateful to be alive and to have this midlife opportunity to shift my energy, recharge my body, and focus on all aspects of my self-care.
	I'm aging. My doctor says it's normal to have health problems as I age. There's nothing I can do about it.		I'm growing. It's normal to go through menopause and I embrace all my body's changes. I will do all I can to support it so I can improve my quality of life, shift into a higher vibration, and move from surviving to thriving.

IMPEDING BELIEF		SUPPORTIVE BELIEF
Menopause is THE WORST! I don't recognize myself and **cannot** handle my exhaustion, hot flashes, night sweats, memory lapses, focus problems, reduced sex drive, and painful sex!! WTH?!!		I am grateful to be where I am in my life and now decide to focus on being healthy and feeling good. I accept how menopause is burning off old energy that no longer serves me. I know this experience will enable me to rediscover myself and pave my new path.
I hate how heavy and bloated I am. I feel so unattractive and, no matter what I do, I **can't** lose weight.		I choose to love myself just as I am, knowing that I am always changing and can grow in my own time into who I wish to become.
I give up. This time in my life is a dead end. I have lived the best part of my life and have already contributed the most I have to give.		It's time to glow! This time in my life is an opportunity to create a new abundant beginning, a soul-aligned mission that will carry me forward to where I want to be. I have lived life as a student and now can truly shine by sharing my experience and wisdom with the world.
What are people saying about me? What will they think if I do what I really want to do, or become who I want to become?		It's time I stopped worrying about what others think and how they've labeled me. Now that I have more freedom, it's time to focus on what I think and decide who I want to be for the rest of my life.
TOTAL		**TOTAL**

*This survey evolved in large part from the six years of work I've done, and continue to do, in The Avatar Course, the self-development program that Harry Palmer started in 1986. The consciousness management tools I've learned and used carried me through multiple traumas. I will be forever grateful that Spirit guided me to this life-saving, life-changing door to so many possibilities. For more information, go to www.avatarepc.com and www.theavatarcourse.com.

SO, I KNOW MY BELIEFS. NOW WHAT?

Once you embrace new positive viewpoints, you'll be ready to explore the who, where, why, when, and how of your future. The more you work on yourself, the more complete you'll become, and the more you'll light up your personal world and the world around you.

While you continue to work on Step 1 by further examining consciousness management, you'll find Steps 2-5 progressively easier. Now that your spirit has guided you to these pages, I'm here to support your self-empowered journey to vibrancy and wholeness. As you open to all the possibilities before you, you'll be guided to those healing modalities that will best serve you. You'll become more able to cope with the stressors that undermine your wellness, and you'll find it easier to commit to the personalized dietary and supplements regimens I will recommend. The other lifestyle changes you choose to make will be equally easier as you learn not to resist them.

As you map your midlife and menopause path, I will help you be kind to yourself and patient with your body. You'll discover confidence and faith that you're transitioning into a magical part of your life, when the experience, awareness, wisdom, healing, and growth you have earned with blood, sweat, and tears (literally!) can mold you into who you're destined to become. It's time for the boundless part of your journey, for you to begin to serve the world in your unique way with your new power, optimism, and love.

Holistic · Experienced
Committed · Compassionate

Erika Dworkin, BCHN, is a lifelong learner, award-winning board certified holistic nutritionist, and wellness guide. She crafts personalized, evidence-based regimens that enable the body to heal itself with a wide selection of natural therapies: diet modifications; lifestyle changes; proven dietary supplements; beyond-organic essential oils; and time-honored metaphysical tools. She makes obtaining quality of life and longevity simple, convenient, and time-effective. To learn the differences between BCHNs and Registered Dietitians (RDs)/Registered Dietitian Nutritionists (RDNs), go to www.vitathenawellness.com.

Erika grew up with an understanding of both natural and conventional Western medicine and, for 12 years, owned her family's well-loved nutrition center that operated for 65 years in Connecticut. There, Michael Dworkin, PD, CCN, a Connecticut licensed clinical nutritionist with a doctorate in pharmacy, formally mentored her.

Erika is passionate about empowering others, especially women in midlife, to pave their paths to their individual levels of optimal wellness. She has done this for thousands by addressing both the symptoms *and* underlying causes of diverse health issues, including hormonal imbalances, inflammation, fatigue, anxiety, obesity, bone and joint challenges, digestive issues (including candidiasis), and cardiovascular concerns.

When you work with Erika, she'll consider your whole being, your body, mind, and spirit. As she gently and compassionately helps you discover your path to wellness, she'll guide you down it without judgment. Feeling into what you're feeling, she'll tap into her resolve to empower you to find relief. She'll listen intently, research thoroughly, and search with an open mind until she discovers innovative answers. As you relax into the awareness that investing in your wellness will reduce your suffering, your collaboration with Erika will foster self-love, confidence, real healing, and inner peace.

860.646.8178

edworkin@vitathena.com

www.VitathenaWellness.com

www.naturalnutmeg.com (Published Articles)

www.wellevate.me/vitathenawellness (Online Store/14,000+ Items)

CHAPTER 4

EMBODIED

WAKE UP YOUR
PSYCHIC INTUITION TO HEAL

Lisa G Roche

"I spiraled into an abyss of dark silence. Little did I know my transformation would begin with a complete surrender—a death and rebirth I had never before experienced."

MY STORY

I came to after having passed out on the table while at breakfast with friends. The last thing I remembered was a squeeze, like a giant hand on the back of my head. Not able to see or hear, I asked for help and tried to stand but fell back into my chair, not able to feel my feet on the floor. The world was spinning, and I was in the center, trapped in an echo of life—a reverb of sound and light with no comprehension of what was happening.

Thinking of those nine months—memories fade in and out, some quite vivid and others a blurry shadow. I remember being shuffled out of the restaurant, my hand brushing the wall and the feel of the textured wallpaper. I remember thinking, *this is bumpy* as if I were defining and describing new information to my brain. I remember the searing pain of sound and light. I remember lying on the floor, begging for death. And then I remember the voice.

We call 2015-16 the forgotten year—a year where the camera of my mind comes in and out of focus, darkness into light, drifting in and out of consciousness. So much was lost, but the miracles remain, seared into my memory as glass plates etched with scenes of divine intervention.

I remember wanting to jump out a window after being prescribed an anti-psychotic that was supposed to relieve my migraine. I remember my husband trapping me in the water closet so I couldn't access any windows while we waited out my urge to feel broken glass cut through my skin. I remember longing for relief from the pain raging in my skull and the deterioration of my body. I remember the conversation with the ENT.

"You want to do what?!"

"Drill a hole behind your right ear. It will relieve the pressure, and then we can explore to see if there's more happening that we can't see."

I was horrified. *Who suggests that?! Are there people in this world who listen to that and take him up on that kind of advice?!*

All these experiences of listening to doctors and trying medications— were miracles that awakened my consciousness to realize the absurdity of modern medicine.

I remember telling every medical professional who would listen that I knew there was a dark mass at the base of my skull. And while every test and specialist insisted I was wrong, *I knew.*

That grey mass—I felt it, saw it, sensed it. I could hear the void and taste the color, but no test provided proof. No mass, stroke, heart or circulatory issues, nothing—so they recommended a psychiatrist and prescribed more medication. Unbeknownst to me, my psychic senses were activating—another miracle.

I remember feeling exhausted that no one would listen. There were tests, doctors, questions without any answers, and then another miracle. My sister offered salvation—divine guidance.

I called her after the appointment with the ENT. Sobbing and gasping for air, I explained how he wanted to do exploratory surgery. I don't remember much of that conversation except for when she said, "I work with a woman whose friend had similar symptoms to yours. She saw this chiropractor, and it turned out she had swelling at the base of her skull. The chiropractor adjusted her and had her take a decongestant. I know it doesn't sound like much, but she's better now!"

In complete desperation, I took her advice, and my life began to change.

There I sat, eyes closed and sound swirling like static pulsations through my head. I felt as if I existed only inside myself, invisible to the outside world, encaged in confusion and chaos. I was completely disconnected until I felt hands on my knees. The chiropractor knelt before me; her touch was pure kindness. I remember the sensation of care and stability seeping into my body like warm honey dripping through my skin and into my bloodstream. With a simple touch, I felt healing.

"This is your atlas. I'm going to take care of you, but if you need to throw up, please tell us because all of our trashcans are mesh, and they don't have liners."

I laughed for the first time in over five months—another miracle.

Slowly, the marbled blob of light and color took form and focus. The doctor, looking at me, cheered, "You can see me!" I remember the relief that ran through me as I took in her face; the miracle of sight was restored. Her voice was clear and at a decibel my brain could manage. The miracle of hearing was restored.

I went three times a week, and while the adjustments helped tremendously, I wasn't able to hold them and kept slipping back into a shell of a person. With each adjustment, a rush of hope: *Would this be the one that made me normal again?* But within days, hope slipped away. Again and again, a repeating pattern that lasted for months.

Until finally, I broke.

I remember the moment so clearly. I had just found a meditation chant, RA MA DA SA, a chant for the nervous system. I was grasping at anything that could help. I fell to the floor and sobbed. Sucked back into the entrapment of a body that refused to heal, I prayed for death. Exhausted, helpless, and hopeless, I begged God to take me, take my pain and suffering, and release my family from the burden of me. I begged, and that's when it happened. In my complete surrender, I heard it—the voice.

Ask for help, and help will come. Have faith. Have hope. Do you accept?

Clear, powerful, commanding, and gentle. The voice repeated its message.

Ask for help, and help will come. Have faith. Have hope. Do you accept?

Confused and yet, in complete trust, I said, "Yes."

Inexplicably, I crawled off the floor and climbed onto the couch. I opened my iPad and found myself in a Facebook group where someone had posted, "It's the Easter season, and I am looking to help someone. If you know of anyone in need, please message me."

My stomach lurched at the words. Tears streamed down my face as I read them over and over again. "I'm looking to help someone." My head was pulsating, and I realized I was holding my breath. I gasped for air and heard that voice again.

ASK FOR HELP.

Shaking, terrified, humbled, and vulnerable, I said yes and asked for help. Two days later, another miracle. Help had come.

She helped me with my coat and down the stairs. She held my arm and helped me walk a few yards before gingerly asking what had happened. I explained, "It's this bone called the atlas. No one's ever heard of it, but I have a wonderful chiropractor and am in physical therapy and slowly making progress."

In an instant, the world went quiet, and I felt that familiar squeeze at the back of my head. The cold air froze on my face as my heart pounded at the inside of my skull. I panicked as I anticipated passing out. But this time, I remained present as time stood still, and everything faded away while I listened. "I know exactly who you should see." And in a blink, the world came back. Cars drove by, and I felt the cold on my skin again, the wind in my eyes. Life turned back on as that voice spoke.

LISTEN. HAVE FAITH. HAVE HOPE.

Sitting at my desk with the number in front of me, consumed with fear and doubt, I listened to my brother-in-law in the kitchen as he prepared dinner. The clanging of pots and pans reverberated through my skull as he tried desperately to be as quiet as possible. Exhausted, I laid my head on my arms and asked if he thought I should call. His answer was simple, "Are you kidding? Lisa, when God sends an angel, you ignore her?" So, once again, I found myself saying, "Yes." I picked up the phone, fingers shaking, and dialed. Not only did someone answer at 7:00 on that Monday evening, but they had also just had a cancellation, and I could go in on Wednesday.

The atlas. The mouth of God. The area of our body through which divine words are spoken. And if we ignore our spirit's call long enough, this area collapses. God will not be ignored forever.

A funny thing happens when you surrender to divine guidance. You heal! That Wednesday began my healing journey. I had been in failing health for months, in a wheelchair, palsy, sponge baths, and dry shampoo. I had no short-term memory and needed assistance to eat and drink. The slightest exertion caused me to pass out. I went from a healthy, athletic, 42-year-old mother and wife to being told that was my new normal and to prepare accommodations. Anger and disgust in our conventional medical system motivated me to follow the signs to about 70% functionality with my first chiropractor. But in faith, hope and complete surrender, I went to a full recovery and beyond. I can honestly say I'm better than I had ever been before.

Convinced the procedure would lop my head off, I lay on the table in sheer panic. Crying and terrified, I told my husband that I loved him. The doctor explained that it would be painless and half-jokingly said, "I'll even count for you. One, two, finished." Click. That's all I heard. A simple singular sound of metal hitting metal. The specialist used a sound wave to adjust my bone. Like a whisper through my tissue, a breath of safety and security allowed the bone to shift and my muscles to accept the new alignment. I knew in an instant that the voice had just moved through me.

From there, everything changed. I could feel the energy moving through my entire being. I felt blood coursing through my arteries and veins. I felt life coming back to nerve endings. I could trace the reawakening patterns throughout my entire body. My husband and I marveled at the red lines that lit up on my skin as blood rushed to heal different areas. Reactivation bounced around my being without rhyme or reason, and I witnessed it in complete awe and gratitude.

As I regained neural function, my brain fog lifted, and I was given clarity of thought again. One day I woke up, and the voice told me I could heal myself.

YOU HAVE THE KNOWLEDGE. USE YOUR SKILLS.

I discontinued my physical therapy sessions and mapped out a recuperation program using the spiraling movements of The Gyrotonic® Method. It was exactly what I needed to increase blood flow and brain activity to find new connections throughout my entire being.

Within three months, the voice told me it was time to be in service of others. I went back to work as a Gyrotonic® Instructor and said yes, as client after client showed up with atlas injuries. I was now a guide and led them to the specialist for treatment. Lives changed as I was then able to practice and share what I learned. One by one, clients had their atlases adjusted and then worked with me to hold their alignment and retrain their bodies.

Not long after, I started to see red spots light up on bodies and the voice told me where to place my hands. I said yes to trusting the higher guidance and witnessed the unwinding and healing of muscle tension under my fingertips. I was re-introduced to Reiki and said yes when the master teacher offered to attune me. And just when I thought life couldn't get any better, things accelerated.

Since attuning to Reiki, the healings that move through me are nothing short of miraculous. Every day, I work with people to release the energy of disease, infection, and trauma. Mysteries and ailments are made simple with divine guidance and intervention. I have a team of ancient healers that work with me and through me to help guide people on their healing journeys. I live in awe of the magic and healing abilities of love. The very essence and energy of love are so simple and yet so profound. A vibration and frequency that truly heals all.

HEAL ONE, HEAL ALL. PEACE FOR ONE, PEACE FOR ALL.

Now, I've been guided to change the vibration of this planet from fear and pain to peace. And I say yes to this next step in my healing journey.

Ironically, my awakening began with passing out; the humor is not lost on me. My hope is that others don't have to suffer as I did. My hope is that everyone chooses to shift from pain to peace. Because when we choose peace, we heal our trauma, observe change and listen for the way forward. We thrive and not only change our personal lives; we change the world.

I was forced into darkness, forced inward to remove all distractions from the outside world. I was gifted with the time of deep discovery, and while at the moment, I was frightened, overwhelmed, and driven to the point of giving up, I'm eternally grateful. My awakening has been an empowering, humbling experience that has not only benefited my overall well-being but has allowed me to connect with others in a way I had no idea existed. Divine healing. Divine connection. Divine sharing.

And now *I* kneel before *you,* my hands on your knees. I'm going to take care of you and if you feel like you're going to throw up—go for the can with a liner in it.

Seriously, I say yes to guiding you on your healing journey, so let's begin by choosing to go inward and wake up your psychic intuition.

THE TOOL

PSYCHIC INTUITION FOR HEALING

I invite you to dim the lights and turn on some vibrational or meditative music. Make yourself comfortable, laying on your back on the floor. Rest your head on a pillow, use a blanket, and support your legs. Make use of any props needed for you to be in complete comfort and peace.

Take a deep breath and feel your spine on the floor. Allow your tailbone to grow heavy, reaching down into the floor and then growing long and downward into the earth. Allow yourself to ground for a few moments while we prepare to move inward.

Take a few deep breaths and notice an area of your body. Maybe it's your back, stomach, or head, a leg, an arm, maybe a foot. Whatever came to your mind first, place your hands on that part of your body.

Allow your hands to rest here and breathe into this area of your body.

Breathe life force energy into this one area of your body.

Open your eyes and take note of the body part that jumped into your conscious mind. This part of you just identified itself as the first place in your body that is ready to release the negative energy stored there.

This is the beginning of Psychic Intuitive Healing. Our bodies need us to go inward and listen for guidance on where and how to release the negative energy that is regenerating and causing dis-ease and dysfunction.

Welcome to your magnificent healing journey. A complete audio version of this meditation can be found in the Spirit Calling Community. Join us at www.spirit-calling.com to continue your exploration of intuitive psychic healing and to surround yourself with a supportive community as you transform from pain to peace.

Every soul has the same purpose: to live in peace. The first step to fulfilling your soul's purpose is to amplify your frequency with self-care. The ultimate practice of self-care is healing your pain and releasing the trauma that lowers your vibration.

Your healing journey is a winding path of self-discovery, understanding, and healing where every step leads to a greater sense of peace. And peace for you generates peace for the world.

Like the very structure of our DNA, peace and healing spiral around each other to combine and create life. What kind of life have you created? What kind of life would you like to create?

Connect with your psychic intuitive healing powers and release the emotions and trauma that deteriorate the human body and hold you back from thriving. Ease your body back into a state of perpetual peace.

Heal your soul.

Lisa Roche is an expert Psychic Reiki Master Teacher specializing in soul healing, helping clients who are ready to experience profound change to heal their pain and live in peace. Through communication with your team of spirit guides and her counsel of guides and ancient healers, Lisa will share transformational messages and facilitate physical and spiritual healing. You'll experience a journey of more peace, health, and abundance by releasing emotions and trauma that hold you back.

Lisa is also the Co-Founder of Spirit Calling, a sought-after, safe online resource and space to guide you through your spiritual awakening with ease, autonomy, and empowerment. Come together with like-minded, compassionate souls to learn and share your experiences.

Find Lisa and her programs at
www.LisaGRoche.com and www.Spirit-Calling.com

Thank you for doing your part to raise the vibration of the planet. By reading this book and implementing the tools, you are supporting your awakening. I encourage you to continue exploring your healing. Awaken, transform, and ascend into the very best version of yourself! Thank you for sharing your energy with me and contributing to the love and peace that fill my soul. Together, we will change the world.

CHAPTER 5

OVERCOMING THE EFFECTS OF ANIMAL-RELATED TRAUMA

A SIMPLE TECHNIQUE TO HELP HEAL YOUR HEART

Kathy Boyer, Animal Communicator, Energy Healer

MY STORY

A decrepit-looking tortoiseshell cat with an ugly, orange mustache wandered into our yard in July 1993, near Yokota Air Base, Japan. Skin and bones, with nipples dangling from her belly, she obviously had kittens and was scavenging for food. Since we already had two cats, I tried my best to ignore her desperate pleas for help. *She's not my responsibility,* reasoned my brain. *If you ignore her, maybe she'll go away and look somewhere else for food.*

Within a week of the cat's first visit, I had a very vivid dream asking me to take care of her. I could not ignore it, and she became my first rescue cat. *Here we go.* From that moment on, I never looked back, and thus began my endless trail of taking in needy cats!

I named her Pretty Girl to detract attention from the hideous mustache above her mouth, and now, after the dream, I just *had* to find her. The next time she appeared, my ex-husband and I followed her, discovering her hiding place in an old, abandoned house. There were four filthy month-old kittens residing in the bathtub.

We embarked on our rescue mission three days later, with cat carriers in hand during a rainstorm, arriving at the old house eager to bring everyone home. *But where are the babies? They're gone.* We looked outside the front door and spotted Pretty Girl carrying them one by one across the street towards another house. I could feel her anguish and fatigue.

Combatting the rain, we hurriedly brought the whole family home to join our two male cats. *They're safe at last and won't ever have to fend for themselves again!* Pretty Girl loved being a mama, and the kittens loved to play. *There is so much joy in our house!*

We planned to keep Pretty Girl, but I was *not* expecting the emotional impact it would leave on her when we gave away her babies. I presumed that whenever kittens were big enough and stopped nursing, you just found good homes for them. The grief was heart-wrenching, and I felt it along with her. It was devastating to listen to her moan through the house, looking for them. *What have I done?*

Fortunately, one of the new homes didn't work out, and three days later, the gold and white male, Spunky, was returned. It was a happy day for Pretty Girl, who doted on him for the next 16 years until they passed away just months apart from each other.

I swore I'd never separate a mother cat from her kittens again, but in 2005, Fuji, a calico who was abandoned in an apple orchard, joined our family. Through unusual circumstances, she got pregnant before she was spayed and had three kittens. At the time, we had eight other cats, and again, it wasn't feasible to keep all three kittens. *But we're keeping at least one.* A good friend of mine adopted the two girls, and we kept Boots, the gold-and-white boy.

I re-experienced Pretty Girl's ordeal as grief enveloped me again, watching Fuji scour the house, desperately looking for her two missing girls. I felt like I was a total traitor because of the agony I caused her.

Meanwhile, Boots, missing his sisters, lost his desire to play, became a loner, and was never the same emotionally.

Where is this extreme sensitivity coming from? A flashback to the movie *Bambi* entered my mind.

As a six-year-old, I stared at the large screen in the movie theater, sobbing uncontrollably when Bambi, a young deer, lost his mother to hunters. The sounds of the gunshot killing her were forever etched in my psyche. *Make it stop!* I didn't think I'd ever recover from the pain of watching the permanent separation of a baby animal and its mother.

This scenario showed up again two years later in the first episode of my favorite TV show as a kid, *Kimba the White Lion.* Kimba's mother died when the ship carrying her and little Kimba sank. Kimba was now alone, trying to adapt to life. *Mother animals and their babies being separated? I'm seeing a pattern here.*

Although not involving live animals, those scenes broke my young, impressionable heart into pieces, well into adulthood. At that time, I had no idea what animal-related trauma *was,* much less how to cope with it.

I've always had a huge love for animals and a sensitivity I couldn't explain until I became an animal communicator 50 years later. I'm extremely empathic and sensitive to the emotions of animals, which has now become my superpower in helping others, both human and animal.

We don't often recognize animal-related trauma or label it as such. As a culture, we haven't valued the emotional impact caused by difficult incidents involving animals, whether it's related to behavior, an accident, or a childhood experience. We're told, "They're just animals."

Or, after one of our beloved companions dies, we hear these well-meaning but callous words: "You can always get another one." We're embarrassed to share our feelings anymore, so we store the grief in our hearts. *How will I ever overcome this?*

It was nearly 30 years after adopting Pretty Girl that I learned about Emotional Freedom Technique (EFT) Tapping, a technique that helps release emotional stress from the physical body. You do it by *physically* tapping with your fingers on a series of acupressure points on the body or in the air on its surrounding energy field. You can also tap on your own body as a surrogate for another person or animal, using *intention,* which I define as the will of the mind directed towards a specific outcome.

For those who like a more technical explanation, these points are along the meridians (energetic pathways running through the body), which in Chinese medicine are associated with specific organs and related to specific emotions—by tapping on these points in a sequential, repeated pattern, stored emotional energy releases from the body, often in the form of a deep breath or sigh.

How does it play out in life? The emotions surrounding that trauma stuck in the body are now lessened or totally gone, and the memory of that event no longer triggers them—the result: emotional freedom.

I learned about tapping when I attended a four-day animal communication conference taught by Joan Ranquet, founder of Communication with All Life University (CWALU).

Joan demonstrated EFT tapping on a rescue dog named Bandit, whose new owner, Michelle was a student in the class. Bandit had a sore on his mouth that Michelle desperately wanted to treat but couldn't get close to because a previous groomer had slapped the dog's face during the grooming sessions. Since most of the tapping points are on or near the face, Joan directed Michelle to tap in the air, just a few feet away from Bandit, with her hands directed towards the tapping points on his body.

The results were astonishing! Bandit relaxed, laid down on the floor, nearly fell asleep, yawned, licked, and chewed. Michelle was now able to touch him on his face! *She didn't even touch his body! I have to learn more about energy.*

After I got home, I immediately tried tapping on Nelly, my horse. We were both distraught, as Jake, my other horse and her companion of ten years, passed away unexpectedly just before the conference started.

I stumbled through a tapping session as I touched her body, barely remembering all the tapping points. The emotional release was immediate: Nelly lowered her head, yawned, licked, and chewed. *This is remarkable. She's never done that with me before. It worked!*

I immediately enrolled in Joan's 18-month online Animal Mastery Program. I had found my soul's purpose—to help animals and their humans!

Part of my training was to practice tapping with homework partners and releasing stored emotions from animal-related trauma. Childhood animal memories popped into my head.

(1) Blacky: When I was ten while playing with friends down the street, my young cat Blacky was hit by a car, breaking his leg. I didn't know what happened until my mother picked me up later in the day and told me, along with the upsetting news, that she had brought him to the vet to be put to sleep.

I was devastated. *Why didn't they save him? Why didn't she come and get me so I could be with him? I'm heartbroken.*

How did this affect me later on? I tried to save *every* animal I came in contact with, no matter what the medical issue. Tapping freed me from the stored anger from Blacky's death and helped me realize that I can't save them all.

(2) The German Shepherd: A fierce-looking German Shepherd lived up the street from us in a fenced yard. *Grrr. . .Woof Woof. . .Grrr* was the sound I dreaded every time he came running toward me. I was terrified of that dog, even before I left my house.

After I tapped through that fear, I started seeing German Shepherds everywhere, beginning the very next day on Facebook with a heartwarming video of one helping a kitten up the stairs. A week later, I saw another one at the park. *I'm not reacting at all! I'm no longer afraid of German Shepherds! I wonder if my cats would mind if I adopted one.*

(3) The Fast Horse: I loved horses, but owning one was impossible since we lived in a small town. When I was 11, my mom found someone in the country willing to let me ride their horse. *At last, this is my big chance! I'm so excited, and I can hardly wait!*

I sat unattended in a saddle on the back of this unfamiliar horse in a large paddock surrounded by a barbed-wire fence—both excited and nervous while my dream was coming true! *I can do this.*

Au contraire! The horse bolted; I held on for dear life, miraculously staying on his back, but came within an inch of scraping my knee against the barbed wire fence! *It feels like my heart flew out of my body.* That was my only flashback—the panic, my knee, and that fence.

The impact? Forty years later, when I bought a horse as an adult, I was terrified of going fast, even at a trot. In my mind, although I was galloping across beautiful open spaces with my hair bouncing in the wind, my body tensed and was gripped by fear instead. *I better change my aspirations of winning the Kentucky Derby!*

Tapping completely erased that fear. I can now confidently go on a trail ride and am comfortable going fast and enjoying myself. *Emotional freedom!*

(4) **Samantha:** My college boyfriend Jeff and I found a sweet, gold-striped female kitten we named Samantha outside our apartment, which didn't allow pets. We decided to take her across Canada to upstate New York, offering her as a playmate to my mom's cat Oscar.

Mom wasn't thrilled, and without telling me, she gave Samantha away to a farm over a mile away. But Samantha found her way back home, only to be given away again to *another* farm, further away, where she (apparently) stayed.

That tore my heart apart. *Why didn't she tell me? Why did she give her away—twice, even after she worked so hard to find her way back home? I feel like I betrayed this beautiful cat. My heart is broken.*

The result? I never *willingly* gave a cat away again, no matter how many I had. The words on my nightshirt echo this: "Cat Addicts Anonymous: I can stop any time I want!"

Tapping relieved me of the stored sadness and anger and gave me a better perspective about having a large cat population. As I age, it's more difficult to take care of more than just a few, but I can help find homes for those in need.

(5) **Pretty Girl–the rest of the story!** My boy Pumpkin passed away in August 2021, leaving me with only two female cats. *My house feels so empty. And I have no male cats.* I gradually started to feel the urge to adopt again. *But from where?*

In October, a friend unexpectedly asked if I would like to adopt the two remaining male kittens from a young, feral cat she was helping. Immediately I was triggered. *How could I even think about separating a mother from her babies again?* I wrestled with this dilemma yet somehow knew these kittens were supposed to be mine.

This time, I used my tools as an animal communicator; first, by talking with the mother cat, who told me, she was worn out and needed time for herself to grow up. I reassured her that her babies would be safe and loved. Next, I talked with the boys and told them of their adoption and that their names would be Simon and Max.

Then the miracle happened! Pretty Girl was appearing in my dreams for almost a month. *What's that about?* I had not yet done any tapping to clear the stored trauma from 30 years earlier. Along with the guilt and regret, there was self-hate. I blocked my capacity to receive love from my cats as much as I tried.

I was cleared of what seemed like a lifetime of trauma in no time! *Why did I wait so long? This was such a simple fix.*

When I brought Simon and Max home, the guilt and regret were gone, and I experienced them as two angelic beings that brought me the purest love I'd ever felt from an animal! *Wow!*

Animal-related trauma can happen in many ways and not always from experience with a live animal. It can be from movies, television, magazines, or even social media.

And then, there are end-of-life issues. I believe this is what we, as pet parents, have most in common. I have lost 17 animals in 20 years, second-guessing every choice I made during their final days, always thinking I'd made the wrong one.

We can forget all the wonderful years we had together, leaving us fixated on the end-of-life scenario. This can prevent us from getting attached to another animal, believing we're not being loyal to the one who passed.

You don't have to remain stuck in the story! With this simple technique, you can move forward with your life as a pet parent! My tool is a tapping script focusing on end-of-life issues, but it can be adapted for any animal-related trauma.

THE TOOL

Tapping Script for Healing End-of-Life Animal-Related Trauma

Preparation:

(1) Choose which animal's death still has the most emotional impact on you.

(2) Write the emotions down on paper that you want to be free from.

Examples:

(1) Regret

(2) Guilt

(3) Can't forgive myself

(4) Selfish

(5) Heartbroken

(3) Write down several transition statements to direct you toward your goal.

Examples:

(1) "I'm sick and tired of feeling this way."

(2) "I'm open to being set free and moving on."

(3) "Maybe it's not my fault."

(4) "I'm ready to let go of all this."

(5) "I allow myself to move through this."

(4) Write down how you would *like* to feel to have this resolved.

Examples:

(1) "I'm at peace now."

(2) "I know I did the best I could."

(2) "I'm okay now."

(3) "I've let this go, and I can move on."

THE TAPPING PORTION: SPEAK EVERYTHING OUT LOUD AS YOU TAP

1. **Setup Statement:** Tap both pinkies together where they attach to the hands, like a karate chop, and say your statement three times.

   Example: "Even though (animal's name) passed away, and I feel so much guilt and regret, I love and accept myself."

2. **Tapping on the Points:** Use the tips of the fingers on both hands to tap. Focus on the emotions of the story as you move from point to point. Do at least one complete round with each emotion you listed.

   Example: One round of tapping with sample dialogue:

   (1) *Inside the eyebrows:* "I feel so much regret."

   (2) *Outside the eyebrows:* "I feel so much regret."

   (3) *Under the eyes:* "I regret my decision to_____."

   (4) *Under the nose:* "I wish I had made a different choice, and I regret it."

   (5) *Under the mouth:* "I made the wrong choice, and I regret it."

   (6) *Under the collar bone:* "I regret what I did to (name) so much."

   (7) *Top of the head:* "I feel so much regret over my choices."

As you go, tapping through all the rounds, you may feel the release in the form of sighs, yawns, or deep breaths. If so, continue on with step three. If not, go back and do some more rounds.

3. **Transition Statements:** Using the transition statements you listed, do several rounds of tapping using the same sequence of points.

4. **Tapping on your *ideal world of emotions* surrounding this situation:**

Do more rounds of tapping using the statements you listed of how you would *like* to feel. You should have a sense of "I'm finished" at the end.

Now take some deep breaths! When you think of this scenario, does it still bring up any of these emotions? If not, you have set yourself free! If so, repeat the process, or move to step five.

5. Follow along with the video: I've posted a free video on my website using this basic end-of-life script you can tap along with. Go to https://www.thepetconnector.com/eft-tapping

If you'd like to book a session to address your specific situation, please contact me—and keep on tapping!

Kathy Boyer, animal communicator and energy healer is a cat mom, lifelong animal lover, as well as musician, and certified vibrational sound therapist. She is a graduate of, and now a teacher for, Communication with All Life University. She has brought her dream of helping animals to life.

Using Telepathic Communication, EFT Tapping, and Scalar Wave Energy Healing, she is truly able to make a difference in the lives of both animals and their human caregivers, improving their relationships with each other in the process.

Kathy is a professional musician who lived in Japan for five years while serving in the Air Force, where she inadvertently started her own cat sanctuary, albeit an informal one. For the next 23 years, she nurtured a consistent population of 8-10 felines, primarily coming from environments of abuse or neglect.

Drawing from her experiences, she particularly loves to help animals who have had a rough start in life to heal from their early trauma. In addition, helping pet parents heal from the difficult emotions after their animal passes is near and dear to her heart, as she has said goodbye to over 17 animals in 20 years.

Her love for animals extends beyond cats. She's been a horse mom for 14 years, and if she had the space, she would bring home every dog, duck, and squirrel she sees daily at the local park.

Her mission is to help the animal kingdom feel more connected to humanity while also helping build better interpersonal relationships between animals and their humans.

Connect with Kathy:

Website: https://www.thepetconnector.com

Email: kathyh@drnetwork.com

To subscribe to her newsletter, send your request
to: kathyh@drnetwork.com

CHAPTER 6

YOUR INNER SHAMAN

TRUSTING AND ACTIVATING THE HEALER WITHIN

Rev. Evangeline Hemrick

MY STORY

Janis Joplin, Kurt Cobain, Jimi Hendrix, and Jim Morrison all died at 27. I guess I'm in good company because it looks like today is my day to die.

I turned 27 years old two weeks before my miscarriage. Thoughts of rock stars my own age dying way too soon filled my mind as I lay hemorrhaging on the cold bathroom floor. None of the doctor's staff seemed concerned that I bled through all the towels I carried into the waiting room with me, barely coherent after losing so much blood.

"Have a seat, Ma'am. We'll be with you shortly."

The nurse seemed cheerfully detached as I told her I had been bleeding for way too long since my miscarriage and couldn't stop. Anyone thinking clearly would have gone straight to the emergency room, but I made it to this office. The front desk staff was business as usual, handing out paperwork.

I think I made a mistake coming here instead of going straight to the emergency room. Is anyone going to help me?

"Go to the bathroom, Honey, and we'll get you ready for your ultrasound."

No one sensed the urgency of my situation as I calmly held onto the walls and made my way to the bathroom.

My vision went all black and white as I fell onto the bathroom floor, bleeding harder than before. I visualized my heavenly rock star line-up welcoming me to the other side.

No rock star reunion happened that day. This was not going to be my day to die after all. Actually, this was the day in 2001 when I arrived, fully present. When I fell to the floor, I had an out-of-body experience that shook me out of my complacency, programming, and conditioning once and for all. This is the story of my ultimate spiritual wake-up call.

The first thing that happened was I saw my body on the floor. It felt so strange to look down at my physical self from a higher vantage point. I zoomed out and saw anything I wanted; the entire room and medical office building were in my sight, and I could also get very close to my body and examine it. Like many others who try to explain their near-death experiences, I was shocked to see what my body actually looked like, crumpled on the floor, compared to what it felt like to be inside that physical container.

It feels good to be free of the constraints of muscles, bones, tendons, and gravity. I feel so light and expansive!

From this liberated vantage point, I saw exactly what I needed to do to repair and heal once I got back into my body. Even though it took years to make all the energetic and nutritional adjustments that were downloaded to me in an instant, I'm still amazed at how those helpful insights came flooding in so quickly. My personal healing revolution began on that bathroom floor, and it's been a wild ride ever since.

How could I have learned so many valuable lessons in a matter of minutes or seconds?

So many a-ha moments happened in what felt like a timeless vacuum. I knew the reason my baby girl chose to incarnate and why she transitioned suddenly. Her soul's mission was to wake me up, and our contract was complete. There was a new level of understanding and peace that came with this realization. This seemingly tragic situation was perfectly orchestrated to get me aligned with my soul's purpose. Perceived tragedies can catapult our spiritual growth and turn out to be our greatest healing gifts.

The next thing that happened was terrifying yet wonderful at the same time. This fierce, strange, otherworldly creature appeared in front of me and filled me with awe.

What are you? My angel? You seem feathery, but you don't really have feathers. There's so much color and light all around you, colors I've never seen before! You're like a gold thunderbird, but your face is unlike anything I've ever seen. You're not human, not animal. What kind of being are you?

My questions didn't get a response. The creature in front of me had no gender, nor was it beautiful or sweet as I supposed an angel to be. This creature had such a powerfully fierce face, like an alien, and it was sending me telepathic transmissions of clear communication. Even though I was intimidated, I felt so much love coming from this being. I knew I was safe.

It is not time for you to leave your body. You have much work to do in order to accomplish your soul purpose. You are here to raise consciousness on Planet Earth. You have to get back in your body now.

The creature talked sternly to me and told me to get back in. From that day forward, I'd never fear death again. Sometimes I even get excited at the prospect of what lies ahead when it's my turn to cross over.

The experience of the other side didn't feel like I went to a specific place at all. Heaven didn't feel like a destination. No, heaven came to me. And you want to know the coolest part of the whole thing? I knew exactly what I came to this Earth to do, without one shred of doubt. From that day forward, I've been passionate about living in alignment with my soul.

The creature asked me a final question before it disappeared.

Would you like me to sing to you now?

Yes! I love you! I answered emphatically, as this weird spirit creature full of gold, feathery light began to sing me into my body. I felt my energy swirling down into my lower extremities. Just a few weeks after turning 27, my spirit was occupying this physical body in a totally new way. Only then was I able to understand how ungrounded and disconnected I had been up to that point.

No wonder I've been so unhealthy with so much reproductive disease! I wasn't even occupying my lower chakras or organs at all.

I wasn't coming back to my body to be the old me I was before. This was a resurrected, reborn version of me, fully embodied and showing up to live as my soul. As I breathed my spirit into my body, I woke to the feel of the cold, stainless steel table underneath me. I was in another room in the medical office, being positioned with stirrups for an emergency D&C procedure.

No one knew exactly how much blood I lost until they found me unconscious in the bathroom. I have no memory of anyone finding me or taking me to another room. "There's no time for pain meds," the doctor said. A dilation and curettage procedure to scrape my uterus was the only thing that would stop the bleeding.

No time to get you to the hospital. Hold on tight! This is going to hurt like nothing you can imagine, but it's going to save your life.

The office staff canceled all appointments, explained to patients there was an emergency, and locked the office door. The doctor was right. Having your insides scraped with a knife with no pain medication is an initiation like no other; it was a necessary rite of passage for me. Somehow I knew I was exactly where I needed to be. Through this excruciating pain, I birthed the medicine woman who lived inside me all along.

Most people called to walk the spiritual path of shamanism have a near-death experience (or a dark night of the soul) where they leave their ego behind and step bravely into service for humanity. I experienced the traditional ego death of the shaman. There was no more fear, no more enslavement to conditioning. All the silly things I spent time worrying about in the past were absolutely gone, like blinders being lifted. With no more fear and uncertainty to hold me back, I found my inner shaman. You can activate your inner healer without having to experience trauma as I did. I teach people how to do this all the time.

So what does it mean to be a shaman? The oldest translation of the Siberian word *shaman* means, "The one who knows." In our modern world, we do not have a designated person to help us balance our physical, spiritual, emotional, and mental health like the tribal medicine person did for the community. Now is the time to be our own healer.

Prior to my near-death experience, I studied Cherokee spirituality in an effort to connect with my ancestry. But the rules of the old paradigm felt too heavy and rigid for me, similar to the legalistic organized religion I left behind. My heart led me to a deeper way of connecting with lineages and wisdom keepers of all the indigenous wise ones, not just some tribes.

I found cross-cultural shamanic teachers who taught me about empowerment, responsibility, effectiveness, flexibility, love, and service. Since stepping into my own power, I've been on a mission to remind people they have the power to heal their own lives.

Twenty-one years after my near-death experience, I think back on all the chronic conditions I have healed within my own body. When people ask me how I healed endometriosis, polycystic ovary syndrome, uterine fibroids, and tumors, along with chronic pain and hormonal imbalances, I can't say I did only one thing to fix all that. I used a combination of energy healing modalities to repair my chakras, entrained my energy field to ground to the earth, and worked on feeling safe in my body for two decades. Intuitive eating was a huge part of my healing process, along with learning how to live in my heart, not just operating from my logical mind. Since healing is a spiral, not a finish line, I will continue to rebuild my body and energetic field with love, patience, and acceptance.

Back in 2009, I was lying on my red shaman blanket on the ground in nature during a retreat. The soft, rhythmic drumbeat catapulted me back to that traumatic miscarriage moment on the timeline, and guess what? That fierce, otherworldly creature who sang me into my body was me all along. What I encountered in that liminal space was another version of my soul, my higher self.

A tragic experience became the most empowering moment of my life. I brought heaven to me and became my own angel. I share this story with you because I want you to know that you can recreate your experiences, turn trauma into soul medicine, and become your own hero.

Did you know your nervous system can't differentiate between a real or imagined event? You can revisit moments in your life and rewrite the script of the events that took place. This is how shamanic journeying works and why it's so effective for healing.

In shamanic journey sessions, you can reprogram your body to hold new memories, replacing trauma with energy imprints of abundance, love, and success. Meditative journeys can happen in the comfort of your own home by yourself, in a session on the phone with a practitioner, and also in a group retreat setting. You can reprogram your nervous system by changing your stories and shapeshifting your life. Using shamanic journey techniques will help you deepen your meditation practice.

Shamanism is about becoming the producer, writer, and star of your own show. The shamans of old were the first neuroscience biohackers. Shamanic healers are empowered because they take responsibility for everything they experience. Are you ready to be the medicine woman or man of your own life? Now is the time to access your own inner shaman.

Once I discovered cross-cultural, global shamanic healing, I was insatiable, eager to learn as much as I could and share that knowledge with others. Twenty-nine countries and counting, my goal in the quest to learn has never been to appropriate ancient cultures or stay stuck in the past. My heart's desire is to live as my own unique medicine and teach others to do the same. This is an expanded way of life, very different from being born into the lineage of a tribal healer. I teach healers how to harness their power, hold their intention, and create positive change through ritual.

Why do we use ritual and ceremony in shamanic practice, and how is it relevant to modern life?

Ceremony provides a container for our intentions. This intention container generates even more power when you share your intention with others, adding the power of community. This is how ceremony becomes a vehicle for effective change. When we use a ceremony, altar, or ritual objects, we give our intention somewhere to go and something to do. It's time to reclaim your power and activate the healer within. Are you ready?

THE TOOL

CREATE YOUR OWN ACT OF POWER CEREMONY

An easy way to amplify your intention and reclaim power as your own healer is to have your own ceremony. The following ceremony is called an Act of Power. Take time to think about the most important goal you would like to manifest right now. Set an intention for what you wish to create in your life at this time.

In this ceremony, you will create two shamanic power objects:

- Death Arrow for releasing and clearing
- Life Arrow for manifesting

Items you will need: one small stick, one large stick, cotton string or crochet thread, paper, and a pen.

Take a walk in the woods. Find one small stick and one large stick. The small stick should be thin enough to burn easily. The large stick should be thick enough to be placed upright in the ground.

The small stick will become your Death Arrow. You'll release anything in your life that is holding you back from achieving your goal with this power object.

Your large stick will become your Life Arrow. You will grow and manifest what you most desire with this sacred power tool.

CREATE A DEATH ARROW

The term Death Arrow simply represents letting go of blockages. On a small piece of paper, write any obstacles, habits, or limiting thoughts holding you back from achieving your goal. After you've written everything that is limiting you, secure this piece of paper around the small stick by wrapping cotton string around it, tying the string tightly. You have now created a Death Arrow. It's time to say goodbye to any blockages that have been holding you back. Burn your Death Arrow in a safe, fireproof container, such as a metal bowl, fire pit, or fireplace. As you carefully take precautions for safety, watch the arrow burn, visualizing the release of obstacles that have been keeping you from your goal. The effects of this exercise are intensified if you say aloud what you're releasing while the arrow burns.

BUILD YOUR LIFE ARROW

Now that you have cleared obstacles from your path, carefully consider what action steps are needed in order to accomplish your goal. Take some time, and write everything you're willing to do in order to turn your dream into a reality. With these written action steps, you're making a promise to yourself.

After you've written your commitments and list of action steps, carefully wrap the paper around your large stick. Secure it by wrapping the cotton thread or string around it, tying it securely. The thread you use can be multi-colored and beautiful. You can also adorn your Life Arrow with gemstones, shells, and feathers. Make your life arrow beautiful and appealing to you, but remember to use natural embellishments. You are giving your Life Arrow as a gift to Mother Earth. Make a commitment to yourself and to the Universe.

Plant your Life Arrow where you can see it often to be reminded of your goal. As you impregnate the Earth with your hopes and dreams, say aloud, "This is my act of power. I now create _____." While placing your stick in the ground, speak your goal as if it were your current reality.

Never underestimate the power of a ritual for one. You can still have a very powerful ceremony even if no one else does this exercise with you. Sometimes it's hard to say our hopes and dreams aloud (even if we're alone), but there is much creative potential in the vibration of our voice.

This ceremony is one suggestion to get you started. Make it your own. Be creative and playful with this tool. There's no wrong way to do a ritual for manifesting and amplifying intention if you put your heart into it. Simply gather a group of trusted friends, and discuss what you want to create and how you want your world to be. It can be as simple as that! All you need is a focused mind and a loving heart to create positive change through a ceremony. Want to learn more principles of modern shamanism that are easy to incorporate into daily life? I'd love to teach you in my foundational shamanism course called Expanding Sacred.

Evangeline Hemrick is a healer, teacher, storyteller, podcaster, death doula, and holistic practitioner. She's been a Reiki Master and Huna Master/teacher since 2003. Throughout Evangeline's 26-year career as an energy healing practitioner, licensed massage and bodywork therapist, licensed esthetician, and intuitive wellness coach, she has traveled the world in search of effective healing methods.

Evangeline became a non-denominational ordained minister in 2008. She founded Evangeline Hemrick Ministries, her own non-profit organization for healers, in 2021. Her professional background as a massage teacher and owner of Elements Day Spa, combined with extensive training in indigenous traditions, influences her teaching and writing. She offers four online courses: a foundational course in modern shamanism, a certification program in energy healing modalities, a death doula certification program, and a minister ordination/priestess apprenticeship.

She hosts and produces The Next Level Healer Podcast. Her first book, True Calling, is a #1 best seller in the massage and holistic healing category on Amazon. True Calling-The Successful Hands-On Healer is a career guidebook and self-care resource for holistic practitioners who want to take their healing businesses to the next level.

Evangeline lives in North Carolina with her husband, son, and their dog Kona where she offers remote healing sessions, intuitive coaching, shamanic ceremonies, and virtual classes. When Evangeline isn't teaching, writing, or working with clients, you can find her playing in her flower garden, making flower essences, or dancing with fire.

Connect with Evangeline:

Website: https://evangelinehemrick.com

Email: evangelinehemrick@gmail.com

Facebook: https://www.facebook.com/evangeline.hemrick

Instagram: https://www.instagram.com/evangelinehemrick/?hl=en

YouTube: https://www.youtube.com/c/EvangelineHemrick

LinkedIn: https://www.linkedin.com/in/evangelinehemrick/

CHAPTER 7

BEING SEEN

LIGHT UP THE HEART OF WHO YOU ARE

Sandra Lee, BS, LMT

"You say surprising or shocking things."

"Uh, yeah." Vera hesitates, a bit uncomfortable.

"Do you want to hear more?"

Intrigued and curious, "Sure, I think so," she says with a tiny self-conscious laugh.

Considering this is a casual coffee shop meeting with a networking acquaintance, it's notable that our interaction takes a knife-straight dive deep into the pool.

"When you were young, you probably got a kick out of shocking people."

"Hah! Yeah, I'm good at that."

"You wield words like a subtle knife, shocking people into taking action. Vera, you're a transformation agent, nudging stuck people out of their comfort zones."

There's that familiar full-body shiver, with the bubbling lift in my heart and welling tears.

Vera and I are deeply connected, sharing this heart space of truth.

The energy is deliciously electric. I call this state "Shine."

With Human Design, I access details that wouldn't normally come up in conversation, and Vera experiences a revelatory flash of self-understanding.

In a few minutes, we go from casual surface conversation to being deeply related, oblivious to the surrounding chatter and milk frothing.

Vera shared a predicament she'd faced in a photo shoot.

"I wonder how that shows up in your Human Design chart. Want to see what the planets say?" And we're off to the races.

This discussion is the seed that grows into a cherished friendship.

Vera profoundly experiences being seen. She shines.

MY STORY

"Your soul requires seeing. But it cannot be truly seen until you are willing to be vulnerable."

~ Lebo Grand

I live for such moments of vibrant aliveness and shine. They add satisfaction and satiety to my existence.

And the journey's taken decades.

Ugh, none of them sees me.

The typical awkward wallflower, I'm painfully aware of being excluded from every group.

Smile this way, dress like her, do that. But it's all just a masquerade ball mask.

My fervent wish for connection and depth plays on repeat. *I want conversations that mean something!*

Beneath my sense of failure sulks, *I hate myself.*

Following high school, my mother's expectations require college. Instead of selecting a university for educational and career opportunities, desperation drives my decision. *Nobody knows me at Caltech, and I can become a completely different person.*

However, Caltech doesn't teach me how to escape myself, loneliness or longing.

So college releases me into the world, chemistry degree in hand.

MY HEALING

For the first time, what to do is 100% up to me.

Stumbling into personal development and healing work, I discover a path to freedom.

I'm bad, and I hurt people. Ouch! That hits a nerve.

This is at the bottom of everything I do and say. Finally, acknowledging what I've buried is a relief.

That weekend at Landmark Education, I grew up and took responsibility for steering my life.

Shit. How often have I allowed my inner six-year-old to flip the circuit breakers controlling my decisions? No more! It's time to take charge.

Navigating the storm of fears and mental chatter that used to overcome me is an odyssey punctuated by tears and triumphs.

Previously a normal massage therapist, with budding awareness, I now develop intuitive abilities enhanced by my chemistry background. *Chuckle. Caltech was the right college, after all.*

Bridging the worlds of science and esoteric awareness, I help my clients visualize what's going on in their bodies. They actively engage in healing physically, mentally, emotionally, and spiritually.

I'm poised to transform my belief in myself and my skepticism about energy healing.

The old mental conversation plays as I write an email to a friend, Jane, about an energy healing modality I've been doing, The Healing Codes.

I'm bad, and I hurt people.
That's not true.
What? Is my mind talking back to me now?

Stunned, I test this bizarre debate.

I'm bad, and I hurt people.
That's not true.
I'm bad, and I hurt people.
After a couple of rounds of this, my mind insists, laughing, *Give it up. It's not true.*

Wow. This energy healing stuff works!

A mountain of self-punishment and negative programming has plagued me for as long as I can remember. Today I realize years of agonizing therapy, personal development, and now The Healing Codes have uprooted rocks and pulled them away from the foundation.

The edifice is crumbling. Finally liberated from imprisonment, glints of freedom shine through the cracks.

I am here.

My intuitive receptivity and accuracy blossom when I discover Biofield Tuning, a modality of healing with tuning forks. I receive words, visions, and emotional states for my clients. I feel temperature changes, tingling, and itchiness. Empathically recalling someone's early life pressures suppresses my breathing like an elephant crushing my chest.

Here's how I describe the way I serve.

Your soul has things it wants you to know, but you're too close to see them. So your soul sends messages to you through me. I serve as your courier.

A radiant beam arcs out of Tamara's heart and lands upon her son, gently caressing and enfolding him, then settling in like rainwater seeping in to awaken the soil. Astonished, I see another beam arise from her chest and bridge over the distance to support and encourage her struggling client. Streams of light fountain from her chest, each nourishing, encouraging, and supporting a cherished companion.

Honored to witness these gifts of love, wonder bubbles within my own chest.

"I see beams of love rising from your heart and going to your children, clients, and other people. You support them with your love."

Matter of factly, Tamara responds. "Yes, I do that. Every day I send people love from my heart."

This is the first time I perceived how people energetically contribute their purpose to the world.

For Tamara, supporting people with bundles of love is routine. My recognition of this generosity rings with rippling waves of truth.

Being witnessed in this expression of her purpose confirms Tamara's inner knowing, bringing conscious recognition to it. With a peaceful, smiling sigh, she settles more deeply into the massage table.

In this momentary blaze of connection, we mutually experience being seen and accepted.

Tamara is glowing. And my heart lifts, my breath catches, and my body both shivers and sweats.

This is shine.

Take a moment to imagine two encounters.

I walk down the sidewalk past my neighbor's yard, seeing the roses that always bloom in June. I pause to wave at Martha and appreciate the flowers, then walk on.

Standing on one foot, I pull on one shoe, then the other, and grab the keys. *Yesterday Martha's rosebuds were practically bursting. They're probably in full bloom.* Stepping onto the porch, I see Martha by the fence. Audibly inhaling, I savor the sweetness. "Oh, they are full and lovely, Martha! Look at that red burst of sunshine. I so wanted to admire the roses with you."

There is a world of difference between these episodes. One is a casual thought-less experience of an event. The other is intentional, thoughtful participation within that shared event. Seeing Martha's roses could be either routine or the highlight of both my day and hers.

Here's the point. Focusing thoughts, emotions, and intentions on any experience enhances it.

Most people feel blah about daily existence, unconscious of making a significant contribution.

Your Human Design chart describes your life purpose. With this understanding, you can amplify your experiences by focusing on them through the lens of your purpose.

Armed with knowledge about the strengths in your chart, you start each day expecting to contribute your purpose through the day's activities, large and small.

You are intentional.

In Human Design, I'm a Manifestor Type and designed to initiate. For years, I was confused about initiating. Then suddenly, I got it.

"Hey, guys. Why don't we get together?" I offer a suggestion, and a few weeks later, we get together for a practice session and lunch. That gathering wouldn't have occurred otherwise. *Wow, initiating is powerful.*

Before this a-ha, I believed my actions didn't matter. Now I'm conscious of being a cue ball and initiating flows naturally within casual conversations. And I see resulting waves of impact upon people's thoughts, beliefs, and actions. Other times I identify situations that need to change, and I thoughtfully plan and start transformative conversations.

By consciously accepting this initiating role, I serve people and live my purpose. Focusing thoughts, emotions, and intentions on providing benefit amplifies the impact.

This magnetizes to me additional opportunities to serve.

I am powerful and have a beneficial impact on people and the world. Awareness of my purpose enables me to be intentional and energetically supports my results. Life is so much more purposeful and satisfying. Compared with my early life, I'm unrecognizable.

From this place of awareness and responsibility, I shine.

Human Design and Biofield Tuning complement each other in my work.

I deeply connect with clients and bring to conscious awareness what's physically and energetically at the heart of their issues. Seemingly unrelated elements pull together to make sense of both their decisions and stuck places.

Many of my clients say, "Human Design makes sense of my entire life!" And they love Biofield Tuning. Something about how I combine these modalities is magical.

"Amy, you just know things and gather all kinds of information. Then you feel pressure to understand it and to explain it to other people."

Until I pulled this from her Human Design chart, Amy hadn't thought to mention the long hours she studied in medical school. "Why did I need to study while my friends partied? But I really wanted to be a doctor, so I studied at home every night."

Amy's extra efforts in understanding make her extraordinary at explaining.

She has many disadvantaged patients who appreciate her special skills.

Human Design helps Amy recognize this irritating personal oddity as central to her blueprint. Perspective adjusted, now she consciously relies upon this strength when serving her patients.

Next, we do Biofield Tuning, "I see you conveying information to people, from your head, through your heart. And your chart shows this."

With the tuning forks, we integrate all of these elements cohesively within her field. Amy's awareness, life circumstances, and Human Design are in alignment.

You want to be seen, and I want to be seen.

We need each other.

I live to share experiences of vibrant connection and aliveness. Shine.

A baby leaves the safety of the womb, and *bam,* the shock of separation hits. Instinctively, she feels compelled to establish stable connections to survive. This is a universal human experience.

A 2018 US Loneliness Index* found that 46 percent of Americans report feeling lonely sometimes or always. The questionnaire measured subjective feelings of loneliness and social isolation.

I write this in 2022, years into an era of profound trauma and isolation that will scar human memory forever.

We need antidotes to isolation now more than ever.

We need each other.

Connection is healing.

Being seen is healing.

Each of us perceives the other more clearly than we can see ourselves.

When we come together in that place, we shine.

Create shine experiences every day by setting an intention to do so. Transform your life, the lives of those around you, and your work.

Intend to connect. Intend to see others and to be seen.

Make this a feature of your approach to every day.

You will attract wonderful relationships, satisfaction, and opportunities.

THE TOOL

Let's explore how you can create shine experiences.

Grab a notebook and pen, a glass of water, and a comfortable, peaceful space.

Set out to gather pearls from within the realms of your mind. In response to your earnest questions, your guidance system willingly offers jewels of wisdom. Cherish these treasures.

As with all endeavors, the intentionality and effort you give this exercise determine the depth of your results.

Here's a personal revelation. When faced with questions like these, I squirm. *I don't have an answer. Get me out of here.* Not allowing myself to dream, I quit, dropping the exercise forever. Stopped by fear of the ugliness that might rear up, I avoid inquiries that threaten to break through my pretense of confidence. *I can't have what I want anyway. So why bother.*

Those limiting beliefs no longer control me.

Take this opportunity to witness, receive, and love yourself!

When you desire to be seen and loved, it's *your* eyes that matter most. It's seeing yourself that matters most. Connecting with yourself is important.

If painful or challenging emotions emerge, pause and breathe. Reclaiming your power from discomforts makes freedom possible.

Be understanding with yourself. Healing takes time.

Open your mind to possibilities. If even one question leads you to increased freedom, the process has been worthwhile.

Fortunately, you're just reading a book, and only you will see your responses. Create a safe space with yourself for witnessing and vulnerability.

Get comfortable and call in your conscious and subconscious minds. Call in your higher self.

"May I gather information contributing to my well-being, happiness, and success."

Question #1: Rate your experiences from 0 = Never to 10 = Always.

Take whatever number pops to mind, rather than thinking about the answers.

Record any thoughts and emotions that bubble up associated with the statements.

_____ I love myself.

_____ I am comfortable and happy with the way I am.

_____ I feel like people see the real me.

_____ I know how I feel.

_____ I know what I want.

_____ I can ask for what I want.

_____ I have the freedom to be myself in my relationships.

_____ I have the freedom to be myself at work and in my business.

Question #2: Consider your qualities, strengths, and skills. Think about what matters to you.

Make lists for each statement:

- I value and appreciate myself and the following aspects of who I am that I do express within my relationships.

- I value and appreciate myself and the following aspects of who I am that I do express within my work.

- I value and appreciate myself and the following aspects of who I am that I want to express more within my relationships and my work.

Question #3: What can I do to create shine experiences in my daily life, relationships, and work?

Imagine the customers and the abundance this will attract to your business! Visualize it happening now.

Breathe. What do you notice?

Thank you for engaging in this inquiry.

You make a difference every day through your relationships and your work.

Now go out there and shine.

IN CONCLUSION

Thank you so much for spending this time with me. I hope it's been rewarding.

Consider how these aspects of being seen show up in your life and business.

* ★ Feeling connected and being seen are fundamental human needs.
* ★ When you experience feeling connected and being seen, you enter a vibrant, energetic, and emotional state of aliveness and freedom I call "Shine."
* ★ Purposefully creating interactions with shine in your relationships transforms both you and others.
* ★ Every day, be consciously aware of living from the heart of who you are.
* ★ Approaching life and business in this way attracts customers and miracles.

How would living with this perspective make a difference in your world?

I look forward to helping you fulfill your life purpose and create experiences of shine, connectedness, and being seen.

I'd love to get to know you. Let's have a conversation about what is meaningful for you and your business. We can explore how we might benefit from working together.

The unique combination of tools I use to assist you is tuning fork sounds in Biofield Tuning and the wisdom of the planets through your Human Design chart.

My intuitive insights help you discover clarity and strengthen your alignment with the heart and integrity of your purpose.

Please go to my website to schedule a Discovery Call and pull your Human Design chart.

Would you like some gifts?

Making decisions wisely is so important! Are you consistently satisfied with your choices? Or do you feel confused and frustrated?

For some clarity, see your first gift, the *Making Powerful, and Effective Decisions Checklist.*

Then experience Biofield Tuning with a *Biofield Tuning Audio for Stress Release.*

Please visit my website: https://MiracleInspirations.com/book-a-call

Awaken the Heart of Your Business!

Breathe.

With love,

Sandra

*https://www.multivu.com/players/English/8294451-cigna-us-loneliness-survey/

Sandra Lee, BS, LMT, is the owner of Miracle Inspirations. She has over 30 years of experience in intuitive energetic work and massage. As a Human Design Specialist and Biofield Tuning Practitioner, she is uniquely qualified to support you in turning your dreams into successes.

You are not an island. Your soul has messages for you. But you're too close to yourself to see them.

Sandra would be honored to receive guidance for you. She loves helping you align with the heart and integrity of your purpose and attract your perfect opportunities.

Sandra's healing journey began with a BS in chemistry from Caltech, a top science and engineering university. Like a medical intuitive, she helps you visualize the "science" of your body. She produces seemingly "miraculous" results.

Sandra is a blogger and best-selling contributing author to Stop Overworking and Start Overflowing: 25 Ways to Transform Your Life Using Human Design, and Abundance By Design: Discover Your Unique Code for Health, Wealth and Happiness with Human Design.

Living in the beautiful Okanagan Valley of British Columbia, Canada, with her husband, Sandra enjoys visiting friends in Washington State. She shares pictures of whole food cooking that inspire her Facebook friends.

Connect with Sandra:

Website: https://MiracleInspirations.com/book-a-call

Facebook: https://www.facebook.com/SandraLeeInspiration

Please visit her website:

- Gifts await you!
  - Do you struggle with decision-making? Read the Making Powerful and Effective Decisions Checklist.
  - For stress relief, listen to Biofield Tuning Mini Audio for Stress Release.

- Request a complimentary discovery call. Sandra loves hearing about your desires, then exploring how your business would benefit from Human Design and the Biofield Tuning.
- Request free Human Design charts.
- Watch weekly video blogs.
- And more!

Awaken the Heart of Your Business.

Live your truth, my friend. Shine!

Breathe,

Sandra

CHAPTER 8

MY JOURNEY TO ME

LEARNING TO TRUST MY ANGELS AND INTUITION

Carolyn McGee,
The Decision Queen, Sacred Haven Living Expert

MY STORY

I finally said, "The common denominator in all these unhealthy relationships is me, and I want to change."

I was heartbroken and frustrated! My boyfriend was not treating me respectfully; he was inconsistent and not making time for me. He expected more from me than he gave. I thought I had healed this pattern and that this time was different. I swore I wasn't dating again until I figured out why this kept happening. *I'd rather be alone instead of dealing with everyone else's dysfunction* became my mantra.

In the years since my divorce, I took classes, went to counseling, and read books on how to attract a healthy relationship. I made lists of what I wanted in a relationship and what I didn't want. Looking at my contribution and the energy that I brought to the relationships never made the list.

After ending that relationship, a friend connected me with an angelic healing circle. Angel energy was created by God to provide messages to humans in a way that we can understand. We, as humans, all have free will, so we can choose to ask for angelic support and guidance in following our soul's journey. We can also choose not to ask and/or not to receive the messages, therefore making our lives more difficult than needed.

I began classes to learn more about angel energy and my intuition but wasn't convinced it was real.

At the beginning of the journey with my angel team, I continued my pattern of doing it alone, not accepting support, and believing I wasn't good enough to be loved unconditionally. I constantly tested my angelic support team.

I demanded, *Show me heart shapes so I know I am loved.* When my angelic team showed me heart shapes in the sky, plants, earth, and in my home I still didn't fully believe. So, I said, *Okay, that could be a coincidence; show me heart-shaped rocks that I can take with me, so I know I am loved unconditionally.* Angels have a sense of humor and do love unconditionally, so I have a collection of 100s of heart-shaped rocks in my home.

As a kid, I loved watching the clouds shift into shapes and imagining the messages from each image. When I started my angel classes, I owned a dog walking company, so while walking a dog, I said: "If angels are real, I want to see an angel in the clouds." As I walked around the corner, the most dazzling and clear angel showed herself to me in wispy white clouds. Her wings were defined and spread out. Her face was beautiful and peaceful. I felt the love radiating out to me from her heart to mine. *You are real! I am sorry I doubted you. I am grateful for your support*—this moment of asking and receiving cracked my wounded heart to start healing.

As I continued remembering how to receive my divine messages, feel them in my body so that I trusted the information, and then took inspired action, my fear sometimes arose.

My strongest senses at that point in time were claircognizance (the gut instinct and knowingness) and clairsentience (our feeling sense). I basically sensed my way through situations, almost as if I was sending out invisible feelers or antenna to help me navigate the world.

As I took my first Angel Communication class to help me understand my intuitive senses and strengthen my skills, I became a bit defensive about how I was connecting. I felt like I wasn't getting it. Our teacher wanted us to isolate our senses to really focus on one sense each week to practice and strengthen that sense. I felt out of control.

The first week was clairvoyance, messages that we see. I was so afraid about what I might see that I did the homework using my feelings and my knowingness. When I woke up the next day, I couldn't sense anything, and my knowingness was also shut off.

I felt like part of me had died, or I had lost a limb. In many ways, I had—I developed a reliance on those two senses without any awareness of the other information available to me.

When I reached out to my teacher, she said, "You are so loved that your angels went to extremes to get your attention." She laughed and added, "Carolyn, trust yourself and trust your angels. Take baby steps and start to notice what you see."

Trust wasn't a word in my vocabulary, so this was easier said than done. I was hurt so many times by friends, family, and myself that I didn't know if I would be safe with this new way of engaging in life.

As the week went on, I noticed images, shapes, and numbers, and I intuitively knew what the message was for me. I started to look for new messages and have fun.

The next week I focused on clairaudience (messages we hear) and noticed song lyrics, paid attention to words spoken around me and even heard a voice that wasn't mine in my head. Emergency sirens brought a message, and my dog barking at certain times had meaning.

In the weeks when the rest of my classmates focused on feeling and knowing, I deeply sharpened my seeing and hearing senses. I gained confidence and started to have fun with the different ways I now received information.

As we entered the last week of class, I started to worry that I'd never be able to sense things again and that my knowingness was gone forever.

During the final class, I said to my peers and teacher, "I am so grateful that I am really seeing things, that my intuition has magnified exponentially, and I am clearly able to hear Divine messages."

Suddenly, I could know and sense again, and *I knew I had four strong senses I could rely on instead of two.*

It became clear that we can slow down the flow of information if we focus too much on one outcome or way of communicating. Yet I still wasn't clear on understanding how I was blocking healthy relationships in all areas of my life. Thank God for my angels and their patient guidance and support.

When I took my master's level angel communication class, we were asked to light a candle, meditate, and journal with a specific archangel each of the seven weeks. The first week was Archangel Michael and a red candle for the root chakra.

Since I still had trust issues and didn't believe I'd be supported, I decided that my root chakra was fine and that I didn't need to follow the rules and meditate with the red candle each day. *I can do it myself* stepped forward to sabotage my connection.

The next day, when I came down to meditate in this closed room, where no one had access but me, the red candle was gone. *Where is it? Where did you hide it? This is not funny!* I searched everywhere for that candle. The holder was there, but the candle disappeared.

I finally accepted that Archangel Michael was teaching me a lesson. He wanted me to firmly understand that I don't need to be alone. I can accept support. It's safe for me to connect and trust my angel guidance—that no matter how grounded I feel I am, I can always connect deeper.

I spent the rest of the week working with Archangel Michael without a candle and felt his loving presence and support. Releasing resentment over the way the message was delivered was healing. The next week, I moved on to the orange candle and the next archangel and worked my way through the balance of the class with gratitude and a much deeper understanding of my connection with the angels. I felt supported, loved, and seen.

Working with that divine energy, God's messengers, I learned to love and trust myself. I remembered that I am a divine being and highly intuitive. Feeling supported, loved, and seen gave me the courage to open my heart even more. I began to forgive myself for the choices I made and forgive others who had hurt me. This returned my energy to me, and my ability to draw in healthier relationships expanded.

It took two more years of deep spiritual development work to fully realize that I was the center of my relationship challenges and why I hadn't manifested my dreams. It wasn't the romantic partners, family, friends, clients, doctors, etc.; it was me.

Seeing the link between my emotions and how I showed up - or didn't gave me the power to trust myself to make choices and connect deeply. Not having that energy of resistance and releasing the resentment, anger, and judgment released the chains on my heart. Accepting my choices, stepping into the responsibility of making decisions, and taking accountability for my actions and inactions was freeing.

Understanding the patterns and themes in all my relationships was empowering. Seeing that my ebb and flow relationship with money was the same as my push/pull pattern with clients, employees, and friends, started the shift into powerful connections, ease, and abundance. My health started to improve as my energy stabilized.

As I shifted my expectations—once I understood that I was the common factor—I started asking: *What can I change within myself?* Instead of: *Why is this happening to me?*

Utilizing everyday situations as opportunities, I started recognizing roadblocks in my life and transforming them into healing moments and healthy relationships. This empowered me to transform any obstacle and manifest the success, love, and happiness I desired and deserved.

One of the biggest gifts of living into the awareness of *"how I show up in one place is how I show everywhere"* was the creation of Sacred Haven Living.

Sacred Haven Living manifested into my life as I trusted my angels, intuition, and myself to move from Massachusetts to North Carolina during the pandemic. Knowing that my divine messages were true, that my life would change for the good when I followed the guidance to move to North Carolina, and my belief that the angels and God always have my back gave me the trust to follow my dream even when it didn't make sense.

Sacred Haven Living is living in and through your heart-space, being centered, peaceful, and joy-filled. It's breaking lifelong patterns of how you show up in life to understand the relationship to yourself, others, health, money, and spirit.

My tool is the first step in awareness of the energy that surrounds us and the messages and healing we can receive from this awareness of energy.

THE TOOL

This exercise is about increasing awareness of your environment and the world that you live in. In each moment, it gives you information, feedback, and guidance to enhance your life.

Using the clairsenses I talked about in the story: Notice what you see (clairvoyance), what you hear (clairaudience), what you sense (clairsentience), and what you know (claircognizance).

I invite you to settle into a comfortable place.

Have your journal close by to write your observations in.

STEP ONE:

Sit with your back upright on your favorite chair, the floor, in your garden or yard, or wherever it's comfortable for you.

Take three deep breaths in through your nose and out through your mouth.

Become and feel centered, noticing that there is an energy in your heart because your heart is the center of the center of the center of it all.

Imagine that there is a pillar of white light that goes from your heart (heart chakra) and extends up through your body, past your neck (throat chakra), your forehead (third eye chakra), out the top of your head (crown chakra) and goes into your own personal star.

This star is the source of inspiration, intuition, and divine masculine energy.

Connect into that and feel comforted.

Then bring your awareness back to your heart and allow that pillar of light to move from your heart (heart chakra) into your belly (solar plexus chakra), past your belly button (sacral chakra) into your hips and legs (root chakra) and out of your body into the center of the Earth.

This is the divine feminine energy, the source of creativity, centering, and grounding.

Now you're centered and completely connected in the energy of creation and the energy of inspiration.

Just breathe that in for a moment and revel in it.

STEP TWO:

Open your eyes and allow your senses to expand around you to see what catches your attention—what seems more significant.

1) Maybe there's a color that really jumps out at you.

2) Or there's an object that you notice.

3) Perhaps there's a sound that captures your attention.

4) It might be you know that you're supposed to look at something.

5) Or you feel the sensation on your skin of I must pay attention to this.

Whatever it is, just pay attention to it and write it down in your journal.

Then ask: What's the message for me?

STEP THREE:

Use your intuitive vocabulary to decode the message for you.

Intuitive vocabulary is our gift of interpreting messages from the Divine in our own unique way. For example, yellow roses for me always signify romantic love, long-term love, and not easy love.

My dad gave my mom yellow roses on their first date; he gave them every significant anniversary after. They had a long-term marriage that they really worked at. It was not easy, so that's the energy of a yellow rose for me.

It's not the same energy for everybody else. If you look up the energy of yellow roses in a traditional flower book, it's all about friendship, but that's not what it means to me.

Your angels and guides will use personal experiences to help you interpret energy.

An example of how the message can be twofold is:

1) I will see a flowing river and be reminded of my childhood, how safe it was, and how fun it was. I loved living at my grandparents' house for the summer and playing by the river. My imagination flowed.

2) Other times I'll see a flowing river and remember the time I almost drowned in that same river. It signifies danger.

These are very different energies from the same imagery. I get to filter what I need to know for myself and my clients at each moment.

STEP FOUR:

Write your notes in your journal on what your intuitive vocabulary/angels/intuition shared with you.

Write freely and joyfully with no filter. Do not read what you are writing—just allow the words to flow.

Have fun playing with this exercise and repeat it as many times as it feels right to you.

You may see/hear/sense/know the same thing at a deeper level or something new,

Look at it with curiosity.

Being in gratitude and acknowledgment of the gift that you receive each time you experience this awareness will open the portal to your intuition and divine connection deeper.

I would love to hear your experiences with your journey and answer any questions you might have. You can email me at carolyn@carolynmcgee.com or connect through social media.

I also have a recording of this journey on my website to help you go deeper. You can find it at https://www.CarolynMcGee.com/resources.

If after reading my chapter and tool you are curious about how you can connect deeper to your angels, divine guidance and intuition, and trust it to take action without second guessing, I invite you to find a time to chat with me.

https://CarolynMcGee.as.me/Inner-Wisdom-Clarity-Activation

Carolyn McGee created of the Sacred Haven for Empowered and Intuitive Living Community, which includes virtual gatherings and retreats, powerful workshops, private coaching, and soul-nurturing VIP weekends. She serves women ready to connect with their inner wisdom, trust it to make empowered decisions, then take inspired action and discover the power of nature's cycles to create a life that lights them up.

Carolyn specializes in amplifying *your* intuitive superpower to listen to, trust, and follow your soul's path to living the most joyful, healthy, connected, abundant, and purposeful life. She has taught thousands of women to trust themselves and their intuition so they can show up in their full power in business and life.

Carolyn is gifted in finding the patterns in relationship to yourself, others, spirit, and money that block ease, flow, and joy and then guiding you to release them.

By showing you the way back to your intuition, she helps you enhance your ability to receive messages and understand your guidance 24/7. This empowers you to take inspired action so that you release second-guessing for good, and you feel 100% confident in making crystal clear decisions.

With a background of 20-plus years in high tech, Carolyn knows firsthand the importance of living from a blend of her masculine and feminine energies.

Carolyn, lead author for the #1 bestselling book, *Inspired Living: Superpowers for Health, Love, and Business,* has also co-authored over ten bestselling books and is a popular radio and TV host, sought-after speaker, and blogger.

To learn more about Carolyn or to contact her, visit https://www.CarolynMcGee.com.

You can join her Inspired Living Community: https://www.facebook.com/groups/inspiredlivingsuperpowerscommunity

Find out about her latest workshops: https://carolynmcgee.com/workshops/

Like her Facebook page: https://www.facebook.com/CarolynMcgeeIntuitiveCoach/

Experience tools from other books and classes: https://www.CarolynMcGee.com/resources

CHAPTER 9

ENERGETIC SELF-MASTERY

TAMING YOUR WILD ENERGETIC SELF

Constance Koch, Animal Communication and Energy Healing

May all beings be happy
May all beings be healthy
May all beings be safe
May all beings be at ease

MY STORY

Presence itself is a sacred moment.

We're moving into a new time; being a lone wolf is not beneficial any longer. It's time to create collaborative healing fields. It's not just happiness we long for, it's purpose and a compelling desire to live for something beyond ourselves. Animal communication and energy tools create healing that ripples out instantly into the collective. When one heals, all begin to heal. Healing is contagious in the quantum field.

I want to share my story of embodiment and the therapeutic power of presence through the art of animal communication. This direct communication is done using telepathy, which is the use of words, pictures, and feelings.

Max, the cat, is the animal that had me commit to learning Animal Communication. I always felt I could help him in deeper ways. I never chose my own animals; instead, I always accepted strays or other animals needing a home or care. Max was my mother's cat. When I visited from out of town, Max always seemed to have an issue that nobody else noticed. Somehow he knew I was sensitive to his needs. Soon as I walked in the door, he'd come by me and eliminate on newspapers or in baskets. He looked right at me and cried. Emergency ER visits found that he had urinary cystitis again. We took care of it immediately. I was honored to know that he knew who he could count on.

When Mother passed, I inherited Max. By then, he was deaf with multiple ailments. The doctors found tumors on his throat and ears. We had a good three years before things got really rough. I had started animal communication, and we could already read each other's minds, so it was the energy tools of acupressure and scalar wave that soothed both of us at the most painful times. It brought some peace until Max looked at me the way he did, and I knew it was time. It was such peace to know exactly when he was ready. I owe that peace to being fully present in my body to sense what Max was saying.

I have always had an animal, a spiritual animal, or nature by my side. That is where I feel best; my energy relaxes and grounds. I prefer one-on-one interaction. Add even one more person, and I lose my ground; my energy can begin to fly. That is what is so dynamic about animal communication; you ground and become neutral by consciously moving aside your own issues. Nothing else matters at the moment but that animal. You become the facilitator, the conduit, through deep listening for the human and then the animal. You're the bridge. Healing often happens just by the animal being seen, heard, and understood. Then that shifts the energy of the person and living situation.

As fate goes, I found Joan Ranquet and her school, Communication With All Life University. Joan's presence is full of grounded peaceful strength; her energy is like a beautiful white pillar of strong, radiant light from Earth to Heaven. She says, "Shift a mindset of defeat into resiliency with detached compassion." Detached compassion is becoming a neutral witness, not engaging in any unhealthy physical or emotional experience of the situation. It's support from a place of stability and empowerment.

I love all animals with their essence of innocence. I cringe witnessing abuse of any kind, animal or human. Helplessness leaves me numb. Compassion fatigue sets in; I withdraw.

For my third act of life, I've finally uncovered my gold treasure. I have met my purpose. I'm aware that my sensitivities are actually my highest gift. My wildly-firing energy self has been tamed to be grounded, relaxed, centered, clear, and receptive. My heart is still wild, but I've learned to bring my energy down to hold sacred space for others. It wasn't always that way.

EYE-TO-EYE EPIPHANIES

Below are a few extraordinary connections with the more-than-human world. These are early nature connections I held dear to my heart and saved as the magnificence and wonders life gives us. These always set my heart a-flutter. I didn't realize they were signs of my purpose for the greater good. Before, I thought these experiences grounded me; now, I know I have these experiences regularly if I'm grounded.

I was in a cabin on a private Canadian island; I thought I heard my friend outside. I came down the stairs, turned, and was eye-to-eye with a moose. It turns out it was a friend, just not the friend I thought. Here I am with a moose. There was no panic, just a loss of words. Looking deep into those eyes, time stood still as we stared into each other's souls. There was curiosity, peace, and joy in that eye-to-eye epiphany. It happens regularly if you're open and aware; other beings come and connect. Animals feel the good clear energy.

While on a boat tour on the Inlet Passage of Alaska, up out of the water, a humpback whale breached and rolled. We were so close that our eyes met; my breath was taken away. Awe-struck! *Look, oh my goodness, there is an infant too.* The ecstatic joy; what amazing beautiful beings! At that moment, the world was full of wonder. Ironically, no one else on the boat saw it.

In Chicago, I frequently would go to commune with the zoo animals. No matter how you feel about zoos, they exist now, and I fully support the health and welfare of these animals. A perpetual learner, I participated in a gorilla research class. For a week, I hung out and observed the gorillas, documenting their behaviors into categories. I came back the next week to visit without a clipboard, and hand-held electronic data device. Sitting on the floor, up close to the enclosure, I could spend an hour at a time quietly watching their grace. I knew not to meet their eyes directly; that can be a challenge in gorilla language. With my head bowed and eyes lowered, a large silverback knuckle-walked directly toward me. He sat, with only the plate glass window dividing us. Slowly, he raised and pointed his fingers gently toward my forehead on the glass. It felt like a direct transmission to my third eye. Reverence, awe, and wonder filled every cell of my being. We are all kin and here to guide one another to the new way of peace and understanding on Earth.

BRING YOUR ENERGY DOWN

Decades later, I'm in an open, flat-topped jeep in Timbavati, South Africa, at the Global White Lions Protection Trust. It was a trip of a lifetime to a sacred site with Joan Ranquet and friends from the Communication With All Life University. We were rolling slowly along the dirt path, looking for the special trinity of white lions. Our patience was waning as we had been circling for what felt like hours. Edgar whispered, "Look!" We saw them far away in the brush and moving toward us. They sat a distance off, grooming and being their regal, sacred selves. The thrill of being in their white, luminous presence is one of the most ecstatic experiences I've ever had. Being in their Christo's presence is truly a mystic self-transcendence; the lions radiate pure unconditional love.

Unexpectedly, in the distance, we heard "Roarr. Roooarr. Rooaarrr" from wild lions in a very near preserve. Our lions responded back with deep and resonating territorial roars. The lions quickly stood up, and all three lions began moving swiftly in our direction, coming straight for us. Their rippling big cat muscles were intimidatingly beautiful and known to be four times stronger than a human's. In a panic, Rachel, who was sitting next to me, leaped up, standing tall, almost climbing over into the seat in front of us to get away. Jumping up with desperate energy is the worst thing you can do in front of a predator. The feeling in the air was electric, trembling, and full of scared anticipation.

I moved my hands around Rachel's waist and gently pulled her back down, whispering, "Bring your energy down!"

As soon as Rachel sat, all energy grounded, bottomed out, and settled; everything went quiet and completely still. Like after a storm, a calm filled the air as the lions continued to move gracefully, powerfully, into their signature triangle. They surrounded our Jeep in a protective mode, one stationed on the front, one on the side, and the last in the back left. There was a supreme satisfaction when we realized the white lions were allowing us into their circle. The feeling was calm, content, and communing with our pride. All it took was being aware of the energy—grounded and calm energy ripples out through the field.

Finally, this experience with the white lions showed me I did have a grounded presence. I helped ground Rachel. Through all the years of energy exploration and personal development, I'm embodied! I control my anxiety and master my energy by fully inhabiting my therapeutic presence. All the years of work paid off; it's given me the confidence to help others and save lives.

THERAPEUTIC PRESENCE

A therapeutic presence allows you to know your energetic self and receive the wisdom of your body, which can pick up the frequency of others.

At a sanctuary, I met a small, blind lamb, Betty, whose caretaker had concerns about how she was doing.

Betty told me, "I love to be inside the house at night. It is so cozy, caring, and safe. During the day, though, I get nervous; the paddock outside is so large with too many workers, I don't know who is there to help."

When I shared this with the caretakers, they got it and replied,

"Yes, the volunteers are in a hurry with a lot on their plate; they move quickly and can be very noisy, trying to get all the work done."

"What if we role play with the staff and experiment with feeling the difference between calm, grounded work and a chaotic, fast work pace? That way, we can actually know what it might feel like to a blind sensitive lamb."

"That's a great idea!" "There is nothing better than personal experience!"

The staff enjoyed the training and became more aware of the effect of energy patterns. As a result, the staff built Betty a mini barn as a safe retreat space while they worked in her paddock. It's all about the energy!

GROUNDED JOY

Energy can become stagnant and cause issues. My friend's two dogs were making trouble in the apartment. I asked them, "What's up?"

They whined, "We're so bored, so boxed in with nothing to do."

As we were communicating, my friend's son, Zach, called and asked, "Hey Connie, what do I do for low energy and phlegm?" I had a plan!

"I'll be right over," I grabbed my spearmint essential oil and headed over. Spearmint has the energy like Superwoman with her hands on her hips, full of confidence and pluck. It's also safer for dogs than peppermint oil—less menthol makes it milder.

"Hi Zach, are you ready? I am going to put one drop of essential oil on a few select acupressure points, Okay?" In just a few minutes, he coughed some, then felt relief and smiled. The dogs sat around me as I was treating Zach. A slight scent of spearmint circled in the room. You could feel the energy rising. The dogs yawned, licked, and released pent-up frustrations. All at once, the room exploded with activity. Zach tossed a tennis ball, and the chase began; around and around they went. We moved the fun outside. Interestingly, Ivy, a beagle boxer mix, did not usually chase balls. They played and played, exuding pure joy! The dogs had ear-to-ear smiles, and so did I. What a great energy stretch.

Animal communication with energy healing is a reciprocal healing gift; the healed heal the healer. I traveled down an awesome road—a twisty, turning road full of deep connections, in pursuit of therapeutic presence. Finally, I've found it; I've found my sacred energetic home. I feel the grounded joy of being an animal communicator, energy healer, and nature mystic; I am here to serve.

THE TOOL

This tool is shared gratefully and with permission from Suzanne Scurlock, founder of the Healing From the Core Curriculum, https://healingfromthecore.com, where the key to healthy full body presence is to embody the six wisdom centers of the body. These are as follows:

The Wisdom of the Legs and Feet: The Gift of Movement.

The Wisdom of the Pelvis: The Gift of Power.

The Wisdom of the Gut: The Gift of Instinctual Knowing.

The Wisdom of the Heart: The Gift of Inspiration that ignites all cells and sparks compassion and love throughout the entire system.

The Wisdom of the Bones: The Gift of stability, clarity, and presence.

The Wisdom of the Brain: The Gift of Integration.

GROUND AND FILL

This ground and fill embodiment meditation is what I credit with enabling me to experience the whole body sensation of being energetically self-contained. Without this, I would never have been in my body enough to get out of my head into my heart to connect with the animals. Even if you feel you're grounded, the feedback is that this soothes and releases aches and makes you aware of every cell. How much stronger of an energy container can there be?

I use this technique for myself and clients; when you're fully present in the moment, the human or animal feels that calm, and it grounds them too. This meditation is from Suzanne Scurlock's, *Healing from the Core* curriculum. Her website is: https://healingfromthecore.com.

This is the beginning, 5 Breath Ground and Fill, part of the longer session of facilitated healing. When you're grounded into the Earth and then fill your body full of a nourishing, nurturing sensation, there is no room for errant energies. I, personally, use the nourishing image of glowing warm amber honey filling and soothing all my body spaces, all my nooks, and crannies. Try it; it is delightfully enriching.

Let's begin. Move slowly through the suggestions and feel the present moment sensations. Linger with each step while slowly inhaling and audibly exhaling when ready.

Allow yourself to settle into this moment as best as you can.

Noticing your breath, the rise and fall of your chest and belly.

Notice your back resting into whatever is supporting you, your sit bones resting on whatever is supporting them, and the soles of your feet in contact with the ground beneath you.

And allow yourself to connect down into the Earth, using whatever metaphor works for you—roots, light beams, rivers of energy, and connecting as deeply and widely as feels comfortable to you at this moment.

We are going to fill our inner energy reservoirs by using breath, as though we have lungs in the bottoms of our feet.

With each inhale, we can fill with whatever nourishing sensation is needed within us.

On each exhale, you can allow whatever you no longer need to leave your system on your breath.

With your first breath, invite nourishing, nurturing sensations to soak into and fill your feet and legs, from the bone marrow all the way out to your skin.

Slowly and audibly, inhale and exhale.

With your second breath, filling your low back, pelvis, and belly...all the organs that are resting there, with this nurturing energy resource.

Take another slow, audible inhale and exhale.

Third breath, allowing this flow to continue on up into your upper torso, chest, heart, lungs, and rib cage.

Take another inhale and exhale.

With the fourth breath, receiving this nourishing flow into your shoulders and down your arms, and into your hands.

Take a slow, audible inhale and exhale.

And to complete the journey, with your fifth breath, allow this river of nourishing sensation to continue on into your neck, head, brain, and all the cells that make up who you are there.

Allow this nourishing resource to flow up and out the top of your head, showering down around you, bathing your skin and the energy field that runs through and around it.

Inhale and exhale once more.

Notice what it feels like to be you *now,* and know that this resource is available to you whenever you need to tap into it.

Begin to feel your feet on the ground and wiggle your fingers and toes. Gently open your eyes and come back to the room. Thank you for engaging.

May all beings be free
May all beings be peaceful
May all beings be happy

Constance Koch, MBA, LMT, Dipl. Asian Body Work, is a nature mystic, animal and nature communicator, energy healer, herbalist, naturalist, and forest connection guide. Her energy modalities include: Reiki, acupressure, Aroma & Floral Acupoint Therapy, Flower essences, Nada trauma acupuncture therapy, EFT, Scalar wave, and Distance Healing from the Core. Currently, she is a teacher trainer at Communication With All Life University.

When the pandemic happened, she shifted to working virtually doing Distance Healing from the Core sessions and online animal communications with EFT and Scalar wave—all perfect for remote work.

Constance lives in Traverse City, Michigan, after living in Chicago, Illinois, for 40 years. She can be found hiking to commune with the gorgeous green nature abundant in this area. She is the caretaker for Juliet, the building's feral cat. When they met, Juliet warned Constance: "I am not yours; we are just good friends." Juliet is a gift!

In Chicago, she worked as an administrator, sponsored program manager, naturalist, and on outreach projects for Field Museum of Natural History, Morton Arboretum, Chicago Botanic Gardens, and Independent Lens (ITVS) documentary series on PBS.

She loves to travel to sacred sites and has been to Machu Picchu, Tibet, Argentina, Hawaii, Alaska, and South Africa. Each visit has a special mystic experience attached to the memories. She's also looking forward to more travel, especially to commune with gorillas, elephants, and lions. Nature is speaking, and we need to listen.

Constance is creating local workshops, walking sacred labyrinths, sharing herbal ceremonies, leading forest communing, and sacred activism projects. Her mission is to use nature communication to work with animals, plants, landscapes and the more-than-human nature to give them a voice allowing their points of view to be heard.

Connect with Constance: conniekoch615@gmail.com

CHAPTER 10

SECRETS REVEALED

YOUR LIFE IS A MEDITATION

Ed Cleveland RMT, Zildjin Gong Master,
Neuro-Acoustic Sound Therapist Master Teacher

MY STORY

The time was near; the final step in completing my 4th-degree black belt was upon me. After many months of dedication, pretests, and intense physical training, I was ready, and the only step left was graduation night.

The celebration that was years in the making was exhilarating—until a late-night request came to help a student with their sparring.

It was the night before a tournament when I was injured. My body cooled down, so when I overstretched and was punched in the groin by an excessively excited and nervous student, it caused a tear that sent me to the hospital.

I had an emergency operation that ended my career as a martial arts teacher. Injured and heartbroken, I felt alone, and on top of all that, my family decided not to make the move to join me in Arizona as we had planned.

I ended up moving back to Connecticut during my recovery time, only to find out my kids were not being taken care of and were even put in jeopardy.

I filed for a divorce and was granted full custody after two years of being tossed between three different courtrooms. At that time, men seemed to be put through the wringer when it came to full custody, so this was a big deal—and came with great responsibility.

Now, it was up to me to create a better quality of life with my son and daughter. I didn't know where to start or what to do, so I began my journey into self-help books, knowing change starts within.

I was drawn to a holistic book and crystal shop in town and prayed for a moment as I stood in front of a wall of books. I closed my eyes and asked, "I have a four and six-year-old, I am doing my best, and I don't know what else to do. Please show me a sign!"

Upon opening my eyes, a book appeared to be glowing, so that was the one I reached for. It was a book on Reiki. Not knowing what Reiki was, I held the book close to my heart and asked, "Show me what I need to know."

My answer was given as a page explaining an energy ball. This made total sense to me as I had once made an energy ball in Karate, so I kept trusting where I was being led.

I pulled this energy into my heart as if it was the right thing to do. Closing my eyes, I sat with the feeling of this unknown presence, somehow knowing something would reveal itself to me as time went by.

Now I felt inspired, and I needed to know more, so I bought the book, read it that night, and went online to find a qualified teacher.

Luck would have it that I found a weeklong, multi-level program happening the following week, and I immediately called to make my reservations for Reiki I, II, and III and reserve my sleeping quarters.

However, I found one thing that didn't feel right from the book, and it had to do with the rule of waiting 21 days between levels. Waiting between levels wouldn't work for me with having full custody of my kids.

So, I called to ask about that rule, as I'm not really a rule person, and the receptionist said the teacher just happened to be walking by at that moment and asked if I would like to talk to her. "Absolutely," I responded.

I shared a quick version of my story. "If life sets this up, then you must be ready," she said. "Life won't give you more than you can handle, and it sounds like this is important for you and the upbringing of your kids."

So, I went all in, and things were never the same. This "all in" mentality, with teachers, classes, knowledge, and wisdom, did not stop. Still, to this day, I'm drawn to older versions of teachings to find the original roots of the subject matter, and I will never stop learning.

THE TOOL

Throughout my studies and practice, I've found ways to share this knowledge and healing wisdom with others. Understanding the basis of the underlying energy of the Universe allows one to use and connect with it on an even deeper level.

The basics of space, presence, and meditation are the foundation for understanding and using this universal life-force energy for healing, guidance, and knowledge. They're the tools that will bring you to peace and encourage self-healing in the body, mind, and soul.

SPACE

Where do we go when we sleep? Is it a space in our brain we hang out in until we awake? Where is this lucid place of REM sleep? Is it a collective secret place beyond our comprehension? Where are you coming from when you awaken?

Asking these questions opens us up to that space to receive wisdom, healing, and guidance, as it's the "nothingness" and "all-that-is" at the same time.

If you're open to this space, you'll be ready to learn and realize your answers have been waiting for you all along. The brain never stops, which is why many people have trouble falling asleep, meditating, or even finding a moment of peace for themselves.

Most of us rely on praying for things to happen and then go about our day without waiting to hear, see, or know an answer has been given. This space provides many ways for the translation of information to be received.

When you allow yourself to be in this space, you feel the energetic nectar of wisdom coming in with answers or creative solutions like honey dripping into your crown. This is also the time to notice if your brain wants to tell you a story, as the brain lives in a never-ending line of "what if."

Sleep apnea, overthinking, stress, anxiety, and even a poor diet can be a problem for many in achieving deep sleep and gives you the feeling of being disconnected.

This is where sound meditation can help quiet your mind, so you get the sleep you need while giving you time to feel the elements move through your body as prana.

Deep REM sleep is how your body heals, and often dreams will reveal information or solutions to life's challenges. Upon waking, pause for a moment, feel, and hold on to the space of "nothingness."

Ask if there was something you needed to remember. Ask to remember the connection from where you went to help keep that line open if you were to need it.

Is this "nothingness" a place that holds all the information of everything and everybody who was ever created? Is that where your answers, creativity, and inspiration come from?

It's that secret, unknown place where your words, thoughts, and feelings become part of your conscious expression. You have to feel the presence of that space within you so you can be authentic and unique in your own vibration.

Take a few breaths, listen in without judging, and hold this pure, precious moment. Bathe in the bliss of creation itself as you surrender all expectations placed on yourself or others. Knowing and understanding the law (or realization) of impermanence—breathe and let things come to you.

MEDITATION

Getting into the space of no mind, no body, nowhere, in no time can be achieved consciously through meditation.

There are many myths about meditation being difficult or reserved for the enlightened, but all in all, meditation is simply focused attention. Allowing the mind and body to detach from physical reality and enter the void of nothingness connects you to wisdom and knowledge and promotes your own personal growth and healing.

My love of merging Reiki and sound healing drew others into this calling, as the requests were flowing in for sessions and a better understanding of these unlimited benefits. As this popularity in knowledge grew, so did the experience that was unfolding with miraculous results.

I needed to learn more, so advanced shamanic studies (with four-hour meditations) were next in exploring altering time and space and learning how to slow the mind chatter.

During another weekend training, lessons came up about using the energy ball in Reiki, amplified with sound and breath. I was in my zone with this exercise and had to stop as the ladies on both sides of me started saying that I was pushing them off the chair!

These were the experiences that led to the wisdom of helping others and understanding more about the human energy field so that we can learn how to manage, protect, and cleanse ourselves.

While facilitating a session, I'm telling your brain a story through the sounds of the elements, helping free your mind from the internal thinking that can create turmoil and repetitive behavior. Personalizing sessions live or online, in many different categories, reaching all ages, assists in realizing that 75% of our ailments are created within our own brains.

These tendencies can lead us to unhealthy external views and thoughts about ourselves and the world. Understanding this can help you master your own feelings and emotions, creating optimal health and abundance while helping others along the way.

Connecting with or creating "space" can take various forms through meditation. A few effective ways to add mindfulness to something you do daily are:

A SHOWER/BATH MEDITATION

This can make your daily routine more meaningful, giving you more peace and adding extended realizations that are in balance with your internal world or that will help your internal world. Ever notice how the most brilliant ideas typically come to you in the bathroom?

Everything you do can become a form of mindful meditation.

For example, walking to the bathroom, turning on the water, feeling the temperature, and noticing how the water runs down or surrounds your body. It's all connected as in the act of cleansing, both physically and energetically.

You may also want to use Himalayan or Epsom salt in your bath, crystals like smokey quartz, or even essential oils, and as you do, connect with the energy, texture, and scent.

It is the journey that is important, no matter how short the time spent.

You're not washing to just get it done so you can move on and get ready in a timely fashion—it's the experience we want to become fully engaged with and present in.

Perhaps we could ask, what's the overall intent here? You just woke up, you want to freshen up to be more alert, and you want to clean your body and warm or cool off your muscles and skin to feel good. So, let's look a little closer and put more meaning behind our actions.

The water from the shower head enters all the different layers of your energy field before interacting with your body.

Think about the saying that water is life. This life-giving element is directly being absorbed into your field, so consciously let it wash away any heavy debris like fears, thoughts, worries, concerns, anger, jealousy, pride, desire, delusion, and the like.

Look at this as the perfect moment to allow the water element to flush away these very things. What emotions are holding us back from enjoying our inner happiness?

Also, the spraying of water introduces or creates negative ions into your space, which can directly amplify your field all on its own. Surrender to letting that water make positive changes within the cells of your body, like rain connecting with the ocean.

Going back to the shower or bath and now that we are all cleaned up, imagine a final purging or release of negative karma while you open the drain.

Think about the way a siphon works, and like a lymphatic drain, everything will work all on its own. Stay present with the tub as it drains, and work in your practice of holding space, to simply release anything that is not in your best interest until the tub is empty.

WALKING MEDITATION

Just like walking up or down a flight of stairs, it's not just about getting somewhere else as a better place to be than where you are at; it's the journey.

Taking each step as a walking meditation, connecting with the earth with each step, allowing the rise and fall of your breath, body weight, lymphatic system, and blood flow as it moves through your body. The millions of different things that need to systematically happen for you to take a step without falling is a miracle all in itself.

From this deep meditative space, feel the winds that sustain your breath and life force, the fire that cleanses and purifies your container, and the water that gives fluidity to your being that flushes away impurities.

Feel the earth from the understanding that all material things come from her, including your physical body, and to where all things will eventually return.

SOUND AND BREATH

This is huge when combined with the mental clarity of connecting to the space-element of nonjudgmental thoughts and the so-hum of your breath. "So" is the sound of the inhale, and "hum" is the sound of the exhale, which also vibrates the thymus gland—boosts the immune system.

This is the space where we begin to add the sound of the gongs and singing bowls into the infinite places that exist between the piano keys that are right next to each other.

This form of mathematical information, or communication, within the complexity of harmonics and micro-tonality, compounds the sounds of the five elements into something your brain has never experienced before.

Yes, we are talking about sounds you would hear from within the womb, sounds of deep earth, the ocean depths, deep space, and even the sounds of the tunnel when transitioning from this life.

It is our life's spiritual journey to learn the language of the mathematical information that can be given or received through our five senses, five elements, five major organs, and five personality types.

When you open and understand that this language has always been available, you will see it everywhere—as it's also the building block of creation itself—and is prevalent wherever you are in service to others.

Simply listening to the sound of your breath or your heartbeat can help connect you with the infinite space that resides within and is an easy way to start practicing mindfulness and meditation.

This is where the gift is. You cannot stop your brain from thinking, so the exercise is to observe for as long as you can without naming or judging your thoughts.

Remember the conclusion of your shower meditation, taking with it all your heavy stuff while giving loving gratitude to the water. Asking Mother Earth to purify this water like the morning dew.

Then add what's called a Dedication of Merit as a prayer, or a quiet moment holding the space of compassion while generating the heartfelt wish that all beings be freed from suffering and that they find the spiritual path to enlightenment for their benefit.

Imagine that you have accumulated merit by engaging in this spiritual practice as it generously gives to the quality or welfare of all beings from the reach of our prayer.

Ed Cleveland is the founder and owner of The Ed Cleveland Reiki & Sound Therapy Training Center located in Hartford, Connecticut.

He is professionally trained in sound therapy as a neuro-acoustic master teacher, RMT, holographic master teacher, medicinal aromatherapist, and national is a award-winning martial arts teacher.

Ed Cleveland earned the title of Zildjin Gong Master after completing several gong camps, sonic theology, the science of sound, and the practicum with the world's leading researchers and teachers in the field of sound therapy, Mitch Nur, Ph.D.

When they resonate throughout the human body, these frequencies induce physiological changes that can be harnessed for therapy and for altering consciousness. Ed brings his skills into his new recordings and music videos created in The Recording Den. The goal is to enable patterns for positive cognitive change.

As a master neuro-acoustic teacher, Ed provides workshops, presentations, and performances in sound meditations for an educated experience in community outreach programs for schools, universities, hospitals, libraries, senior living centers, holistic centers, and yoga studios, with appearances on public TV, and various podcast discussions.

Ed is committed to delivering sounds that ease your stress while helping your body's natural ability to heal itself for those in pain or who have a serious illness and to help speed up recovery time.

Ed will help motivate people to learn healthy practices while teaching you the hows and whys of energy healing and sound therapy to create your experience with wisdom, enthusiasm, and inner awareness.

This development and presentation is a combination of research, studies, and direct experiences that made him an expert in the field of sound therapy/sound healing and neuro acoustics teachings.

You can learn more about Ed Cleveland and his training center at 555 Asylum Ave. Apt #409, Hartford, CT, 06105

Connect with Ed:

Facebook: https://www.facebook.com/EdClevelandSoundandReikiTraining/

Email: EdReiki3@yahoo.com

Website: www.edclevelandsoundhealing.com

CHAPTER 11

REIKI MEDITATION TO IGNITE YOUR INNER HEALER

TWO MINUTES TO PEACE AND HEALING

Lori Pieper, Total Well-Being Coach, Reiki Master

MY STORY

The most stressful and humiliating event of my professional career set in motion my most profound healing experience and ultimately sent me on an amazing spiritual journey that changed my life in unforeseeable and wonderful ways.

It began when a friend called me from Australia and said, "Lori, the Aussie offices are looking for a pre-sales systems engineer. You interested?"

"Yeah, right," I said, thinking he was joking.

"Lori, I'm serious. You're perfect for the job."

Being logical, I replied, "It sounds amazing, and I'm flattered you thought of me, but really I can't." Meanwhile, deep inside, my soul was screaming: *Yes! Sign me up!*

I have dreamed of living in Australia ever since reading *The Thorn Birds* in high school. And even though my heart burst with excitement at the idea of moving to Australia, my logical brain just couldn't see the possibilities.

I now know that when my heart is leaping with joy, I'm in alignment with the Universe. And when my choices align with the Universe, solutions the brain cannot begin to imagine will appear as if by magic. And in just over three months, I was at the airport, checking in for my flight to Australia.

As I approached the airport check-in counter, it hit me. *Oh shit! I'm going to Australia for two years!* My heart skipped several beats. My knees got weak. My stomach started to churn. My hands started to shake. *What the hell was I thinking?*

It all seemed like a dream. Three months ago, I was emphatically saying, "No, I absolutely can't move to Australia for two years." Yet here I am three months later, about to hop on a plane.

What the hell? I quit my US job, rented my house, and I won't see friends or family for another two years. Was this really a good idea?

My chest tightened with anxiety. It was hard to breathe. *Why am I doing this?*

For the past three months, I didn't have time to process my decision. It felt so right at the time, and things just flowed. But now I was terrified.

"Ma'am," The attendant said.

"Oh, sorry. What did you say?" I was so distracted by my fears I hadn't heard her tell me my luggage was too heavy. She handed me an empty box to offload some clothes from the over-stuffed luggage, and I was on my way.

Great, like anything from that box will survive the flight, I thought as I headed for the gate. *Crap! I hope I made the right decision.*

THE PROJECT THAT DAMN NEAR CRUSHED ME

I didn't have a chance to destress from my move to the other side of the globe before I got my first project. The project was to demonstrate our reporting software to a potential client using software I hadn't used in two years.

"Here's the list of features the prospect wants us to demonstrate," the sales rep said, handing me a sheet of paper.

"Great!" I replied.

"You need to demo the features in the order listed there."

"Seriously? These features are pretty random. They're not in any logical order. Historically, if we demo in this manner, our chances of winning a deal like this are slim to none," I explained to the team.

"Yes, but this is what the client wants. We *have* to do it their way."

The discussion went on for quite a while. This was a big deal for this sales rep, and he continued to push back. I wanted to make sure we were doing what was needed to win the client. Finally, the managing director agreed with me, and I set out to create a kick-ass demo using a logical workflow to demonstrate the software.

In the next three weeks, I worked on learning the software, building a demo, and finding an apartment. The software wasn't cooperating, and I had a lot of trouble getting certain features to work. I had no time to find an apartment. Stress was compounding.

Holy shit! What have I gotten myself into?

Relax, Lori. Breathe. You've got this. You are smart, and you are capable.

It didn't help that stress kept me from sleeping. I was tired, frustrated, and I didn't know anyone here in Melbourne I could talk to yet. I felt so totally and completely alone. My heart was in pain, while my brain was in chaos.

I struggled to appropriately manage my time, and before I knew it, it was time for me to demo to the client. I felt neither prepared nor confident.

I am smart. I am capable. Time to shine!

Through the demo, I gave the client a vision of a typical workflow using our software, pointing out the client-required features as I demonstrated. Things were working, and I felt good.

After about five minutes, the client stops me and asks, "When are you going to show us the features from the list we gave you?"

"I am pointing them out to you as I demonstrate them. Do you need me to run through anything again?"

The gentleman looked at the checklist and pointed to the first bullet. "Yes, where did you show how to schedule a report?"

"I'll do that in just a moment, sir. I am currently creating the report, and then I'll show you how to schedule it. I'm demonstrating the features as you would use them in a typical workflow."

"Can we just follow the bullet list, please?" He asked with impatience. I hoped the customer didn't sense my virtual eye roll.

What the client wants, the client gets. I managed to muster a smile and say, "Of course."

Crap! This is going to be a disaster.

Here is where it all goes to hell-in-a-handbasket, and my career flashes before my eyes.

The first bullet was to schedule a report. No problem. I right-clicked on the report, and my heart sank. My hands began to shake. My stomach and bowels churned. I felt the blood leave my face and extremities as I realized I was showing how it worked in the *old* version. I couldn't remember how to do this in the *current* version I was demonstrating.

Okay. Take a breath. Don't panic.

You got this.

Dammit, Lori, think!

But, my lungs wouldn't allow me to take a deep breath, and my brain melted out of my ears and oozed all over the meeting floor. Meanwhile, the client's executives glared as they waited impatiently for me to do something.

I froze. For the first time ever in my career, I totally froze. One of my colleagues had to take over the demo. Tears were welling up in my eyes.

Don't cry here, Lori. I begged myself.

Shit! Will I get fired?

My career is over.

Where the hell is that hole I desperately want to crawl into?

I felt my 5'9" stature wilt to about three inches as I relinquished my seat at the computer and let someone else finish the demo. My first month of a two-year gig in Australia, and I failed miserably!

I was able to outwardly maintain my composure while in the client's meeting room. As soon as I got in the taxi, I cried heaving, uncontrollable sobs. I cried all the way home and well into the night. Luckily it was Friday, and I had the weekend to pull myself together.

Saturday morning, I woke up with red puffy eyes, crusty with dried tears. I felt the protection of the soft, cozy covers that smelled flower-fresh from fabric softener. I was afraid to leave this safe haven but knew I had to.

I failed my team with my first assignment. I talked the team into letting me create a workflow demo instead of following the client's instructions. I ruined any chance we had of winning that client. *Shit! How do I show my face in the office again?*

I probably would've cried some more if there were any tears left.

Oh, God, please, tell me what to do.

What? Did God just say, *Lori, you need a pedicure?* I think He did! I know He did!

That sounded perfect. A little less self-criticism and a lot more self-compassion are just what I needed.

REIKI DISCOVERED

This place looks nice, I said to myself as I opened the spa door. I could immediately feel the peace and calm spilling over me as if someone was giving me a warm, welcoming hug.

"It'll be about ten minutes, Ms. Pieper," the receptionist said. "Please have a seat."

While in the reception area, I looked at the other services they offered. A Reiki flyer caught my eye. *Ree-icky? What is that?* I had no idea what it was, let alone how to pronounce it.

"Ms. Pieper, we're ready for you. Please follow me," the receptionist called out.

I grabbed a "Ree-icky" flyer, put it in my backpack, and followed the receptionist. She seated me in front of a hot soapy tub of water. The smell of sweet lavender in the water was already helping me chill. I dipped my feet into the water and felt my stress begin to melt away.

Oh yeah! Now we're talking! This is exactly what I need. Good suggestion, God!

When the pedicurist arrived, we exchanged the usual pleasantries. I then held up the flyer and asked, "What's this Ree-icky all about?"

"To start, it's pronounced *Ray-key*," she smiled.

"Oops!" I laughed. "The flyer says we all have an innate ability to heal, but our daily stressors block that healing. Can Reiki really remove energy blocks and make way for deep healing? 'Cuz I could sure use some of that!"

"Absolutely, and healing can be physical, emotional, or spiritual. You will love it."

The pedicure was wonderful, and as I left I made an appointment for a Reiki session the following weekend.

MONDAY ARRIVES

My hands were shaking, and my stomach ached as I approached the office. I took a deep breath. I had to gather my courage and go in. I knew the news of my failure spread throughout our small office. I lost a $70K+ deal for the sales rep, and he had a right to be angry. Others in the office might be more compassionate, but I had no illusions of him showing any compassion.

Okay, Lori. You know you need to talk to him and apologize. Put on your big girl pants and do it now!

I walked into the sales rep's office. The daggers in his unblinking eyes stopped me dead. This was not going to go well.

"I know I screwed up, and I'm really sorry. I take full responsibility, and this will never happen again. I promise."

"I know it won't," he scowled, "because you are never going near another customer of mine again." And I didn't.

I did work with the other sales reps in the office and redeemed myself, but I always felt uncomfortable around that rep.

REIKI MAGIC

It's Saturday, and I return to the spa for my Reiki session. The Reiki Master asked me to lie on the table and relax. I did as she asked. I think. My hands clutched the sides of the table for dear life, for fear my arms would flop off and hit her.

"Relax," she reminded me. "Now, close your eyes. On an inhale, imagine you're breathing a golden white light into your lungs."

I do as instructed.

Wait, is it more white light or more golden light?

Or maybe equal parts of white and golden light?

What the heck does a golden white light look like?

I'm an engineer, for crying out loud! Give me the specs!

Yep, that's how my brain works. I wondered if I'd ever be able to relax.

As it turned out, this was the most amazing and pivotal moment of my life! My body tingled as the stress melted away. At the end of the session, I truly felt like a new woman. I floated off the table. I felt so light. It was as if mystical fairies lifted me off the table and held me suspended just above the ground.

Wait! What is this? A laugh? Happiness?

It seemed foreign to me. It had been months since I had a good belly laugh. I felt the freedom an eagle must feel as they soar high above the earth, allowing the breeze to lift them up. Reiki lifted me up, and I was grateful.

A week later, I signed up for Reiki training.

You may expect me to say I completed my training and became a Reiki Master in record time or some other magical story. Nope. Quite the opposite. I took the training but didn't feel like it stuck. I knew the strength of Reiki, but I didn't believe in the strength within myself. I sensed something was missing. I just didn't know what.

Two years later, and back in the States, I'm again working too much, stressing too much, and forgetting how good inner peace felt. Then a series of synchronicities led me to become a Reiki Master and have as much confidence in myself as I have in Reiki.

It started with yoga. I enjoyed the yoga poses but wasn't into the spirituality. I was too driven at work and didn't have time for that. Then I walked into a studio where I felt such peace come over me, and I knew I was home. I was so moved I signed up for their teacher training. I began appreciating the spiritual aspects of yoga even more than the physical.

Soon after, I went to a Chopra seminar. We learned the Chopra signature Primordial Sound Mantra (PSM) meditation. I tried many times in the past to meditate but failed, believing I couldn't do it right. The Chopra training cleared up the myths that kept me from thinking I couldn't meditate—the biggest myth being, "clear your mind." That gives false hope of being able to stop your thoughts during meditation, and that's impossible.

With proper instruction, my meditation practice flourished. Through this, I manifested my perfect job. I had more compassion for myself and others. I had more clarity in making tough decisions. And the list goes on.

When the Universe decided I was ready, another series of seriously crazy synchronicities brought me to Reiki training again. Instead of the weekend training, which is the norm, this was a yearlong course. We were taught Reiki as its founder taught it—Reiki as a spiritual practice first, with a side-benefit of healing.

My meditation and Reiki practices soared, and so did my spirituality and confidence. I now feel that energetic connection between my clients and me. That is what was missing before. I realized the energy from my heart and soul needs to drive the bus in healing, not my brain. Only then can I truly serve my clients.

In 2016, I received my Reiki Master certification. I provide my clients with a safe, supportive, and relaxing space where their inner healer can thrive.

I continue my spiritual practices and further my Reiki and healing education via books, seminars, and networking with other like-minded healers. I particularly enjoy learning about the science behind how and why it works.

THE TOOL

Two key things to remember about healing, both physically and spiritually:

1. Your inner healer is powerful and knows what's needed to heal.

2. Stress weakens your inner healer.

Reiki is a powerful tool for reducing stress and activating your inner healer. Everyone has an innate ability to heal. Stress impedes this ability. It's even attributed to many of the chronic diseases of today.

The below meditation will help you to relax and will give your inner healer space to work.

You can do this anywhere. I have done this in airports, in the grocery line, before having a difficult conversation, etc.

REIKI MEDITATION TO IGNITE YOUR INNER HEALER

To begin:

Set your intention for healing. You can make this intention as general or specific as you want. Have faith that the energy and your inner healer know how to do the rest.

- Close your eyes if it's safe to do so.
- Inhale slowly through your nose, expanding your belly.
  Expanding your belly when you inhale is important physiologically. It signals your nervous system that all is well, triggering relaxation.
- Exhale through the mouth with a sigh.
- Repeat the above two to three times.
- Keeping your eyes closed, breathe normally.
  Be mindful of expanding your belly on the inhale.

Now combine the breath with a visual of bringing healing light into your body, as follows:

- On the inhale, imagine you're inhaling a bright white light through the nostrils and bringing it down into your abdomen, a few inches below your belly button.
- On the exhale, expand that light throughout your body.
- You can also send that light to a specific area that needs healing.
- Continue for two minutes or longer.

Your overall health and well-being can improve dramatically by doing the above breathing exercise occasionally throughout your day. This makes sense because this helps you get out of fight-or-flight and into rest-and-restore. It is in rest-and-restore where healing occurs.

Continue the exercise for a longer period of time for added healing. Studies show it can take 15-20 minutes for you to completely return to a healthy balance.

Remember the above is to help you relax. Don't stress over making it perfect. Struggling puts you back into fight-or-flight mode, which impedes healing. If you struggle to envision the white light, that's okay. Just having the *intention* will work.

FINAL THOUGHT

Be easy with yourself. Trust in your inner healer. It's wiser and more powerful than you can imagine. Take time to relax throughout your day. It's a game changer! You deserve it!

For the top five *easy* de-stressors you can do anytime, visit my website.

Lori Pieper is the founder of Journey to Inner Joy. She's a certified Chopra Total Well-being coach, Chopra PSM meditation instructor, Reiki Master, Yoga instructor, and Chopra Perfect Health: Ayurvedic Lifestyle Instructor. Lori brings the magic of a unique blend of healing practices and life-changing wisdom to you through Total Well-being coaching.

Lori's passion is to help people improve their health and well-being. She enjoys serving her clients who are at a crossroads in life and need to find the clarity needed to make decisions in alignment with their heart and soul.

Fifteen years into her 30-year career as a computer systems engineer, she watched the World Trade Center towers fall on 9/11. A deep longing to serve others bubbled up, and she knew there was a greater reason for her existence. Her journey to clarity was beautiful, necessary, and worth it—and expertly prepared Lori to understand and serve her clients.

As a coach, Lori uses her training and deep intuition to assist her clients on their journey. She listens with compassion as she guides them through soul-searching practices, giving them clarity to make decisions that are right for them.

"Do I change careers?" "Do I start my own business?" Scary questions like these become easier when the answer comes from the soul. The brain and ego will often give fear-based answers keeping you from making the brave choices needed for your well-being.

The deep introspective work used in her Total Well-being coaching has helped Lori's clients in many unique ways: decluttering their homes, deciding to go back to school, applying for and getting that promotion, managing work stress, and so much more.

This is your life. It's time to live it with clarity, choice, and passion.

Connect with Lori:

Website: https://www.journeytoinnerjoy.com/

LinkedIn: https://www.linkedin.com/in/loripieper/

Facebook: https://www.facebook.com/JourneyToInnerJoy

CHAPTER 12

REIKI FOR LOVE

IGNITING THE LIGHT IN YOU

Dr. Makeba Morgan Hill

MY STORY

A DAY TO REMEMBER

My new favorite masseuse had just done her thing. The massage was much-needed and absolutely amazing. I rolled off the table, got dressed, and made my way to the door. On the short stroll to my car, I looked up at the morning sky and noticed it was a little cloudy and unusually warm for an early February day in Atlanta. My steps were light. I felt like I was being lifted on a cloud that was the afterglow of the session. I felt great!

I need to ground myself now, so I can focus!

I sat in the car for a couple of minutes before starting the engine. Just a few days before the massage, I discovered my ability to communicate with spirits. As a newbie, I spent much of my free time communing with them. It made sense that I would call upon them immediately after my massage.

How could I go an hour without checking in?

I said aloud, "Hey, spirits, I missed you guys. Does anyone have anything to say before we get on the road?" To my surprise, I received a message that changed my life forever. God spoke to me. It was February 5, 2022, a day I will never forget.

THE MESSAGE

God said to me, *I sent you to Earth to show people that the only way is the way of God, that you are a disciple of the Lord, and that you are the truth. You will be a light for many, and you will be a joy to be around. People will love your spirit because you will be so bright, and God will show through you in so many ways.*

I gasped and exclaimed, "Holy cow," as the tears began to flow. My spirit guides, whom I became familiar with only days before, said, *Breathe, Makeba! God is always with you.*

Thoughts swirled in my mind. *I'm not super religious. How could this be? Why me? Really? No way! Am I losing my mind? No, really? This is crazy!*

For 48 years, I searched for my purpose, and at that moment, an amazing clarity enveloped me. I am to bring love and light to humankind. My passion for bringing joy to my small circle and also to the world at large was ignited.

It was time to get to work.

"How?" I said, "What is the path?"

THE JOURNEY

It's difficult for me to talk about what led to this point, mostly because it involves delving into a marriage that should have never been. I married my ex-husband because I had a child with him, not because we were in love. I wanted my child to grow up in a two-parent home because I didn't. My parents separated when I was 11, and I took it hard. I didn't understand why they weren't together and why, all of a sudden, I had a broken home. I blamed my father and judged my mother. I vowed that would never happen to me.

At 28 years old, I suffered from my second real bout of depression and anxiety. My mother lived in New York. I was in Atlanta. She worried about me. When she called me, she always asked, "What's wrong, Keba?" All I could say was, "Nothing."

My college sweetheart and I broke up. He was the love of my life at the time. After having a few failed short-term relationships after the breakup, I didn't have the words to describe the panic I felt.

I'll never find love again. I'll never have kids. I'm destined to have a failed marriage like everyone else in my family. I'm not good enough, smart enough, pretty enough.

It was the ultimate negative self-talk. I was so focused on my grim future and perceived inadequacies that I was barely present during my late twenties. I was totally in my head and felt lost.

Around that time, I met Tim at a birthday barbecue for a guy I was casually dating. He said, "Hey, dance with me." I said, "No. I'm here with the birthday boy. That might be a little awkward," and laughed as I smiled coyly. Tim was cute, so we talked, laughed, danced a little, exchanged numbers, and started dating, eventually.

It was a rocky relationship from the start. I didn't love myself when we met. My confidence was low, and I was looking for a relationship to make me whole. I didn't know where I stood with him. We never formally declared we were a couple. A year and a half later, after several breakups and make-ups, I discovered I was pregnant.

My father urged me to do the right thing, while my mother reiterated her mantra over and over again, "You know you don't need a man, right?" It didn't matter that my ex-husband never told me he loved me during our courtship or that we had a shaky dating relationship. I married him anyway. At the time, I didn't think I could do better. I married a man who would never truly, fully love me. I did this because he asked, and I wanted to do the right thing for my daughter.

Tim proposed when Meredith was a couple of weeks old. I planned the wedding hastily because I didn't want him to change his mind. We got married seven months later, and I quickly realized I had made a bad decision. I thought things would be different once we were married. I thought he'd declare his love for me. I thought we'd be a good team. I thought we'd spend time together. I thought my needs would be fulfilled. I thought I'd adjust or that he'd change, but he didn't change, and neither did I. I remember him shouting, "Why did you marry me anyway?" And I recalled thinking: *I have no earthly idea.*

Intimacy was always an issue with us. I did lots of research during the marriage, and it was clear to me that we were in a sexless marriage. If I didn't initiate sex, it rarely happened. It was like he was afraid of me or like he wasn't attracted to me. I often thought, *what is wrong with me?* I tried to make myself more attractive to him, but it never seemed to work. Eventually, I accepted it and just dealt with it. I stayed with him for our daughter. I wasn't happy. I didn't feel loved. I didn't feel heard, seen, or understood. We walked on eggshells around each other. It tore us both down.

Fast-forward 14 years—my daughter and I had a conversation that went something like this:

"Mom," she said, "I don't feel like Daddy loves me. He doesn't see me or hear me. He doesn't pay me any attention. He always seems so annoyed with me."

Disgusted, I could relate and said, "Really? That's how I feel. You shouldn't feel like that, though. He's your father. He loves you." I married him so she could have a relationship with him, and it backfired. I felt so stupid.

That's when I realized the issue was deeper than my romantic relationship with my husband. He didn't know how to love us because he didn't truly love himself. And I stayed for my daughter because I didn't want to be a failure. *I chose this life, so I should just stick with it.*

By then, I had grown a callus around my heart. It was numb. My back ached in the heart space because of the pain. I felt helpless. As an empath, it felt odd not to feel anything for my husband. The anxiety I felt over the years crept back up. I needed a return to love.

THE AWAKENING

We made it to my daughter's high school graduation. She was heading to college. *What will I do now? She gave me purpose. She was my joy—my company keeper.* My internal light felt dim and desperate, to be honest. I tried yoga, meditation, isolation, associations—anything to stay busy and protect myself from the lack of love at home. I was doing alright, I thought.

One day an old friend called. He was in town and wanted to meet to talk. He said, "Keeb, it's been a long time! How've you been?" I said, "I'm living."

We had a history. He knew me well a long time ago. My lack of enthusiasm was palpable. He looked deeply into my eyes, searching my soul. He tilted his head and said, "What's that mean?"

We walked and talked. We laughed and cried. We were both going through similar things at home. He reached for my hand. The sudden surge of energy I felt when our hands touched sent what felt like a jolt of lightning through my body. I was nervous. I thought I might be having a heart attack—literally—my breathing was sporadic. I felt lightheaded. The dead battery in my chest was suddenly recharged. I remembered what it felt like to feel again.

When I encountered my friend that warm summer day, and he touched my hand, my heart chakra opened. That moment ignited my healing journey. Neither of us knew that at the time, but it was truly a blessing. That was Reiki.

That was the beginning of my personal enlightenment and a return to self-love. I'm sharing this story so that you, too, may move further along on your path to enlightenment using Reiki as a self-healing tool.

THE TOOL

ENLIGHTENMENT

After that encounter with my friend, I began to write again. I began to listen to music and see in color again. I could see beauty in the mirror. I was more attuned to the energy in others. I realized how sensitive I was to negativity and how bruised I was by it. I searched for ways to nurture my energy and made a decision to put myself first. I was so open. *Something has to change!*

I asked my husband for a divorce. I'm not saying divorce is the answer for everyone, but it was the answer for me. It was a turning point for me, and it led me to the practice of Reiki.

WHAT IS REIKI?

According to the dictionary, "Reiki is a healing technique based on the principle that the therapist can channel energy into the patient using touch, to activate the natural healing processes of the patient's body and restore physical and emotional well-being."

We are energetic beings. All humans can move and transfer energy within, around, and amongst ourselves. The practice of moving the universal life energy, i.e., Reiki, in a person's body doesn't require special training. We all have the power to be a vessel of energy.

Reiki is an amazing tool used to move the universal life force within one's body. It helps with chakra alignment so people and animals can do the work to continue their own healing. Training and attunement allow us to be stronger, more directed, and more knowledgeable about the practice. Therefore, training or working with a trained practitioner is highly recommended.

HOW CAN REIKI HELP?

As a Reiki practitioner, I can sense when chakras are out of sorts. With the power in my hands, I can unstick stagnant energy. I'm told that during a session, my clients feel heat, tingling, and/or a sense of calm. Some cry to release pain or uncertainty. Some cry joyful tears because they understand why they feel the way they are feeling. They leave my table with recommendations and a way forward.

Many Reiki practitioners, including myself, call upon God, the Universe, spirits, and/or ancestors to guide our hands as we practice this work. It's serious business! During my practice, I call directly on God to help me assess and guide my clients. He is always eager to help. He wants to connect more with his people. My practice allows deep connections with God, the inner soul, and the spirit realm. These connections are a constant reminder that we are not alone, even when we think we are. *We are not alone.*

REIKI FOR LOVE

When I became a Reiki Level 1 practitioner, a whole new world opened up to me. I began practicing self-healing at least once a day and could immediately feel changes in my body. Self-healing connects you with the Self. When I hover my hands over my body, I say: *Hello, Self. I love you, and God loves you, too, and there's nothing you can do about it.* I'm immediately calmer, my intuition is heightened, I can manage my sensitivity, and I can be present for others. Practicing self-healing facilitates self-love.

Reiki with others connects you at the spirit level. An early example for me was after scanning my daughter's body and consulting with God and the spirits; I was able to open and align her throat, heart, and sacral chakras. She was having trouble in college, and during our session, I was able to get clarity on her future career. We learned what school she should attend. I was able to share insights about her soulmates and other spiritual connections. We cried together so deeply during that session. Our spirits were united, and our love for each other amplified!

Since then, I have done the same for many people. I give people practical exercises to maintain alignment and facilitate their healing. You can do it, too. Reiki is an effective means of gaining alignment spiritually, emotionally, and physically, and since love is the universal antidote, that is my focus.

FOR YOU, WITH LOVE

Do you ever feel lost or alone? Do you ever feel that you're not worthy of being loved? Do you ever feel the people around you who are supposed to love you are just not cutting the mustard? Do you worry so much about the future and finding love that it cripples you sometimes? Have you gotten so used to not feeling that you think it's normal? You need love. We all need love. We need love in the same way that we need food and water. Don't deny yourself.

Below are a few exercises you can do to help reignite the light in you.

QUESTIONS

Ask yourself the following questions. Be honest. How do you feel about your answers? Are there obvious areas that need improvement? Do something about it. Find it within yourself to love yourself and others.

SACRAL CHAKRA ASSESSMENT - WHAT'S YOUR PLEASURE?

1. Do I make room for pleasure in my life? When and how do I do this?

2. Have I experienced bliss and/or pure ecstasy lately? Why or why not?

3. What am I passionate about? What makes me tick? Am I able to engage in activities that bring me great joy?

HEART CHAKRA ASSESSMENT - WHO DO YOU LOVE?

1. Do I have conditions for myself to receive love and acceptance? If so, what are they? Why?

2. Is there something I need to forgive myself for? If so, repeat in the mirror three times, "I forgive you for _____," and mean it.

3. Is there something I need to forgive someone else for? If so, do the same here. Just because you forgive doesn't mean you have to forget, but forgiveness saves your soul.

4. What will make my heart sing? Search your soul.

MIRROR WORK

Incorporate positive self-talk and basic Reiki hand movements into your daily routine. This is best done first thing in the morning, preferably as you're preparing for the day.

1. Stand in front of your mirror.

2. Look deeply into your eyes.

3. Look at your face, then return your gaze to your eyes.

4. Say, "Good morning, Beautiful. Today is your day. You are special. You are loved. You are blessed."

5. Take both of your hands and hover them over the top of your head.

6. Breathe.

7. Move your hands down to the front of your face. Your palms should be facing you, and fingertips should be hovering in front of your third eye, i.e., the center of your forehead and your palms should be toward your chin.

8. Breathe.

9. Place your hands over your heart with your right hand close to your body and the left hand over the right.

10. Breathe.

11. Ask God for love, guidance, support, forgiveness, and fun in your day. Amen.

NEXT STEPS

These self-healing activities are a start. There are many other ways that you can get your energy moving and make your way back to love. This is what I want you to do right now.

- Remove toxicity from your life. This is a big step. Be careful with whom you expend your energy.

- Pay more attention to what you put into your body. Eat healthily. Drink water.

- Speak up. Make sure you are clear about your needs so that people understand.

- Don't accept bullshit.

- Accept the fact that you deserve to be loved in a way that feeds your soul.

Love is not a fairytale. Have faith that love is out there, it's within you, and it's all around you. Remember, the greatest love of all is the love found inside of you. Light it up!

 **Dr. Makeba Morgan Hill,** affectionately known as Dr. Makeba, the Doctor of Love, wears many hats, as do many women. She is a writer, a Reiki practitioner, a yogi in the making, a health care executive, an entrepreneur, a friend, a mother, a teacher, an extreme cat lover, a believer that children are our future, and a child of God.

Dr. Makeba owns Dr. Makeba & Friends Healing Hands, which is a holistic wellness center based in Atlanta, Georgia, that specializes in modalities to facilitate balance in the body, mind, and soul for humans and their pets. Using the power of love and light generated through her Reiki energy work and her spiritual connections, she helps souls experience much-needed breakthroughs in all aspects of their lives.

As an empath who cares deeply for others, Dr. Makeba has been drawn to non-profit caring and learning industries throughout her career, where she has most often served in strategic planning or executive leadership roles. She earned a bachelor's in Healthcare Management from Florida A&M University, a Master of Health Services Administration degree from George Washington University, and a doctorate in higher education at the University of Georgia.

A believer in continuing education, she recently earned her Reiki level II certification from Althea Lawton-Thompson's Living Life Limitlessly program. She's currently a student of Radiance Sutras School of Meditation to become a certified meditation instructor, and she is also working on becoming a certified sex and intimacy coach. In addition, Dr. Makeba founded and runs Havenly Hills Cat House, a volunteer organization dedicated to the care and keeping of community cats entrusted to her neighbor in Atlanta.

Dr. Makeba is doing her part to bring love and light back to the world. Love is the secret sauce.

Connect with Dr. Makeba:

Website: https://drmakeba4love.com/

LinkedIn: https://www.linkedin.com/in/dr-makeba-morgan-hill-7598394/

Facebook: https://www.Facebook.com/DrMakeba4Love

Twitter: https://twitter.com/DrMakeba4Love

YouTube: DrMakeba4Love

https://www.youtube.com/user/MMHill1

Linktree: https://linktr.ee/drmakeba4love

You are light! You are love! You are blessed!

Love & light,

Dr. Makeba

XXOO

CHAPTER 13

BEING DITZY IS DIVINE HEALING IN ACTION

TAPPING INTO 5D ENERGY FOR HEALING

Denise M. Simpson, MEd

MY STORY

Peggy called, "I saw your new book *Inspired Living: Superpowers for Health, Love, and Business* on Amazon. Congratulations!" She asked if I knew Cathy, who is in her new certification program. I do, so I promised to make a warm introduction for them.

"Mike thinks you're ditzy," Peggy told me. "I'm starting a year-long program working with the superconscious mind. He hopes I don't become like you." While shocked at first, I realized what a great compliment being recognized for who I've become is—a beacon for advanced methods of healing beyond traditional western medicine.

"It's okay. I don't have to prove myself to him. I am more centered now. He's just not ready for fifth-dimensional (5D) healing," I chuckled.

Peggy then told me Mike was dreading his upcoming knee replacement surgery. I asked why. "Well, he had a car accident in his 20s, he died, they got him back, and then his leg didn't work right," she rattled off this shocking news like it was her shopping list.

Peggy continued telling me how his knee would just give out going downstairs. Mike went to physical therapy for a year to heal physically but never addressed the emotional wounds he suffered. He would 'soldier on' stoically. On the job as a realtor, he spent four decades going up and down stairs.

By not addressing the emotional, mental, as well as physical aspects of a trauma, our bodies carry it in cellular memory. We call these energy blocks, limiting beliefs, and repressed emotions. Now the damage is done, Mike's mobility is compromised, and he's in pain. At 70 and retired, his knee is bone-on-bone, so surgery is indicated to repair his body. This is a third-dimensional (3D) healing approach.

The third dimension is our everyday physical reality of width, height, and length—all matter we interact with, including our bodies and minds. Most western medicine utilizes physical and bio-chemical treatments to fix a problem. A drawback to 3D medical approaches is that specialists work on diagnosing one part of the body but lack an integrative approach for the whole person. One treatment may adversely impact another area, and another pill is prescribed. 3D treatments are useful for life-saving interventions but are time-consuming, expensive, and often cause side effects from drugs and surgery.

3D western medicine is more about treatment than healing, and its value is questionable for curing the emotional root level or the long-term quality of life.

3D therapy may take years for psychological analysis using the cortex and neocortex but doesn't teach patients how to access the subconscious, which drives 90% of behavior. "It only goes so far with checklists and coping strategies," according to Margie.

Margie called me after spending thousands of dollars in therapy for years working on her traumatic family upbringing of alcohol and drug abuse. She described family fights, overwhelm, exhaustion, and the need to overcome her anger, sadness, and frustration in life. She sounded stressed and really wanted to change her patterns of negativity and improve her financial resources. In the background, I could hear angry voices and the f*ck word used repeatedly. I cringed.

These are all 3D problems to fix; most are external, while her mindset is internal. Self-care will be crucial so she can neutralize the stress response in the mind to actually get in her body to experience energetic sensations. Only then will she develop an awareness of fear and learn how to soothe it for peace.

The inner voice of fear to survive creates chronic fight or flight stress. Currently, about 95% of the world's 7.5 billion people live this way. Most can't think beyond survival. Their goal in life is protection and gaining basic necessities. Using force over others is dominant. Love is a balance sheet, not an unconditional flow. These are outmoded paradigms. It's time to evolve as four percent of the planet have learned to do—they've mastered their mind and can skillfully shift the energies of the body-heart-mind-soul on the quantum level. The result—tranquility and limitless options, vitality, easier flow, and manifestations. They harness personal empowerment.

Margie continued talking about her dreams beyond a life of pain. She's ready for more, and I know methods beyond 3D repairs, but I didn't always.

What is energy? Does Reiki work? It's just imaginary, isn't it?

One weekend in 2010, I learned the answers.

I saw Reiki performed at health expos beginning in the 1980s, but I didn't believe it was real. It looked to me like people waving their hands around in mid-air or touching a body doing—nothing. But then the person would sit up smiling, relaxed, and happy. *Huh, so what's actually happening?*

After winning the high bid for two people to certify in Reiki Level I and Advanced Level II from the NH Public Television Auction, I invited my college friend Lisa to the first training weekend. She asked, "Do you think it really works? Will we be able to do it?" Her questions mirrored the skeptical doubts in my mind. *What are you getting yourself into?* I wondered as we arrived.

It was a weekend that changed my life.

Upon arrival, our Reiki master Melissa greeted Lisa and me with a huge smile, dogs barking happy greetings, and two horses in a paddock whinnying. The sun shone on the garden, and birdsongs filled the air. I immediately felt at peace.

"Welcome! I'm so glad you're here!" Melissa exudes warmth, generosity, and love as she embraces us in a huge bear hug.

Introductions are made with four other classmates. We begin learning about the chakra system: 10,000-15,000 years of mind-body wisdom from the Sanskrit, Chinese, and Indian traditions. We compare Eastern to European scientific methods, which are only 500 years old. *Wow! I never thought of healing like that.* Mind-blowing perspectives began.

Fourth Dimensional (4D) healing adds time to 3D for healing past, present, and future. The chakra energy system processes the frequency of information and radiates our electromagnetic field, known as an aura. Just like the Earth, our bodies have a Torus field of electromagnetic energy. Our atoms are held together by gravity, a universal force in the cosmos. Keys to 4D healing are the client's intention to allow themselves to heal. Noticing sensations, thoughts, emotions, temperature, pressure, and vibration in the body is key. Channeling energy through the body is key. Quieting the ego to connect inward to the heart and soul is key. These keys work—naturally.

Contrast this with limiting 3D methods fostering dependence on the external authority (doctor, therapist, or expert) who performs the healing, creating the need for treatment after treatment. "Physician, heal thyself," Jesus said (Luke 4:23), meaning go inward. You have the power to imagine your desired state of being. Connect to Divine Love to make it so.

Melissa instructs us, casually accepting my questions with their underlying challenge of "prove it." She is patient with me, using grace and humor. I relax to actually allow the learning.

Lying on a massage table, I feel funny with four classmates watching while Melissa demonstrates hand placements for the chakras up and down my body. When she is over my lower abdomen, Melissa stirs her hands around and—*whoa!* I feel like she is using a whisk in cake batter on my guts. Sensations are getting stirred.

Interestingly, she has trouble finding my second chakra and then locates it off to the side. She finishes, and I describe my sensations. Melissa asks about my right ovary, "Did you have surgery? What about tumors?"

Stunned, I answer, "Yes, I did have surgery for endometriosis and years of trouble with fibroid tumors and an ovarian cyst. How do you know?"

She just smiles knowingly. "You'll learn," she states. *Okay, you've got my attention; maybe there is something to this after all.*

More mind-blowing moments happen throughout the weekend. The most convincing is when six of us sit in the sunshine with pillows on our laps to represent a person for long-distance healing. Joe volunteers his sister in Washington state because she is so far away. He calls to ask her permission, and she says, "Yes. I guess so. Do you really think it will work?" *Yup, I'm not the only one who is skeptical.*

Melissa leads us through the process as my hands move over the pillow. I peek at one point and think, *if anyone sees me now, they'd think I am crazy.*

During the lesson, I sense warm and cool tingling in my palms over very specific areas. I can't make sense of the undeniable sensations. Afterwards, some say they didn't really feel anything. I'm afraid my answer won't be good enough, but Melissa looks deeply into my eyes, encouraging me.

"Well, I did notice…," and I speak.

"Denise, that's great. I sensed…," and Melissa described where she felt energy warmth or congested energy blocks, and it matched. "Joe, call your sister and see what she noticed."

"Joe, I'm not sure what you did, but I feel so much better. Nancy sounds happier and excited even. I haven't told you yet, but I fell the other day and sprained my right ankle. I've been lying in bed with pain, but now it's way more comfortable. And my heart pain is lessened too. Whatever the group did, thank you! This is the best my ankle has felt."

Joe knew Nancy had a heart condition but was shocked about the fall and her ankle. She reassured him, and they promised to talk later.

Holy smokes! How could this woman I didn't know, sister to a man I just met, feel anything over 3,000 miles away? Clearly, something had happened. And I was just waving my hands around in the air over a pillow. *Huh, Reiki works.*

The last day of the training, Melissa talked about auras being the energy field around a person and how we all have the capacity to sense them. Some people can actually see rainbow colors. We are all born with intuition, but for most of us, it is misunderstood, or unacceptable, so as children we shut it down to be loved.

"Wait, are you saying…?" And with that, I delve into deep memories of being five years old and seeing dancing lights around my bedroom ceiling. My mom couldn't see them or answer my questions, so she snapped, "Denise, there's nothing there. Go to sleep!"

I cried myself to sleep, misunderstood and confused. I never mentioned them again. But now, here I am at 50 years old, getting answers. Melissa instructs me to soften my focus as she stands against a beige-colored wall. Voila! All of a sudden, I can see a green glow around her. It was magical, like a light turned on. I start crying from the joy, the bliss, and the wonder of it. I cry for my little girl reclaiming a natural gift and, more importantly, being accepted for it. My heart expanded.

We celebrated all we learned, and I left transformed. A whole new world opened up to me personally, spiritually, emotionally, physically, and for my coaching business. There was light around the flowers, trees, horses—everything. The world was glowing, and so was I, sensing love all around me.

Energy is real. Energy medicine is real; it works. And if it's imaginary—I'll gladly embrace it over the toxic side effects of pharmaceutical chemicals that tax our body's natural abilities to heal.

I continued training with Melissa to obtain the Advanced Level II Reiki certification. Energy healing became less weird and more factual. My inner skeptic was convinced with illogical proof. A metaphysical perspective makes perfect sense to me now and is what I teach my clients—and it changes lives.

Energy is love. We're a universe of walking love in our bodies. Every cell pulsates as molecules dance, swirl, crash into each other, and break apart. Just like the cosmic Big Bang, there are micro bangs within our bodies every nanosecond as cells grow and die. Love supports life; life is love.

"Miracle healings" occur when there is a powerful energetic shift. When love exists, there is no room for imbalance or illness. Disease is the condition of out-of-whack functioning. Energy healing works with the vibrations of the body and outside the body.

Our bodies have meridian or acupressure points which are bio-electric gateways into the body, mind, spirit, and beyond. The brain operates on beta, theta, alpha, delta, and gamma waves. I learned to skillfully shift them to access subconscious programming. You can practice too; it's worth it for greater possibilities in life.

Tapping with meditation, hypnosis, crystal or sound healing, or breathing work on the body-mind level—they shift your brain wave states—for stress reduction, resetting imbalances, and allowing the heart to open to connect to Spirit. Shifting into theta, alpha, and especially gamma is the key to reprogram the subconscious. The Body—Heart—Mind—Soul, this is the magic formula to heal beyond 3D repairs.

My holistic journey moved me into the fifth dimension (5D), where consciousness expands without limits. For a decade, my certification trainings included various modalities: the Emotional Freedom Technique™, hypnosis, Soul Entrainment™, and six years certifying as an advanced facilitator of Evolutionary Mystic Meditation™, and more.

The quantum field is often referred to as the "realm of unlimited possibilities," Infinite Awareness, Oneness / Harmony, The Nothingness that Creates Everything, Universal or Source Energy, Infinite Wisdom, or Galactic Consciousness. These are labels for that which is label-less. Working with clients, I refer to it as "Beyond the Beyond: across space, time, and dimensions." Sounds ditzy, right?

What is energy? Does Reiki work? It's just imaginary, isn't it?

Now I have answers. The skeptic is satisfied. Now I regularly play in the quantum field across space, time, or dimensions connecting to soul purpose, life mission, Akashic Records, and clearing ancestral patterns. Tapping into the inner voices of the mind and channeling the Divine is strenuous work and blissfully easy. Sure I look ditzy, but oh, what a gift it is! I'm living an extraordinary life and so do my clients. It is possible, and you deserve it too.

Clairvoyance, claircognizance, clairaudience, clairsentience, and even clairgustance abilities are all turned on to tap into. My leading edge of training is Full Spectrum Healing™ for even greater quantum field 5D healing capacity.

Learning to channel higher frequencies was an adventure. My body had to calibrate to transmit the higher vibrations through my body. At first, it was scary—like sticking my fingers into an electrical socket and leaving them there. I cried with discomfort, with emotional release of old traumas, and I cried in pure bliss. I reverently honor the sacred transformation and responsibility of being a divine healer. It birthed my Courageous Heart— for this journey "is not for sissies," as my mentor and big brother Alan Davidson used to say.

So when Peggy told me her husband Mike "thinks you're ditzy," I understood it was his fear talking. He's resisting going deeper into his soul's journey so judging me is his ego's way to protect himself. He's really saying, "No thanks. I'll stick with 3D, thank you very much." And that's okay. I release him on his journey in his time, his way. I'm free to provide services to Margie, who's eagerly awaiting healing on the 5D level.

I overflow with joy at the seemingly miraculous results my clients experience with a 5D reprogramming using Tapping, hypnosis, a Soul Purpose clearing, Ancestral clearing, Akashic Record process, or more technologies.

Yes, energy medicine using 5D creates mind-blowing results with unlimited possibilities. Energy medicine is soul-mind-heart and body medicine. And I've transmuted being ditzy into a Divine healer. Now that's a legacy.

THE TOOL

1. Realize that your body is designed to heal naturally. Take care of it using basic 3D approaches by accessing a Sacred Self-Care Planner at https://go.denisemsimpson.com/resources

2. Access Your Brain Waves for Courageous Success

    It is possible to discover, deprogram, and then reprogram new, up-leveled capacities for what you can create in your life versus the limited, negative beliefs you were socialized into. To up-level, you need to learn to master your mind versus having the mind control you with fear, doubt, and limiting beliefs.

There are five brain wave frequencies with unique functions, characteristics, and ways to access them. Discover what's possible by working with them.

	Beta	Alpha	Theta	Delta
Hz	12-30	7.5 - 12	4-7.5	0.5-4
Consciousness State	Waking	Dreaming, day-dreaming, eyes closed	Deep meditation, light sleep, the REM dream state	Deep Sleep, dreamless sleep. Non-awareness
Access to:	Alert, logical, critical reason, executive function	imagination, visualization, memory, learning, and concentration	the subconscious mind. The twilight state between Alpha drifting off to sleep and coming out of Delta, deep sleep.	Unconscious, Gateway to Universal mind
Activity Level	Daily activities	light meditation, program mind for change, success	Vivid visualizations, great inspiration, profound creativity, exceptional insight as well	Access the collective unconscious for downloads of inspired action and information
Emotional / Physical State	Stress, anxiety, restlessness	relaxed, detached awareness	The voice of Theta is silence, deep spiritual connection, and oneness with the Universe	Completely detached awareness... there is no mind, there is no body
Mind State	Monkey Mind, chatter, Inner Critic, Doubt, Fear etc. Or could be Success Team voices!	Gateway from conscious awareness into subconscious. Intuition is more clear and profound with 7.5 Hz frequency	Your mind's most deep-seated subconscious programs reside at Theta.	Deep healing and regeneration occur without effort

3. Tapping is my 'go to' tool because it works shifting from beta to theta/alpha states. Evidenced-based research proves its effectiveness over placebo or pharmaceuticals for trauma and most diseases, plus it's fantastic for raising your vibration for success. It's cost effective

with no chemical side effects and naturally creates good-feeling hormones to reduce cortisol and adrenaline.

Learn to tap watching my YouTube video: https://www.youtube.com/watch?v=8aL2sXNXMt4&t=8s

Denise M. Simpson, MEd, CCH Coach - Healer - Author - Speaker

Living an extraordinary life after depression, stress, grief, loneliness, debt, job loss, etc., is possible. Women professionals and parents are challenged these days by so much, and our hearts are weary with worry. You can't fix these with what you learned, but you can learn the best of 40+ years from Denise's education, training, experience, wisdom, and divine guidance. Denise teaches skills immediately applicable for the rest of your life.

I'm Denise M. Simpson, and I've been there - divorced, depressed, grief-stricken, harassed in a corporate job, feeling broken with too many tearful nights, no joy, and no purpose. So I dove into healing: Tapping, hypnosis, acupuncture, yoga, meditation, crystals, essential oils, homeopathy, Reiki, and writing. I committed to heal my family wounds and corporate harassment because I either got better or I got off the planet.

My hero's journey led me to become the Courageous Heart Coach. It takes courage to live, to heal, to change my mindset, to change nutrition, self-care, and to communicate boundaries. It takes courage to stop people pleasing and say "No" to them and "Yes!" to me. It takes heart opening to live my soul purpose as a coach.

Denise is "delightfully creative, cleverly quick-witted, compassionate, and a charismatically brilliant sage of a soul" who helps women transmute trauma into thriving, evolve their mindset for empowerment and embody courage for inspired actions. The results are stress reduction, improved health, sacred self-care, more energy, a calm mind for better sleep, communication, boundary setting, mature nourishing relationships, better sex, money flow, business expansion, book manuscript completion, and more fun, joy, and pleasure in life. Denise as a coach holds clients with love, respect, and compassion so that they feel safe to transform. They learn new truths about their True Self beyond what they thought was possible. She helps you discover and fulfill the greatest hidden potential within. Clients experience true transformation in shorter timeframes than expected.

Denise has unique intuitive insights and is "an amazing channel" for soul messages. You will be able to navigate mid-life or soul awakening to achieve your heart's desires with courage, confidence, and celebration. Denise shows you how to make an impact, create abundance, and leave a legacy. This creates a life worth living.

Denise brings to Courageous Heart Living and Courageous Heart Writing her unique combination of award-winning training, coaching, creativity, intuition, and 5D evolutionary energy psychology technologies. She studies the newest in energy psychology tools and quantum energy healing technologies. She holds two Masters degrees, plus a lifetime of certifications. She is an Advanced Certified Facilitator of Evolutionary Mystic Meditation™. Denise is a #1 Amazon Best Selling author of *A Muse Your Self Writing* and four more anthologies. She loves to sew quilts, kayak, and garden with Tucker, Chase, and Harley, her cats, in the yard.

Connect with Denise on:

Website - https://denisemsimpson.com

Email: denise@denisemsimpson.com

Facebook - https://www.facebook.com/DeniseMSimpsonMEd

LinkedIn - https://www.linkedin.com/in/denisesimpson/

Twitter - https://twitter.com/DeniseMSimpson

Instagram - https://www.instagram.com/denisemsimpson/

Books:

Author signed copies are available for purchase on

https://go.denisemsimpson.com/resources

Inspired Living - Superpowers for Health, Love, and Business

The Great Pause - Wisdom & Blessings from COVID-19

The Great Pause Journal

A Muse Your Self Writing - How to Overcome Writer's Block

CHAPTER 14

HEALING WITH HERBS AND TEA

PREVENTATIVE SOLUTIONS FOR WELLNESS BEFORE AND AFTER COVID

Vera Halina LMT, CCH, RYT

MY STORY

As I go back in time, hindsight is 20/20. I was coming into the world at a time of social unrest in America. In 1965 the Watts riots went on for six days between people of color and the police.

I was born to a white immigrant mother and a Native and African American father, living between two worlds. Biracial, mixed-race, bi-cultural, interracial, and multiracial are the words that have described my existence here in America.

I can tell you that I have always felt that I was here on Earth, placed between worlds.

Looking back, I realize this was important to be born this way, as it allowed me to understand the dark and light much more vividly than most.

I also remember the moments as a healer, as a child.

Coming into the world was a very dark time. I was born in a Catholic hospital.

They mostly gave women drugs, and instead of assisting in natural labor, instead of helping the mother push, the doctors and nurses pulled me out.

My mother woke up hours later, extremely sick, and they did not let her see me for over a week! She lay in that bed crying for me, as I must have been longing for her.

Without a mother's touch for the first week of my life, I was alone. Just thinking about this brings me to tears.

She dragged her body down the halls to find me when she began recuperating, begging the nuns to bring me to her. I cannot imagine the pain she suffered, but I know what suffering I endured; over 50 years later, I continue to attempt to heal these deep-seated wounds from the past. Years later, I was in awe while a healer friend of mine did a biofeedback scan on me; she let out a gasp as she looked on the screen and said, "All your organs were in failure as a newborn baby!" This observation gave me another point of view on the story my mother told me.

As an infant and toddler in 1966, my parents were legally allowed to finally be married.

On June 12, 1967, in <u>Loving vs. Virginia</u>, the United States Supreme Court unanimously (9-0) struck down state statutes that kept black people from marrying white people.

The marriage did not last but a few years. I ended up being more of a caretaker for my mother. She was terribly ill and could not leave her bed because of severe back pain and other internal pain. She had a complete hysterectomy before the age of 30. I was young, but I knew I had to help.

I remember cleaning, cooking, and preparing food at ages four and five.

As far as I can go back into my memories, I have always been a nurturer, trying to heal and make life better, starting with my mother.

As an adult, I wanted to escape from my small town and travel the world. The only obvious way I could see myself doing this was to become a travel agent.

After college, I worked as an executive travel consultant for 15 years; in my last five years in the industry, I worked as an international travel agent for United Technologies.

During this time, I experienced life-altering events.

I had two major car accidents. A friend lost control of the car while I was on the passenger side, and a few months later, I was hit from behind by a drunk driver.

I was driven away by an ambulance and the cars taken on a flatbed tow off the highway. I ended up with lacerations, dislocations, and extreme soft tissue damage—it was incredible that I walked away alive and without broken bones.

I also discovered I was two months pregnant! I was utterly traumatized. I spent over a year in physical therapy. Within that time, I had a beautiful daughter and began to work nightshifts so I would not miss any of her "firsts."

I was exhausted, but it was all worth it.

As she grew up, I was more comfortable with us traveling the world.

Any time I traveled, it was mandatory to make appointments for healing bodywork. Unknowingly, this is when I felt drawn to healing powers.

My friends and family were curious about healers—it was entertaining.

Every time I spent time with medical, psychic, and spiritual healers, they always told me I had a gift of healing. I was confused; every time I heard it, I was like, "Who? Me?"

I was not in touch with my energetic side. I had a healer once say, "You have a huge black energy blocking your third eye." I had to laugh as I had no idea what she was saying. She said, "I will give you a chart and help you clear it." This was my first introduction to Chakras and energy centers.

After 15 years of working two to three jobs at a time, I also put my own physical and mental healing on hold.

I began getting the feeling of burnout.

Healers would come in every week to my jobs to do ergonomic therapy (as we had to remain seated for over eight hours a day). Chair massage therapy was my mini refuge.

My therapist was also a teacher at a massage school. He listened and understood my suffering and knew the chair massages benefited my body and spirit. He told me to check out the school and said, "This could be a career path for you."

This same week, my mother ordered a package from the same school. I knew this was a sign from the Universe to check it out. They had weekend workshops, so I signed up and never looked back!

After two years of study, I learned different forms of healing, working with energy, how muscles and bones work together, and the Chinese theory of pressure points that activate healing. I felt blessed to receive as many massages as I was giving, which shifted my health like no other modality.

I wanted to keep learning more about healing, and the Asian healing arts intrigued me. In 2000 I graduated from massage school and was so happy to be able to get out into the world and share my gifts.

During that same year, I received a diagnosis of fibromyalgia. Even though this is a horrible, chronic disease, at least I could put a name to all the pain I experienced.

My fibromyalgia diagnosis and education brought me down a rabbit hole of natural healing. I realized it was a chronic condition and that natural medicine would be the way to go for a lifetime of recovery.

Clients come to see me due to a recommendation from their doctor.

Doctors recommend massage for anxiety, lupus, multiple sclerosis, fibromyalgia, Parkinson's disease, and a great deal of other chronic illnesses.

One client said, "The doctor said to get massages, or we will have to start you on high blood pressure medication. It scared me enough to find a massage therapist that would help me, like you!"

In school, Asian medicine was 25 percent of what we needed to learn to pass the national massage therapy exam. I recognized learning the Asian arts were the way to go, continuing my healing practice by learning more about Traditional Chinese Medicine (TCM).

The Chinese herbal medicine made sense to me, as fibromyalgia is widespread muscle pain that disturbs sleep, creates headaches, joint pain/ stiffness, and other symptoms that need attention. Based on TCM, our bodies change yearly, seasonally, daily, and even hourly.

Years after working as a licensed massage therapist, I became a Chinese herbalist. I wanted to share so much information, but I found a great amount of resistance.

I heard from patients that they were on so much medication they were concerned about interactions.

Some folks never took any medication and were worried about herbal tablets (concentrated dried herbs used in tea). So, after years of pushback against the tablets, I decided to create my own medicinal herbal tea company.

Most people I have encountered love the taste of tea but do not understand the healing benefits. The herbs in tea make thousands of combinations, and each herb has its own individual medicinal properties.

My tea line has over 25 blends that use different herbs for different ailments.

It all started when my great-niece stayed with me for a week. It was a long time since I had a six-year-old with me all day and night. I was thinking, *I hope I am up for the challenge.* Knowing I would have to keep a strict routine, I felt confident until my niece left me with an extensive list of directions on giving her daughter allergy medications daily. She loaded my apartment with packs of tissues and a bunch of processed lunch foods.

I was concerned about providing this small child with pharmaceutical medications. She loved having tea with me. Our nightly ritual before bed was a bath, stories, and tea with local honey. I also ensured she had fresh fruits—like berries and oranges—for high Vitamin C, which helps decrease allergic rhinitis and the irritation of the upper respiratory tract caused by pollen from blooming plants. I knew healing started with a clean diet full of fresh, live foods and local honey providing local pollen. I made chamomile tea because, as I learned growing up, it is an excellent tea for relaxing the nervous system to help with sleep. As an herbalist, I also learned about its immune-building qualities, providing immunity to several common allergies. My niece quickly had less sensitivity to seasonal allergies—her symptoms went away almost overnight.

My name, "Aunty Berry," was born that week. She called me Aunty Blueberry or Aunty Strawberry, or whatever berry she could think of at the time. Seeing her happy and not dealing with congestion or a runny nose all day brought me joy.

Genuinely free from her condition, her mother came home and was in a panic that I did not use up her medications. I explained, "We ate fresh fruits and veggies, lots of raw, living foods, and nightly teas to help her with allergies."

Two weeks later, my phone rings; it is my niece on the line saying, "Aunty, what exactly did you make for her?" She was concerned as her symptoms had returned. I gave her the recipe, and the rest is history.

The tea company was my way of continuing to do the healing work at farmer's markets. I made tea for clients, friends, family, and for small gatherings. Tea is a fantastic way to share my love of herbs and the wisdom of plants.

As a Chinese herbalist, I decided to work with tea as an uncomplicated way to help the public understand herbal remedies. In TCM, most medicines taken orally are the fastest acting, including tea. I recommend tablets in my Chinese herbal consultation that have a mixture of two to ten herbs. When creating my teas, I have an ailment in mind with herbs that target various symptoms of an illness or disease. I make formulas for cold-induced disorders. These disorders appear when an external pathogen or invasion of something cold gets deeper into our systems (example: nervous, lymphatic, endocrine) and embeds themselves. The pathogen creates a weakness in the system.

I grew concerned about the long chronic symptoms of COVID over the last few years. I know the acute stage has been traumatic for us all, but I knew there would be lingering symptoms that most western doctors are not equipped to deal with, except for continuing to treat with pharmaceuticals. Western medicine is great for acute onset disease, but not for the long term.

According to Traditional Chinese Medicine, COVID is cold dampness in the system.

It attacks the pulmonary and respiratory system and produces fever, cough, myalgia, or fatigue, and as we know, cases of COVID can be mild or life-threatening.

There are stages of the disease, beginning with prevention, early stage, later stage, and recovery.

Prevention of diseases and treatment are core tenets of TCM practice. Using herbal medicines for COVID includes herbs and supplements in the prevention stage (blocking diseased pathogens and with asymptomatic patients). If any signs show up, they may look like: sore throat, fever, and cough.

Think of herbs like elderberry (Sambucus); there are so many benefits to ingesting this herb. The berry and flower of elderberry have antioxidants and vitamins that help your immune system protect you from airborne pathogens (COVID, flu, common cold, allergens).

Elderberry helps calm inflammation, lowers stress, and can also help to protect your heart.

When experiencing early-stage COVID (mild flu-like symptoms like headaches, muscle, and joint aches), think of herbs like echinacea.

Echinacea (coneflower) medicine has been passed down for centuries to treat influenza. These beautiful purple flowers grow everywhere, especially in the spring and summer.

One of the natural phenomena of plants is they show up when we need them the most.

Echinacea works by stimulating and controlling the immune system. It also has antibacterial and anti-inflammatory properties to help fight upper respiratory infections.

In later-stage COVID (pneumonia symptoms including nausea, vomiting, or diarrhea), as with any deeper stage of disease, treatment is more complicated than taking an herbal supplement, but it is an innovative idea to continue taking herbs to lessen the symptoms of the disease.

An herb called Poria (fu ling) is a mushroom that goes deep into the immune system. COVID will linger deeper into the protective organ layers if the disease process continues long-term.

In Chinese medicine, we call this a lung and qi deficiency. Poria was utilized in clinical studies to lessen fatigue, fever, dry cough, chills, and gastrointestinal symptoms.

The recovering and healing stage of COVID requires the support of numerous herbs and supplements. A clinical study used a combination of herbs and minerals (quercetin, green tea, cinnamon, licorice, and selenium) with enormous success.

Green tea has so many healing properties. It is effective in killing bacteria in the mouth. The Japanese have used green tea as a gargle after meals for centuries. I often suggest people gargle with it for protection or early-onset sore throat. Green tea catechins reportedly have the possibility of preventing influenza and infections.

These herbal examples are a few of thousands that can boost the immune system, releasing the exterior to continue pushing out the pathogen.

Science still has not figured out how to stop the spread of COVID.

The recommendations still include using face masks inside and in large crowds and keeping hands clean.

Based on years of use, I have used the Thieves formula of cinnamon, cloves, lemon, rosemary, and eucalyptus oils to keep in a spray for hands. It can also be used as an aerosol to breathe in an unsafe place for infection to spread.

The Thieves Oil smells warm and healing, and the properties of the herbs are antiviral, antibacterial, antimicrobial, and anti-fungal. Children and adults love the fragrance and the security of knowing the plants protect their health. Due to immune deficiencies, some patients and children benefit from this protective formula, especially when they cannot receive vaccinations.

Research and laboratory settings must continue with the more intensive scientific study of herbs, teas, and TCM herbal medicines outside of China, as potential treatments for COVID and other strategies for prevention and wellness.

For decades, my practice of using herbs in tea has continued to support the healing of my fibromyalgia symptoms and my clients' diseases. I am a believer in herbal teas as medicine in the treatment of diseases. Herbal teas have phytoactive components that show antiviral and immune-building properties which have shown up repeatedly as effective in the research for herbal medicinal use.

Medical professionals and consumers should consider these herbal combinations and formulations to protect their health. They are inexpensive and good for the environment, have zero side effects, and can be applied daily for continued protection from whatever new strain of pathogen comes our way.

THE TOOL

How to Make the Best Immune Tea on the Planet

2 Cups of Water

1 Cinnamon Stick

1 Tablespoon of Ginger

1 Teaspoon of Turmeric

Stir, bring to boil, and Simmer for 10 minutes.

Add one tablespoon of lemon juice.

Optional one teaspoon honey (local). Strain and Enjoy!

You can also watch my YouTube Video for instructions:

https://www.youtube.com/watch?v=1sHidmWnJfA

Vera Halina created Aunty Berry teas and is a sole proprietor of Aunty Berry's Apothecary and Cafe in Stonington, Connecticut. The cafe allows her to be creative in teaching the public and professionals continuing education credits for their professional licensed healing careers. Classes include tea tastings, herbal remedies, and internal and external healing herbal medicines.

Vera Halina is a perpetual student. She just finished her degree at Pacific College for the only Medical Cannabis degree in the Nation. She has been a licensed massage therapist and independent business owner since 2000.

Her love of Chinese herbalism brought her to the CT Institute of Herbal Studies.

Since 2008, She has studied with two Chinese Masters and continues to study in Tui-Na (Chinese medical modalities, including guasha, cupping, acupressure, Reflexology), Reiki, Shamanic Energy Healing, Aromatherapy, Crystal Healing, and Biofeedback.

The company started with the goal of raising the world's vibration to show people their power to evolve and heal. The value of preventative care and medicine is most important to her. Her passion for helping others heal and learn how to empower themselves gives her the greatest joy.

Her mission is to create a bridge between Eastern and Western medicine through education, exploration, and an artisan approach to nurturing the consumer's health and wellness.

Her hobbies are crafting with her grandchildren, traveling, biking, hiking, and yoga.

Please visit www.auntyberry.com to contact Vera Halina or check out the store, which includes the immune tea, all her other medicinal teas, and the Thieves oil.

Take a class or visit Aunty Berry's Apothecary and Cafe for old-fashioned treats and, of course, have some tea!

CHAPTER 15

MOVING WITH MOON MEDICINE

A LUNAR CYCLE TEMPLATE FOR HEALING MIND, BODY, AND SOUL

Theresa Pride, DPT, Energy and Movement Practitioner

MY STORY

I remember when I could zero in on exactly where the pain was located during an initial physical therapy evaluation.

"Here?" I asked.

And the patient on the table widened their eyes and nodded. Or exclaimed, "How did you *know* that?!"

I know because anatomy is part of my expertise. As a Doctor of Physical Therapy, I spent years learning about the body inside and out, dissecting human cadavers, and taking grueling exams to test my knowledge and the integration of that knowledge.

I was also usually on target because I could feel the person's energy and emotion radiating from them—something I didn't understand at first and not something taught in school. As I began to hone this gift of clairsentience, I started to teach my clients about their emotional and energetic connections to their physical pain.

Weaving this holistic way of healing into my practice was incredible. I couldn't believe my sheer fortune in helping others heal, not only their bodies but being able to provide tools for their lives and relationships with themselves and others.

The number one question that came up in sessions was, "When?"

"When do you have time to do all of this, Theresa?"

I proudly whipped out my phone to display my 23 different alarms. My morning routine had ten, just on its own:

5:00 a.m.: Wake up and live your best life!

5:15 a.m.: Shower

5:25 a.m.: Get dressed

5:35 a.m.: Coffee/Shake

5:45 a.m.: Affirmations

5:50 a.m.: Chant/Prayer

6:10 a.m.: Education/reading

6:20 a.m.: Expression/Writing

6:50 a.m.: Planner/Day ahead

7:20 a.m.: Leave the house

I would either receive exclamations of how organized I was or the somewhat disinterested, "That's neat." But one response completely threw me off.

"You can't be serious."

I looked up, startled. *Yes, I use these alarms every day,* I thought to myself. I had read every productivity book out there. This technique worked! The explanations and words of defense never made it past my lips, and we awkwardly continued the session.

This linear and strict structure did hold me up for some time. I tackled the perceived issue my patients had with integrating a holistic approach as a time management one—a productivity project.

Then one beautiful summer day, I was standing in line at Target, ready to check out. I was slightly flustered because I decided to get a handheld basket rather than a cart. It was heavier than I intended and rested awkwardly against my enormous pregnant belly.

I began sweating and noticed the basket starting to slip.

I'm not putting this on the floor, I thought. *What is taking so long?!*

My brain started to search for an out as my heart beat a little faster. I leaned forward and to the side to see what the hold-up was.

Pop!

I straightened back up immediately. Warm liquid began to seep into my pants and down the insides of my leg. A wave of electric heat rushed over my body.

Did my water just break? But it's early! What should I do? I can't believe this happened at Target.

My mind rushed. Somehow, I stayed calm, and no one seemed to notice. Would you believe I still checked out? Exactly four hours later, my first child entered this world with a full head of thick hair and a set of pipes to outdo Celine Dion.

And exactly two months later, I wrote to a support group about how disenchanted I was with everything I learned about time management—the routines, the alarms, and the early mornings.

Hot tears streaming down my cheeks, I poured out how every podcast, book, and time management technique was completely failing me. None of it prepared me for the sheer unpredictable nature of an infant.

No one warned me your time is no longer your own.

Where was the book that wasn't so masculine? That championed productivity from the perspective of a new mom?

Perhaps it existed at the time, but I didn't find it. I did, however, catch a podcast that described tracking your menstrual cycle and suggested it closely aligned with the moon cycle.

That caught my attention. I had never heard that before! My cycle hadn't returned yet in postpartum, so I squarely took my focus to the moon cycle.

I always had an affinity for the moon, searching the sky for it on my long and late commutes. I never really considered her effects on myself and others.

I dove into it all—learning the cycle of the moon, uncovering her energy, learning the history of lunar calendars and how our ancestors used the moon to guide events in their lives, and understanding the seasons. *That's exactly it! I'm in a season.* The relief was palpable.

I was also getting my first real introduction to astrology.

Being equal parts science and spiritual, I ran an experiment. One that would permanently change the way I lived, worked, and healed.

For five months, I tracked my energy. I did the best I could to release the expectation that my life would return to a routine any time soon. I began to recognize the massive identity shift that comes with parenthood.

So while I tracked feedings and diapers, I also noted how I felt. Was today a high-energy day? Low energy day? Similar to asking patients to rate their pain on a scale of 1-10, I would rate my energy level.

I included little notes like sleep patterns, if I had dreams, if something flared up in my body, or times I felt more sensitive or demotivated.

After I gathered all of that data, I went back and overlaid it on the moon cycle for those same months. I found that my energetic patterns and body sensitivities closely aligned with that of the moon cycle.

I was floored.

This completely changed my entire perspective. I finally understood the question "When do I fit in healing?" was less about managing time on a masculine 24-hour cycle and more about managing energy on a cyclical monthly pattern.

What if we could be more proactive? What if, instead of giving disjointed home exercise programs, mindfulness practices, and journaling prompts, I followed the energy of the moon cycle?

The question stuck with me. I've dedicated my career to helping others acknowledge and heal their bodies as well as the emotional and neuroscience connections. We are complex beings and full of emotion. Our emotional state can also affect chronic pain and inflammation. Being able to acknowledge, examine, process, and express those emotions allows us to engage healthily with ourselves and our relationships. Emotional pain, especially from difficult emotions like shame, fear, anger, and anxiousness, can get suppressed and trapped inside our physical selves. There are typically three levels to this—physical, energetic, and recurring trauma.

Let me give you an example. When I was young, my mother had a romantic partner who was verbally and physically abusive. Fear and shame were popular emotions invoked in me around this person's presence. I taught myself to stay out of the way and stay small so as to not draw attention and, therefore, potential harm. I buried my fear and shame deep inside. Eventually, anger was the primary emotion, as this person remained in our lives longer than I cared for them to be there.

I pressed these feelings so deeply, along with the ingrained coping mechanism of clamming up and shutting down any time there was conflict. This presented on those three levels as:

Physical: I cowered my posture to shrink my tall frame. I tensed up all over my body any time I was actively trying to hide. I often looked down and kept my head low. I experienced horrible intermittent chest pain from middle school into college that never had a medical explanation despite extensive tests.

Energetically: Fear, shame, and anger took up residence deep in my soul, specifically my sacral and heart energy. This would block my ability to love myself; I struggled to develop meaningful relationships in adolescence and early adulthood.

Recurring trauma: Until we process and heal the repressed emotion and physical/energetic effects, the body produces chemicals that mirror the original stress and inflammatory processes with the simplest action of having a memory. Before working on this healing journey around this person, even hearing her name brought up in conversation would slam my mind and body back to my younger self.

This ended up looking like unexplained chest pain and advanced osteoarthritis in the majority of my joints by age 22. The protective posturing alone led to back pain and headaches and deeply affected my confidence going into my college years.

So you see, it is not enough to just address the physical manifestations of our pain. I learned very quickly in the traditional physical therapy field that it was never going to be enough for me to only focus on the physical realm. It has a place, absolutely—but for chronic pain, having the option to include healing emotionally and energetically is supported by evidence and is my chosen path to work. My heal-code was born.

What the moon cycle did was bring a beautiful template to the table to embed my methods. I'll break down what it looks like to move with the moon's medicine and heal the mind, body, and soul.

THE TOOL

First, a little background on this gorgeous cycle.

There are eight main phases of the moon, with four being more well-known and what I'll describe here: new moon, first quarter moon, full moon, and third quarter or last quarter moon.

NEW MOON:

For the new moon, we experience a fresh cycle with this dark side of the moon. This is most associated with the shedding of the uterine lining and the first day of the menstrual cycle for those that experience one. It is a lower energy time and time to plant seeds and intentions. Common activities around the new moon are rest, intention setting, journaling, meditation, visualization, and connecting with your higher self/divine feminine.

FIRST QUARTER MOON:

At the first quarter moon, we experience increased energy for attraction and relationships. There is a swell of energy to take action on our intentions. It can also be a time of self-doubt if the to-do list is piled too high or our determination begins to wane. Common activities around the first quarter moon are: executing ideas, meetings, networking, being more visible, connecting with close relationships, attraction rituals, protection work against self-doubt, and realigning to-do lists.

FULL MOON:

In the full moon phase, we are called to honor our progress and celebrate. This is when our ancestors would harvest their crops and gather. The full moon can also be a more emotional time for many, creating a push/pull energy. It is the time most associated with ovulation in the menstrual cycle. Common activities around the full moon are: gathering, celebrating, gratitude journaling, charging crystals, and releasing work after the moon has passed peak fullness.

LAST QUARTER/THIRD QUARTER MOON:

Towards the end of the moon cycle, we find ourselves at the last quarter moon or third quarter moon. Here, the shadows are forming, and the moon is on its way back to the beginning of the cycle. It's a time to release and let go of what is no longer serving us. Common activities around the last quarter moon are release rituals, soaks/baths, shadow work, transmutation work, tough conversations, and removing toxic or unhealthy people or situations.

This is the legwork of utilizing the lunar cycle to your advantage. This is where I began and what sparked a deeper understanding of cyclical living. Merely understanding the energy of each phase and how it might affect you and those around you creates an awareness and a sense of peace.

At this stage, I ask clients to track and tune in. I highly recommend getting a moon journal. How does your energy align with the moon cycle? Can some activities be shifted to support your life better? Can some things be eliminated? Allow yourself to observe for a cycle or two. No pressure, no expectations. When you make a determination to heal, and especially a determination to heal on the levels of emotional, physical, energetic, and spiritual, it may be daunting at first. Try to start with understanding your energetic blueprint and natural rhythms. This sets the stage for moving with the moon while layering in the healing work you desire and deserve.

So now, you've been tracking in a moon journal and are as in love with the moon as I am, right? It makes me smile to know how many people I've turned on to healing and moving with the moon. Following the main phases and introducing small rituals and routines may be exactly what the doctor ordered. However, remember when I said this season of learning turned me on to astrology? That is because the moon's orbit naturally passes through the 12 astrological signs. This is where it gets really juicy and exciting.

The moon is a fast-moving celestial body, so she passes through the energy of an astrological sign every two to three days. This becomes another layer of the energetic field we experience during that time. Additionally, each sign rules a certain part of our bodies anatomically. During the energy of each sign, our body, energy, and the collective are responding.

As an example, perhaps you are noticing decreasing energy, some difficult conversations coming to the surface, your mind on overload, and your intestinal area inflamed. This could happen at several parts of the month, but this scenario would be heightened during the last quarter moon in Virgo. Approaching this part of the cycle, I recommend a client try some energy and crown clearing meditations, process the conversations with a therapist or trusted friend, and give attention to the intestinal area, which is ruled by Virgo. My favorite movement sequence to gently massage the internal organs is a rotation and twist session designed particularly for Virgo energy.

Another example would be, noticing your heart energy needs some attention, yet you're feeling high energy. It may feel like a push/pull energy, and your emotions may be heightened. This sounds like a full moon in Leo, ruler of our heart, chest, and upper back. My recommendation for this energy would be to engage in a heart-centering meditation or breathwork and do some chest opening exercises. My favorite movement sequence for Leo energy is on the foam roller. Your chest and upper back have never felt so good as after a Leo movement session!

Do you see the layers of healing? It's truly fascinating, and I'm so grateful for this template. It guides my lifestyle, personal healing, workouts, business decisions, family interactions, home management, client dealings, and how I process the world around me.

You can always download a quick complimentary guide with all of the signs, their hallmark energy, and their anatomical connections at the https://myhealcode.com site. But here is a rundown of each sign and a suggested way to move with the energy.

When the moon is in:

Pisces: Known for intuition and emotion, ruler of the feet. Grab a towel and place it around the ball of your foot. Pull gently towards your face for a calf and foot stretch.

Aquarius: Known for humanity, hope, and progress. Ruler of the circulatory system. Engage in getting your heart rate elevated with a cardiovascular workout, like swimming, biking, or walking.

Capricorn: known for structure and career/business, ruler of the skeletal system and joints. Low-impact weight-bearing movement like yoga or pilates is a great fit.

Scorpio: Known for transformation and forgiving energy, ruler of our excretory system. Core work and exercises that support the pelvic area are my go-to's for this energy.

Libra: Known for fair and balanced energy, ruler of the skin, kidneys, and lower back. I love incorporating balance work in standing, sitting, and/or kneeling.

Virgo: Known for order and its focus on health. Ruler of the intestinal tract and digestive system. Gentle rotation and twisting exercises activate this energy beautifully.

Leo: Known for individual creativity and fun, the ruler of the heart, chest, and upper back. Chest-opening exercises and stretching on a foam roller are perfect for this energy.

Cancer: Known for emotional and nurturing energy, ruler of the lower chest, diaphragm, and stomach. Diaphragmatic breathing and breathwork sessions do well for this energy.

Gemini: Known for communicative energy and learning, ruler of our central nervous system and brain. Try more complex movements and choreography, like in a dance or kickboxing class.

Taurus: Known for money and material wealth type energy. Ruler of the thyroid, vocal cords. Deep chin tucks and gentle neck stretches before vocal exercises honor this energy.

Aries: Known for confident and action-taking energy, ruler of the head and face. Did you know there are whole face muscle workouts? Give it a search; they're really fun!

Sagittarius: Known for wisdom and understanding, ruler of the hips, thighs, and sciatic nerve. A wonderful way to decompress the low back is the legs on the wall pose in yoga.

If you are anything like me, this uncovered a beautiful world for you. To recap:

- Get a moon journal. Any notebook will do, or you can use the My Healcode Lunar Healing Guide.
- Track your energy and see how it aligns with the moon cycle.
- Create your own template for accessing healing with the moon cycle.
- Add in layers and experiment with moving with the moon as she orbits our planet and passes through other energies.
- Most importantly, have fun! Embrace the seasons as they come.

The moon cycles deeply healed this former productivity addict and guided me through the identity change of parenthood. My sincere wish is that it can be a similar experience for you.

Theresa Pride, DPT, is a recovered productivity addict who teaches others to heal with the moon's medicine through movement, energy work, and aligned strategy. She uses her extensive knowledge of the body from a background as a professional dancer, pilates mentor, and doctor of physical therapy to guide healing in the body. As a certified quantum energy healer, she utilizes energy medicine to provide a whole-person healing model. Founder of My HealCode, Theresa aspires to help others crack the code to their unique energetic blueprint and capacity for healing both on and offline. Theresa resides in Atlanta, Georgia, with her husband and three children, where they enjoy the numerous trails and river activities.

CHAPTER 16

THE HEALING POWER OF FENG SHUI

YOU HAVE THE MAGIC INSIDE

Pat McGrath

We need our energy for health and well-being. But sometimes, our environment can slowly drain it away—drip, drip, dripping until we have nothing left. I know because it happened to me.

MY STORY

I felt an energy surge as I walked into the condo we looked at—a renovated mill building in a historic New England town with 14-foot ceilings, a huge open floor plan, massive windows, and multi-leveled floors leading up to the bedrooms. It even had a balcony. *How cool is this?* Lots of creative energy. A good omen for our new life, both of us starting over in a second marriage.

We set up the art tables in the living room. High ceilings mean big things, right? Not so fast. Yes, exciting things happened. The work we did took us on a short trip to Boston for two Emmys in cartoon commentary. My husband is the cartoonist, and me—the writer. It was fun until I got burned out. Neverending deadlines finally took their toll. But was the work getting to me? Not entirely; it was also my space.

Ten years after we moved in, I was done. Like the ceilings, my life suddenly felt too far away. Whenever I sat on the couch, no matter what was happening in the room, my attention jerked up and out the windows as if I wanted to touch the sky. I didn't. I wanted to sink down into the cushions and chill out. But the energy in the room never settled down. Neither did I.

At a time when I needed grounding, I was floating instead. My attention was constantly pulling away from where I was sitting or standing. Nothing felt casual. Every chore took a herculean effort. It wasn't possible to open the door and shake out a rug. You rode the elevator down two floors. Heaven forbid you forget your keys or your phone and the elevator dies. Bad day all around.

Inside, leaving the lower level meant climbing stairs, a lot of stairs. Four steps to the laundry, four steps to my office, seven steps to the balcony, and 25 steps to the second floor. The nightly trek to our bedroom? A 14-foot climb. I'm getting exhausted just writing this.

If you don't agree that the energy of a space can affect behavior, let me tell you how many times, on a first visit, kids tall enough to see over the balcony get inspired to speak to the masses. They wave to their pretend audience, "Ladies and Gentlemen!" They act out; adults are more subtle. Grown-ups pause, fighting their inner royal. It's so predictable it's funny.

Maybe you grew up like me, in a large family crowded into a small house with no room of my own. All I knew about space was there was none. I had no place for a desk, which was okay since there was no desk anyway. My siblings and I took turns doing our homework at the kitchen table around sticky bits of peanut butter and jelly sandwiches. I remember my grandma noting my stress and whispered to my mom, "She's sighing."

Since our family grew faster than our space, we squished together while our parents talked about raising the roof, literally. We stepped over each other in the living room while watching TV. Like riding the subway, finding a seat was often difficult. Sharing a tight space teaches you how to pretend others don't exist despite breathing their air—a handy little New York survival skill.

The good news, though! My life changed as I got my own room. A great blessing to me since I was the only girl—assistant Mom. I was reborn. Doing homework was so much easier. Being able to focus without interruption was a gift. Plopping my stuff down, knowing it wouldn't be touched, was another gift. I felt confident and prepared for my after-school activities. I was free as a bird.

Fast forward as wife number two, I slowly went numb as my new space overwhelmed me. My life took me from one extreme to the other. From no space to too much space, and all of it vertical. Once again, my surroundings were stressing me out, but for very different reasons. Instead of feeling claustrophobic, I was free-floating. Like a balloon losing its air, my life was blowing in the wind. Yet I still didn't understand how the energy of my space was contributing.

My husband chose this space. For him, the open floor plan and unique architecture meant freedom from mowing grass and shoveling snow. Condos have people for that. At first, I agreed, but then I watched him mindlessly step over the stinky garbage bag in the entryway. *Uh oh, he didn't even see it!* My heart sank. Where he saw inspiration and creativity, I saw more work for me.

In 1928, author Virginia Woolf wrote, "A woman must have money and a room of her own if she is to write fiction." What she failed to mention, however, was how to set up a room once you finally get one. Especially one of this scale and floor plan. I didn't want to write fiction, but I was unhappy, wanting more satisfaction. *Somebody, please, show me what to do!*

Hope arrived when I hired a Feng Shui practitioner. I read an article in a local newspaper where she reported on how environmental energies could affect our lives. As she explored my space, I couldn't believe how her words revealed insight into what I experienced every day. *How can she possibly know me? We just met!* Apparently, the energy of my space was speaking to her. I was all ears.

Her immediate comments? Separate home from work by converting one of the bedrooms into a studio and an alcove into an office for me. Wow, my tense shoulders fell to their normal position as opposed to wrapped around my head. As we continued, she pointed to too much artwork crowding the walls, making it hard to breathe. Gasp. By contrast, the huge white walls created a sense of snow blindness. I rubbed my eyes. My body was coming back to life just talking about this.

Minutes before, when she arrived and noticed the half-bath/laundry area just inside the front door, she asked, "Are you spiritual?" "I think so." But what has spirituality got to do with the laundry? I later learned she was using the Bagua, or Feng Shui life-map, to comment on how certain areas of my life were negatively impacting my space. Huh?

My inner cynic reared up as she told me the drains of the sink, toilet, and washing machine were depleting the energy I needed for my own spirituality. *Okay, I'll play along, but only cause I'm paying her.* Many months later, after I made the necessary changes to that area, (which I won't reveal here because they're sacred), I became interested in spirituality. She was right, I loved it.

There's a saying in Feng Shui, "Where attention goes, energy flows." Over time the Feng Shui changes she recommended for my home gave meaning and purpose to my space, and my life changed for the better. I learned to:

- Place area rugs in the big open spaces. Their shape and design attract our attention. As a result, the space is now defined as a living room, dining room, and entryway. Magically, as the space became clarified, so did my brain. Clear space means clear thinking. Aha! My mind instantly relaxed.

- I hung a mirror (of appropriate scale) to bring a "dead" corner back to life. Instead of avoiding that area of the living room because it drained the life out of me, the energy of the mirror now draws me in. It's more fun to be there.

- And, since colors represent the energy of nature, I painted selected walls green, terra cotta, and soft yellow, which continues to remind us of our inspired trip out west. It's amazing what a bucket of paint can do for our soul.

The scale of my space hasn't changed, but the feeling has. It's more intimate. It's no longer distracting, demanding, and exhausting. It feels comfortable and supportive. I'm organized. Life has more ease and flow. I have the energy to focus on what matters. My relationships, my creativity, and my work are now rewarding.

THE TOOL

When we think about ways to support ourselves, we might turn to the family and friends we trust. My intention is to show you, dear reader, how the energy of your space can also be a powerful tool for feeling supported. Feng Shui affects us in deep and profound ways because its principles are based on nature. When our space radiates a sense of well-being, so does our life.

Here's an example: We know what it's like to stand next to a rushing waterfall. Exciting and dynamic. Good luck trying to sleep next to one. If sleep is an issue for you, as Feng Shui practitioners, we look for bedroom energy that is calming and restorative. Generally speaking, and I'm being facetious here, there are no waterfalls in bedrooms.

However, since Feng Shui is about energy and everything is energy, it's the energy of artwork, furniture, light, computers, and televisions which can either mimic or mitigate the same effect of a powerful waterfall. Have you ever seen a poster of a rushing waterfall above someone's headboard? I have. That woman had a terrible sleep problem. Can you guess what the Feng Shui recommendation for this woman could be? Of course, relocate the poster to some other room! It's easier for us to be objective, but she couldn't see it.

As I work with women, I often hear stories of how they decorated their rooms when they were little girls. They chuckle as they remember the rainbows and unicorns. Years later and, all grown up, those same women can't even remember what makes them happy. Like them, it never occurred to me as an adult to concern myself with what surrounded me. Why would I? I had no idea my environment had any effect on my life.

Over time my wants and desires got buried under what I thought I should be doing. Eventually, even knowing what I wanted was a challenge. Sadly, I discouraged myself from wanting because I didn't think wanting was okay. In the Feng Shui process, I learned how to take a good look at what I wanted and then sync up the energy of my space with me. It was the most significant step I've ever taken towards jumpstarting a new mindset.

STUFF, A CAUTIONARY TALE

Living in an abundant society can make saying no impossible. As a result, we can end up with a lot more stuff than we ever thought possible. Or worse, stuff that is meaningless. My grandmother bought one dress a year in her day. Should I feel guilty when I buy, own, or collect? *No, as long as I'm mindful about it.* What I've learned is having lots of stuff doesn't make us happy but having stuff that truly lifts our hearts does.

Whether we know it or not, we interact with everything in our environment all day long. We clean it, dust it, polish it, repair it, paint it, fix it, sit on it, listen to it, or just notice it as we walk by. But if that interaction makes us anxious, depressed, or unhappy, maybe it's time to investigate why.

Some of our stuff can carry bad memories or remind us of tough times. The right stuff can inspire us, help us find inner peace, and help us rediscover our joy. Letting go of the wrong stuff makes room for all those good feelings to influence our life. When my Feng Shui practitioner asked me the stories behind certain items in my own environment, she encouraged me to let go of the ones with bad memories. I cried with relief.

Somehow, without knowing it, I held on to things that drew me back to a time when I felt less-than. It's not helpful to have our stuff exacerbate our own doubts and negative self-talk. Letting things go with awareness and intention taught me how to address my own needs without feeling guilty. The fact is, the more we support ourselves with good energy, the more energy we have to pursue what we want, including helping others.

LET YOUR SPACE HEAL YOU

Don't you feel better after a hug? Hugs can charge us up and make us feel capable of doing great things. It's how I felt after I made the Feng Shui changes suggested to me. My space was giving me a hug. I no longer felt tortured and distracted by my surroundings. My spirit was lifted, and my soul was healing. As my space gained meaning and purpose, so did my life.

I'm quoting one of my favorite teachers, Denise Linn, author of Sacred Space (and many other books on space and spirituality): "If it feels good, it's good Feng Shui." In other words, what feels good to you lifts your spirit. Bringing your spirit into your space emboldens you and brings out the magic which has been buried inside.

HOW CAN YOU START YOUR OWN PROCESS?

If you find yourself wanting to shift the energy in your home but can't figure out where to begin, here's a suggestion: start with your front door. Your front door is actually the face you're putting out into the world. Take a good look at yours and ask yourself these questions: Does my front door make the statement I want? Does it feel welcoming, or does it turn people away? Does it make me happy when I come home at night? Does it make me want to go inside?

Once you address the answers to your own questions, determine which changes you want to make, and I insist those changes make you smile. Smiling raises your vibration, which allows you to walk through the world confident and ready to share your presence. When you enter your home through your front door with a smile on your face, it means good things for you and your family. When you leave through your front door with a smile on your face, it means good things for you out in the world. What could be better?

Pat is an experienced Feng Shui practitioner passionate about teaching the subtle and profound ways our space can help heal our lives. She believes that since we all embody heaven on earth, Feng Shui is the missing piece in the mind, body, and spirit experience. To her, acknowledging our presence is emboldened when we're conscious of where our presence is actually located.

She holds a Bachelor of Arts from Trinity College, Hartford, CT, and certificates in Feng Shui from The New England School, spiritual counseling from The Psyche Institute for Higher Learning, and Meditation instruction from the McLean Meditation Institute. She is a contributing author for *Fast, Fierce Women,* edited by the University of Connecticut's distinguished professor, Gina Barreca, and *The Energy Medicine Solution,* created by Jaqueline M. Kane. You can find her "Musings" blog on her website: https://www.patmcgrathhealing.com/

Connect with Pat:

Email: mcgrathpat316@gmail.com

Website: https://www.patmcgrathhealing.com/

Cell: 860-490-3016

CHAPTER 17

A CRYSTAL PATHWAY TO HEALING FROM CHRONIC GUT PAIN

Elizabeth Waugh Duford, MSW, CCM,
Certified Crystal Master Healer

MY STORY

Have you ever been so hopeless about your health that you didn't feel like you could go on with life? Have you wondered whether living with chronic pain was just your fate and nothing would ever help? I have.

For over ten years, I struggled with horrible pain in my gut. I was chronically nauseous, my stomach felt like it was on fire a lot of the time, and I had serious bowel issues. I started reading about common digestive disorders and decided I would try changing my diet first. I gave up caffeine, red wine, chocolate, spicy food—the works. It made no difference in my pain level, and I was sick of bland food (and so was my partner—there are only so many nights one can eat millet and plain chicken), so I sought out a GI specialist.

Here's what the first doctor I saw said:

"It's GERD (gastroesophageal reflux disease). Take these prescription medications that prevent acid from entering the esophagus."

I took those pills. My stomach still hurt all the time.

The next doctor said:

"It's IBS. Make these changes to your diet and take these prescription medications. But also stay on the ones you were taking for GERD."

I made the dietary changes. I took those pills. My stomach still hurt all the time.

"We need to do an exploratory endoscopy to see if you have an ulcer or Celiac disease."

I went through the endoscopy. They didn't find anything. My stomach still hurt all the time.

You're getting the drift. Next, was a colonoscopy (if anyone has had one, you know the prep for it is worse than the actual procedure. I thought I would vomit from the stuff they make you drink). Next, I went through a study where I had a camera down my throat for 24 hours to monitor acid, and I felt like I was choking the entire time. Each procedure made me feel more hopeless because they yielded absolutely no answers.

Sometimes I was in so much pain, all I could do was lie in my bed with a heating pad on my stomach. I was miserable. I was depressed and irritable all the time. I had to drag myself to work. I declined invitations to dinners, coffees, and parties because I didn't enjoy eating anymore. I isolated myself from my family and my friends. I sank into despair.

Finally, I was referred to a specialist at a GI clinic at my local hospital.

He told me I had a neurological condition called functional nausea, where the brain sends messages to the gut that there's something wrong, and the gut responds by vomiting—even though there's not actually a problem. The gut has almost as many nerve endings as the brain, so much so that the gut is often referred to as "the second brain." This doctor explained that an old-school medication for depression was used to treat functional nausea, and prescribed Remeron.

I took those pills. And they helped! I was ecstatic. But the side effects were another story. I gained almost forty pounds in less than a year, which is common with tricyclic antidepressants. My blood pressure skyrocketed. I didn't know what to do, but I felt certain that more medication could not be the answer.

I thought about my session with the psychologist who worked at the GI clinic. She asked a lot of questions about my childhood and my mental health history, including questions about sexual abuse and assault.

"Elizabeth, if you are willing to share, have you experienced sexual abuse or sexual assault? I realize this is a difficult question, and you don't know me, so there is no pressure to answer."

I took a deep breath and found my courage.

"Yes, I was sexually abused when I was seven years old, and then sexually assaulted in my early twenties." I held back tears, feeling the shame that arose whenever I spoke of my experiences.

"Those experiences are actually quite common in people who have chronic gastrointestinal pain," she said gently. "There's no clear reason why this kind of pain is connected to these experiences, but we know from lots of research that more women than men struggle with digestive disorders, and a large percentage of the women have experienced sexual violence."

"I have done a lot of therapy about trauma," I told her. "But nothing has really helped with my stomach issues."

"One thing that has helped a lot of our patients is a mindfulness practice, and I encourage you to check out the mindfulness-based meditation program at Duke. Are you open to that?"

"I am open to anything that might help," I replied, but inside I was wary about another treatment approach that might not work.

As a social worker who has served people in crisis situations for almost twenty years, I'm very aware of how much trauma affects our mental health and our coping strategies. So many of my social work clients had significant trauma histories. I often felt like I was putting Band-Aids on their current situations because without healing from the past, their present lives couldn't improve, at least not past a certain point. I considered the large number who had chronic physical health problems, including my younger clients— diabetes, high blood pressure, chronic back pain, and, yes, gut problems. I also started thinking about how my own trauma manifested in my life, including in my physical health. *Could there be a way to shift that trauma out of my body so I could heal from my gut pain?*

Eventually, I pushed past my doubts and enrolled in the program at Duke. And it helped! The breathing techniques and the meditations taught me how to notice my pain and let it pass by, rather than getting attached to it. But I was still in pain. I really wanted to find something that would make the pain go away or reduce it significantly.

I decided to dive further into holistic approaches since Western medicine had largely failed to help me feel better. I tried acupuncture, herbs, essential oils, therapeutic massage, and yoga. They all made me feel healthy and improved my mood, and I was grateful, but the gut pain was always there in the background, like a rattlesnake waiting in tall grass, waiting to strike. I could never fully relax. I might have a few days or even a few weeks of relief, and then I'd find myself vomiting or doubled over in pain. I started to hate my body. *Why couldn't it just deal? Why couldn't it just heal? What was wrong with me?* I was in a state of hopelessness and totally unsure of what to do next. *Is this my fate forever?*

It wasn't until I discovered Reiki and crystal healing, and the ways they could reduce inflammation and release negative energy, that I started to heal. My energy skyrocketed, and I slept soundly. Meals could be joyful again, and I was less irritable with my family. It was an amazing shift. I ended up signing up for Reiki courses, as well as enrolling in a class to become a crystal healer.

I learned that the physical pain we experience is often because an energy center in the body isn't working properly. We have seven energy centers in our bodies that are called chakras. Chakra means "wheel" in Sanskrit, and they spin like tops along our glandular system. When a chakra is spinning too fast or too slow, that can cause distress—mentally, emotionally, physically, and/or spiritually. My digestive issues were related to the sluggish movement of my heart, solar plexus, sacral, and root chakras. Once I learned how to re-balance my chakras using Reiki and crystals, my life improved dramatically! And, if you are struggling with chronic pain, your life can get better too.

THE TOOL

In this section, I'm going to share the crystal path for healing chronic gut pain with you. If you're unfamiliar with how crystal healing works, the main thing to understand is that crystals, like all things on Earth and beyond, have an energetic vibration that resonates at a specific frequency. Our bodies also have an energetic vibration, and there are crystals that interact most effectively with our personal energy field. When we identify those crystals and place them on our bodies, they can help to relieve and soothe discomfort of all types. The crystal path for healing chronic gut pain focuses on addressing the physical manifestation of our energy imbalances. That said, many physical symptoms can be traced back to emotional distress, which is often uncovered during Reiki and crystal healing work.

The crystal path to healing chronic gut pain involves three steps:

1. Identifying where your pain is and using a breathing technique to tune in to that part of your body.

2. Selecting crystals to work with through your own intuitive process.

3. Practicing the Meditation for Gut Pain.

If you're struggling with chronic pain of any kind, it's vital to listen to your body. It's yelling at you! It desperately wants your attention and care. And pain will only escalate when it's ignored, as I learned when I dealt with gut pain for ten years. While I will continue to focus on healing for the gut, the techniques can be applied to any kind of chronic pain.

I know this sounds silly, but the first step towards healing is to talk to the part of your body that hurts. The body never lies. Identifying exactly where pain is in your body and sending deep breaths to that place is the first step toward healing. When you're clear about where your pain is, inhale, imagining cool, white light flowing into your nose. Send that healing breath to the painful part of your body, and hold it for a count of three, imagining that the cool light is penetrating the painful area. Then exhale for a count of three. You can repeat this several times as you more deeply settle into your body and ensure that you have identified the area that needs healing.

Once you have tuned in to the location of your pain, experiment with integrating crystals into a daily pain management practice. If you've never selected crystals before, here are some suggestions for determining which crystals resonate with your body's energy:

- Visit a crystal shop and notice which crystals you are drawn to. Go and pick up one of those crystals and hold it near your gut. Notice whether you experience any sensation or emotion. Does the crystal feel cold or hot? Does your hand tingle? Do you feel a sense of contentment, or are you experiencing an energy surge? If you have a strong positive reaction to a stone, that's one to keep. There's no "right" way to interact with a crystal, and don't worry if you don't feel anything—it might be that none of these crystals have much of an interaction with your own energy field. There are thousands of crystals out there to try!

- If you can't visit a shop, you can find crystals online, and again, notice which ones you enjoy looking at. One easy way to figure out which crystal to use is by color because each of the chakra centers in your body corresponds to specific colors. The chakras that are most often unbalanced when you experience gut pain are the solar plexus (immediately under your breastbone), the sacral (about three fingers-width below your belly button), and the root (on your perineum). The solar plexus corresponds with the color yellow, so yellow stones will work best; the sacral with orange, so orange stones will work best; and the root with red or black, so those color stones will work best. I usually add a heart chakra stone for good measure since our distress about physical pain tends to trigger strong emotions. The heart chakra is in the middle of the chest, and heart chakra stones are green or pink.

Once you have selected some crystals that resonate with you, start to integrate them into the breathing technique we already discussed. Lie down in a comfortable position, either on the floor or on your couch or bed. Breathe deeply into your gut, again imagining the cooling white light, breathing in through your nose for three counts, holding for three counts, and exhaling for three counts. Repeat this until you feel your body start to relax. Then place the stones you have chosen on the chakras that run along your digestive system—heart, solar plexus, sacral, and root. If there is a certain symptom that bothers you most, such as heartburn, you might just focus on your heart and solar plexus chakras. Continue to breathe deeply, sending your breath slowly into each chakra area. Notice if you experience sensations from the crystals—such as vibrations, a feeling of heaviness, or a change in temperature. If anything increases your gut discomfort, remove it immediately.

Now deepen into the following meditation:

MEDITATION FOR STOMACH PAIN

Once you're settled, close your eyes. Take a deep breath in through your nose and out through your mouth. Inhale for a count of four, and exhale for a count of four. Try to keep your breathing at this slow pace.

As you inhale, imagine that you are breathing in peaceful, soothing, cool light.

As you exhale, imagine that you are breathing out all your pain and discomfort. There is nothing for you to worry about right now in this present moment. All there is to do in this moment is breathe. Feel your pain slip away with each exhale.

If your mind drifts to feelings of discomfort, be mindful. Notice it without judgment, and then bring your attention back to the breath. You are strong and can handle anything life throws at you. Notice how calm you feel as you sit and breathe.

Open your eyes and take this feeling of relaxation with you.

After you've finished your practice with the crystals, take a few minutes to journal about your experience. Note your responses to the crystals and whether you experienced a reduction in painful symptoms after using them. It's possible that one area felt soothed while another did not. That's how you'll know that the crystal you placed on that specific chakra was the right one for your body's needs. Continue to try different crystals, journaling about the sensations you experience each time until you start to feel relief. It may take some time to find the best combination of stones to soothe your pain, so keep trying!

It's important to pay attention to your emotional reactions as well as your physical reactions to the crystals. You may notice that some big feelings come up as you start releasing your stored-up physical pain. Often our physical pain is associated with negative personal experiences, including trauma, that has been stuck inside our bodies for a long time. This was certainly the case for me when I finally started feeling better in my body— my heart and mind were overwhelmed by my emotions at various points along the way to healing. There was so much being released, and there were times I felt like I couldn't go further, but I was able to gently push through my fear and continue my healing journey. I wish the same for you as you explore the crystal path to relieving chronic gut pain, or any other type of ongoing discomfort.

I recommend checking out your local crystal healer or Reiki practitioner to help you engage in deeper healing work with crystals. And you can, of course, continue to experiment with using crystals yourself! You don't have to be experiencing hard times to use them. I find that spending time with crystals regularly, even when I'm feeling content and well, keeps me in a more positive, lively, and focused place. And the good news about crystals is that they will never harm you—their energy works with your own in a gentle way to restore balance and give a sense of well-being. Use them in good health and peace.

*Note: The crystals that have worked most effectively for me to soothe gut pain are green calcite, which soothes nausea and reduces inflammation, on my heart chakra, citrine; which helps to stop vomiting, on my solar plexus; and carnelian, which regulates digestion, on my sacral chakra. Sometimes I also add a root chakra stone, such as hematite, for grounding and calming myself!

Elizabeth Waugh Duford, MSW, CCM, is a Reiki practitioner, crystal healer, and social worker. For 18 years, Elizabeth served in leadership roles at nonprofit organizations, including a domestic violence program and a shelter for unhoused people. Frustrated with putting Band-Aids on problems often rooted in past traumatic experiences—and dealing with her own painful autoimmune disorders—Elizabeth decided to shift her focus toward holistic healing in 2018. Elizabeth studied the Reiki method of natural healing and obtained her second degree certification in 2019. She also earned a Crystal Master Healer Certification in 2021.

Elizabeth's small healing practice, Love 360, focuses on working with individuals to recover from chronic gut pain. Her system for soothing pain has produced transformative results for her clients. She also leads monthly workshops on crystal healing. Elizabeth has spoken to local and national small business groups and women's organizations about crystal healing for well-being, as well as appearing regularly on the podcast "Breakthrough or Bust."

Elizabeth is a member of the Associated Membership of Massage and Bodywork Professionals. She lives in North Carolina with her husband and four children.

Connect with Elizabeth Waugh Duford:

Website: www.love360inc.com

Email: elizabeth@love360inc.com

Instagram: https://www.instagram.com/crystalmama74

Facebook: https://www.facebook.com/Love360inc

CHAPTER 18

QUIET THE MIND

THE FORCE IS WITH YOU

Alana Heim, CPA/PFS, CFP®, Certified Human Design Specialist

"May the force be with you."

~ Star Wars

"You were the chosen one! It was said you would destroy the Sith, not join them. Bring balance to the force. Not leave it in darkness," Obi-Wan Kenobi cries.

"I hate you," Anakin spews venomously.

"You were my brother, Anakin. I loved you," Obi-Wan replies as Anakin catches fire.

If you've seen the original *Star Wars* movies, you know Anakin Skywalker is Darth Vader. When you view the prequels, you witness the demise of Anakin Skywalker, the sweet, innocent boy filled with hope and promise for the force to find balance.

Yet he falls. Hard. Into the darkness. Lost in confusion and fear. With all hope, love, and light—gone!

One of my greatest fears is that my light path detours into dark treachery. The part of me keeping this fear alive is simple. My mind. *If a part of me is dark, will I make hurtful choices? Will I manifest negativity? Will darkness consume me like it did Anakin?*

These fearful thoughts ruminate in my overloaded and stressed-out mind if I allow them. Maybe you know this situation well. The more these thoughts come in, the more they take over life to create the dreaded fear. And I know better! I know I *should* stop the thoughts, but here's the million-dollar question. How?

MY STORY

Movies depict stories as if created by imagination alone. They fill my mind with many hard candies to suck on—new concepts, ideas, dreams, fairy tales, and even nightmares. For me, I witness these stories as realities. They're glimpses of realities that have truly occurred somewhere on a timeline or in a dimension where the impossible is possible, even if it feels impossible right here, right now on planet Earth.

I watch *Star Wars* knowing and thinking, *This is real.* Somewhere, I have *lived* this. I see the crossover of how this fictitious story either depicts current reality or a version of a possible future.

The more I read books written by Dolores Cannon, a hypnotherapist-turned-author detailing hundreds of past-life experiences, the more something awakens in me. The stories she shares within *The Convoluted Universe* series piece together Earth and universal histories never shared in the archives. These stories spark feelings of deep inner knowing within me. *This is real.* I can't put a finger on it, and I don't have proof. I just *know.*

As I read her stories about Atlantis, truth waves flow through me. *I am from Atlantis.* Then my mind kicks me to the curb of doubt, wanting proof I'd rather not retrieve. *Was I in Atlantis? Hmm. Maybe.*

When I ask this question in an Akashic Record reading, I am told, "Yes. You were a healer in Atlantis. Your name was also Alana."

Even as the words leave her lips, pulsating energies surge in the palms of my hands. A deep knowing reverberates in my body. At this moment, my heart reveals I'm here for purposes my skeptical mind struggles to comprehend. My soul essence yearns for its inner healing fire to be ignited.

My intuition knows I possess healing gifts, although my mind doesn't want to acknowledge this. *You've been in the financial industry for 20 years. Sure, you left to support your clients financially using Human Design. Now you think you're going to add healing arts to this mix?*

Yes, mind, I am. And I have.

While sitting at my desk, I noticed the pens I bought when starting my business. *Chuckle.* They say *Atlantis.* A memory sparks that I named my oldest daughter Tayla because of the television series *Stargate Atlantis.*

The healing fire within me ignites the energies in my hands. *Hey mind! How much proof do you require? Is that enough for ya? 'Cuz guess what? I am a healer!*

A SERIES OF UNFORTUNATE EVENTS - 2/2/2022

Humanity is facing times of accelerated change. Everything I know is changing—the planet, systems, family dynamics, and who I think I am. No longer am I required to shut down my gifts, settle for less, and get lost in what once was. Consciousness is evolving to reach the destined heights I've not yet experienced.

Are *you* ready? I certainly thought I was.

The power of these energy shifts transpiring on the planet is mind-blowing. It's like time races past in a blur. Events occurring in my life happen so quickly. It's like they happened years ago rather than yesterday.

I have grown so much since beginning this journey of awakening—learning to trust myself and my intuition so I can evolve into the best version of myself.

Imagine my surprise when the powerful vortex of 2/2/2022 took me into the depths of my being I didn't know existed. I awoke expecting the day to be powerfully positive and magical. *I am so happy and grateful for this day to usher me to the New Earth.*

Yet the day doesn't end up as I expect at all.

A series of beautiful events fill my morning. From connecting to nature during a charming walk to having a wonderful in-person meeting to engaging in a fulfilling call with like-minded, spiritually evolving companions—I receive exactly what I want.

Then a series of unfortunate events occur—no big deal. *I've got this.* And I do.

My dinner order at a drive-through is wrong. Although I catch the mistake, waiting out front unravels me. I wait patiently. Time ticks by. I become restless. After 20 minutes, I'm confused. *They said they would bring it to me. Why haven't they? I'm still waiting!*

In the past, I would have just gone home. I finally decided to act.

As it turns out, no one was ever coming. My burger sits alone on a tray, rather than in a bag, on the counter. *They forgot me.*

Anger flares as I exit the building, food in hand, sliding into my car; all bliss is gone. An Anakin alter ego appears and takes over my body.

Driving home, the tightness in my body spreads from my neck and shoulders into my gut. My voice goes hoarse and raw from hysterically roaring like an enraged lion. All energy rushes from my eyes, throat, pores, and cells. A stream of tears clogs my sight, leaving me unable to see clearly.

Pure rage courses through me. And I don't know why.

Although I faced other challenges this day and handled them with love and calm, now those energies are nowhere to be found. *This was supposed to be a magical day leading to ascension! I should never have left the house. Why is this happening?* My scattered mind presses for answers.

Racing along the road, I glimpse the bike cop, parked off to the left, turning on his lights. Immediately I know it's about to get worse. *He's coming for me.* "Nooo!" I scream and wail. And he does.

Speeding ticket in hand, I engage more with this unknown dark side of myself. Screams reverberate off the car windows during the agonizing journey home.

Tears fall effortlessly and abundantly for the next hour as I curl up shuddering on the couch. I'm a wretched mess seriously stuck in my head. *Who am I? Why is this happening? Am I manifesting darkness? Why did I leave the house?*

I appreciate that my family comes and loves me. My children tell me the affirmations I often recite to them, "You are loved. You are safe. You are wise. You are strong."

They wrap me in their arms and hug me tightly.

And I let them.

Over the following days, an odd calm washes over me. You know how after a storm, the sky opens to reveal the sun, maybe even a rainbow, and there's a stillness in the air? Yeah, it feels like that—something massive released allowing spaciousness to grow inside of me.

As I ponder the events, little flashes of epiphanies ignite in my mind. These revealing insights grab my hand, leading me down a path of knowing what needs to change.

I become aware of how *unaware* I was. My mind and emotions hijacked my ability to be fully present, dominating me and my actions. During the rage, I was no longer me—the me I know myself to be—calm, smiling, and grounded.

A-ha! The answer floats into my awareness as gently as a feather dancing with the wind.

Hara! I breathe. *I know the how!*

A SERIES OF FORTUNATE EVENTS - 2/22/2022

This realization reminds me to get out of my head. My head overthinks everything, mindlessly flowing on autopilot. An autopilot I never intentionally set, since it plotted its course based on my observations before age seven. My chattering mind keeps me from being grounded and centered in my body.

You may be thinking, *My mind is never quiet either! There's a way to silence the mind?* Yes! Stick with me, as the tool I share at the end of the chapter supports you with this very concept.

The technique of Hara comes to me naturally when I need it, whether I'm performing remote energy sessions or working out at the gym. In Hara, I'm fully aware of all my senses and am present in the moment. However, I realize: *Why am I not doing Hara every day?*

Now I practice this technique everywhere, every day. During client calls, while engaging with my family, even driving.

In Hara, I'm simply present, grounded, and alert to my surroundings. My mind is quiet. All monkey mind chatter is gone. I'm in the field of potentiality, holding an intention and allowing it to manifest as God determines.

Hara keeps me in a state of calm, where instantly I know when I get pulled out. Like when a thought drops in. Or when an irritation bubbles up. Practicing Hara every day allows my awareness to discern the moment I have jarred away from feeling blissful. This supports me in being prepared for my next big test.

It's 2/22/2022. I deem this day to be another New Earth portal day.

During a client remote energy session, cries come from downstairs. My husband is home, so I continue my session. Upon completion, I move to my desk to jump on a client call.

My husband informs me, "Hunter hit his head." With the kids on a two-hour snow delay, they decided to "ice skate" with socks on the wood floor. "He seems fine, but he's complaining. I'm just going to let him stay home."

An hour later, I jump off my call and check on Hunter. I'm alarmed to find him lying in his bed amidst his own vomit.

"Babe! I thought you said he was fine! He's vomited and clearly has a concussion!" I shout with worry.

We move Hunter to the bathroom. We undress him and place him in the tub. His incoherence is frightening. His groans and words are slurring and choppy. "I. Owww. Take clothes. Uhhh."

Intense fear plagues my breathing. Worry seeps into my mind. This pulls me out of Hara. *Focus Alana. It's going to be okay.* Instinctively, I use a hand gesture (mudra) to recenter myself and quiet my mind. I breathe calmly, thankful for being present again.

As Hunter lays in the tub, I sit with him, sending energy. I ask his guides and angels to support him. My husband runs off to call our pediatrician. Hunter mumbles, stirring restlessly. My baby no longer feels like himself.

Fear wells up in my eyes, causing thoughts to flood my mind. *What if this is really bad? What if it's a traumatic brain injury?* I'm drifting in and out of Hara.

I interrupt my mind, commanding, *Stop! Focus on what you want!* I return to Hara.

We move him to the couch so he can rest. I sit, holding my clear intention; *He is well, all is well.* I continue asking his guides and angels to support him with the best possible outcome. I run energy protocols at his head.

I maintain Hara, keeping myself fully present. Flickers of fearful thoughts attempt to break into my mind. I hold my intention with focus and determination.

For the duration of the experience, I remain calm and aware. I trust all is well.

And thankfully, it is. After he's seen by our pediatrician, by the early evening, Hunter is more his usual self. I am grateful for maintaining my calm and holding my intention.

Here's what I realize: my heart and body radiate more love-light when I trust them. And this is amplified when I quiet the voices in my head.

You see, the mind complicates, well, everything! It dumps you into the abyss, leaving you feeling insecure about your desires, choices, and actions. It weakens your ability to trust the force within you.

So, let's take the Hara exit to get off this "mind" highway.

THE TOOL

"If only I could quiet my mind." "It's so loud in there. How do I shut it up?" "I feel scattered with thoughts exploding like fireworks in my head." My clients share their mental dump sites with me all the time.

We learn the "if only" way of thinking from the voices outside of our heads. Mother said, "If only you'd clean up after yourself." "If only you were good at math." Or here's the real buzz kill, "If only you were more like your sister." Oof.

These thoughts swirl in your mind delivering a gooey bowl of melted soft serve. *If only I was good at math. If only I didn't mess up everything.* The thoughts jumble, so you no longer remember who said what or the exact words used. The mess in your mind is as muddled as the colors of ice cream in the bowl.

This same sticky mess creates an undesirable intention. It leaves you feeling confused and doubting you'll ever manifest what you want.

When it comes to manifesting dreams, being clear about what you want is key. It's important to quiet the mind to allow your heightened senses to leap at opportunities that present because you are aware and ready.

Cultivating inner peace occurs instantly when you silence the mind. Using the technique of Hara allows you to do this. You're fully present within your body, connected to Source and Mother Earth. There is no past or future. There is only consciousness in the moment.

Exercise:

Wherever you are, you can implement this exercise. You could call this an active meditation; however, it is a state of BEing.

Please practice this exercise daily, as often as you can throughout the day. Allow yourself to become unconsciously competent at using this technique. Your ability to manifest will ignite!

Step 1: Get Grounded

- Get in a comfortable position.
  - ○ If seated, sit on the edge of your seat with your legs hip-width apart.
  - ○ If standing, keep your legs hip-width apart, with your knees soft.
- Pick a spot to stare at and keep your eyes open for the duration of the exercise.
- With the tips of your fingers, touch your *tan tien* (located approximately two inches below your belly button).

- Take a few deep breaths through your nose. Imagine a ball of light the size of a golf ball beneath your fingers.
- On your next exhale, imagine a beam extending from your ball of light. Send it deep into the core of Mother Earth.
- Visualize Mother Earth sending bright, intense light back up to your *tan tien*.
- See this beam expanding brighter, a flashlight becoming a spotlight.
- Allow your feet to grow roots like trees. Feel the light climb your feet and legs.
- You're now fully grounded.

Step 2: Enter Hara

- Allow the light energy to move up through your perineum, up your spine, and out the top of your head, connecting to God/Source/Sun.
- Using hand mudras, place your right hand in front of your throat and heart, pointing straight up, centered in front of you. Place your left hand pointing downward, directly in front of your groin. Both hands are vertically and horizontally aligned.
- Continue staring at the point you chose.
- Notice how grounded, centered, and focused you feel. Notice your mind is silent. You are calm, clear, present, and aware.
  - This is the void. This is where you set intentions for manifestation.

- Notice how heightened your senses are.
- Set your intention—whatever you'd like to manifest. Hold Hara.
- If thoughts pop in, you've left Hara. Make sure you're still grounded. Reset your hands. Breathe.
- As you become more comfortable holding Hara, it's okay to drop your hands when you practice.

Breathe. How do you feel?

This technique is powerful. Hara is the key to unlocking access to the void. Here there are no thoughts since you're no longer floating in the auric field. You're consciously present, spiritually centered, and physically grounded in the earthly plane. You are completely still in the now moment, aware of what is. The past and future are nonexistent.

Manifestations occur more rapidly because you transfer the cosmic light energy to Mother Earth, and she returns it to your physical body. This allows you to *be* with the potential of *all,* grounding your intention into the earth and manifesting it into form based on the intention frequency you set. Anything is possible in this state. Anything can be made to manifest.

When you pause the busyness in your mind, you power up your awareness and ignite your spark of light in the realm of possibility. You're stronger than you think. Allow the *how* for your intention to magnetize to you through your Source connection.

During my son's scary concussion situation, Hara allowed me to calmly attract my desired outcome. Keep practicing. You can do this too!

Remember, the force is with you. Always.

If additional Hara alignment, healing, and support are needed, you're invited to learn more at:
https://www.ProsperityAlignment.com/hara-resources

Alana Heim, CPA/PFS, CFP® (sounds like Anaheim), is the owner and soul essence of Prosperity Alignment, Inc. serving as a cosmic prosperity activator. She guides you through navigating the energetic currents beneath your business, life, and money, so you flow consciously within Source's river of infinite prosperity.

Alana is a certified public accountant, a personal financial specialist, and a Certified Financial Planner™. Grateful to have exited the typical financial industry, you'll now find her bridging the spiritual and strategic aspects of currency. She applies her planning and intuitive abilities with clients using tools such as Human Design, neo-shamanic remote energy healing, sound channeling, and Quantum Alignment System™ training.

Alana is a 3-time best-selling contributing author to *Abundance By Design: Discover Your Unique Code for Health, Wealth and Happiness with Human Design, What's Money Got to Do With It?,* and *Stop Overworking and Start Overflowing: 25 Ways to Transform Your Life using Human Design.*

As a 1/3 Emotional Projector, she guides you to recognize the yin and yang, motherly and fatherly, forces within you to ignite your inner child with courage and boldness. Alana is on a mission to apply her Atlantean healing powers to expand prosperity consciousness, so humanity gets it right and reaches New Earth on the organic matrix timeline.

Alana is from Atlantis and now lives in Reno, Nevada. You'll find her living in Hara with her husband and three children.

Ready to connect?

You are invited to connect with Alana:
https://www.ProsperityAlignment.com

Additional Resources:
https://www.prosperityalignment.com/hara-resources

CHAPTER 19

UNIVERSAL WHITE TIME

LEVERAGING THE POWER OF DIVINE LIGHT AND LOVE FOR AUTHENTIC HEALING AND AWAKENING

Bradford W. Tilden, CMT, MM, UWT,
Composer, Vibrational Healer

I want you, dear reader, to trust yourself enough to literally follow your dreams. Do you have what it takes to trust your intuition and the Universe completely, despite seemingly insurmountable situations like a terminal diagnosis? I tell you, it's not only possible but inevitable when you say "yes" to your greater truth. I know this because I said "yes," and in saying yes, my true healing and awakening began.

MY STORY

"I'm sorry, the second test also came back positive. I can give you some information to help you understand your condition. Many people now live long lives with HIV thanks to new medications. You don't have to view this as a death sentence anymore. . ." The clinician's words faded as a bizarre sensation I can only describe as icicles of dread, like frozen slow-motion daggers, began trickling down into my crown chakra. The cold frigid truth of my situation was sinking in.

Fear, the invasive poison, still hung in the air at this epicenter of the AIDS epidemic, San Francisco. I sensed its ghostly presence in the Castro since moving there in January of 2005. It presented itself as a silent absence, a psychic wound in the aftermath of a bomb.

It was a typical sunny day, and a quick decision to get another free HIV test. I was stopped by a perky volunteer health advocate on the sidewalk of Market Street. I didn't imagine my day would come to this; my life would come to this. At 26 years old, I didn't ever think I'd join the ranks of the victims of the pandemic. Living or dead, I was now one of them, shouldering the burden of loss in a twilight of grief.

I started to cry.

The tears surprised me because I realized I was crying for the man I was sleeping with, not for myself. But I was weak and in shock, and I never reached out to him again after that day. I'm sorry. Please forgive me.

The clinician tried to console me from his seat across the table. His whole demeanor shifted to pity and sympathy. It disturbed me more than receiving the positive test result. In fact, it made me sick. *I don't need your pity. I don't want your pity.* I got up from my seat abruptly and left the all-too-tiny room with the all-too-tiny version of my dead reality behind to be pitied and consoled.

I am not my diagnosis.

I stepped back into the sunlight and felt a huge burden lift from my heart. My greatest fear had come true.

What now? All that anxiety and worry dissipated and for the first time, I felt empowered and in control of my life.

What was I waiting for? The diagnosis gave me context, a new purpose, and direction.

What do I have to lose? It's time to start living my life. Courage and strength surged from within. Faced with my own mortality, these were my initial thoughts and feelings.

I responded in a number of ways in the days and weeks following the diagnosis. For starters, I cut off anyone who showed any amount of pity for me after I disclosed my new status to them. I didn't need that energy in my field.

I didn't seek medical attention. I chose to take my health into my own hands and began to research natural cleanses and nutrition. I was thankful to have learned of AIDS alternative theories *before* I found out I was HIV positive. It gave me hope that people were using holistic approaches to maintain strong immune systems and live long, healthy lives with HIV without pharmaceuticals.

I also reassessed my life. I was at the tail end of a six-month temp-to-hire position. The weight of the "cubicle job" was becoming heavy on my soul. I was commuting for someone else's nine to five dream.

One evening, I mustered the courage to have a conversation with the Universe. I looked up to the stars from the balcony of my apartment and said, "I know I'm meant for greater things. I'm ready to put my trust in you, dear Universe, to always be guided, supported, and protected. I'm ready to take my leap of faith."

I resolved to quit my job and work for myself then and there. A soft, warm breeze picked up, carrying the fragrance of frangipani flowers across the balcony. That luscious tropical scent at once confirmed and blessed my prayer.

The next day I gave my notice. My simple plan after quitting was to focus on music composition and performance and support myself by working as an independent licensed massage therapist. But the Universe had much bigger plans.

I met up with a friend the following day. He's one of the most gifted psychics I know. He can name the top cards of a Tarot deck before turning them over with 100% accuracy. I listen to what he has to say. When I disclosed my HIV status to him, all he said was, "Some people get illnesses for Karmic reasons." The words resonated with my soul. Then he handed me a flyer for an open house for a school of sound healing. "You might want to go check this out."

Sound healing? I had no idea such a thing existed! I was struggling to merge my two professional interests of massage and music. Sound healing sounded like the perfect keystone to the arch of my temple. The open house was the next day.

I went.

I noticed the cosmic irony that the sound healing school was located in a building I walked past every day on my way home from work for the previous six months. It took an HIV diagnosis to get me to pay attention and walk through that door.

At the open house, a woman was playing with a crystal bowl and sharing how she healed herself of breast cancer using her voice, crystal bowl, and her faith alone.

My heart blossomed. Without a doubt, I was meant to be there.

I enrolled on the spot.

Over the next few months, I experienced numerous healings and spiritual awakenings at that school. I connected with my guides, could hear them, and, more importantly, was listening to their guidance. They encouraged me to purchase an Amethyst Biomat from one of the teachers and become a distributor. I did without hesitation. (The Biomat is a healing device the size of a yoga mat that generates negative ions and far-infrared heat lined with amethyst crystals.)

Soon after, a different teacher invited me up to Santa Rosa for an 11/11 Portal sound healing celebration. I was only able to attend because another friend asked me to watch his car for the week while he was in Hawaii. I brought the Biomat, hoping someone there would purchase one. No one did, even though they all happily took turns laying on it that damp, dreary day.

Just before I was about to leave, the teacher handed me a pamphlet for a woman who teaches something called *Universal White Time Gemstone Healing,* saying, "Maybe she'd be interested in buying one."

I took the pamphlet and saw this woman was located in a small town called Aptos, just south of Santa Cruz. I only had my friend's car for a few more days. I called her on the spot and made plans to drive down the next day.

The drive to Aptos was long. I had time to reflect on my circumstances. It has been three months since the diagnosis, and already my life has completely shifted. I have felt divinely guided ever since I quit my job. At the same time, doubts gnawed at me. *What am I doing driving two and a half hours in hopes of selling a Biomat to a woman I've never met?* But still, I trusted my guides and my intuition as I pushed forward into the unknown.

At last, I arrived at the woman's address. As I slowly drove up the long, steep, winding driveway, I noticed several redwood groves. I sensed the energy shift. It became quieter as if protecting a secret. I drove on in silence. After what felt like an initiatory ascent, the scene opened up to reveal a majestic hexagon-shaped house pronouncing itself atop a clearing amidst the forested terrain.

How odd, I thought. *This seems familiar.*

I parked in the driveway. Nervousness began to creep in.

I looked around the yard for some establishment and found it in the lushly blooming kale in the garden next to the front entryway. I breathed in the fresh garden scent laced with the cleansing hint from the redwood pines standing guard like sentinels at a holy shrine. Nerves calmed, I found the courage to approach the front door. Deep breath in, pause, then I knocked.

The door opened.

"I had a dream about you." These first words came out of my mouth the moment I saw the petite little woman standing before me.

"Oh yeah? Prove it," she replied somewhat indignantly.

After a short pause, I stated, "You have a 32-year-old son who rides a bike." I didn't know how I knew her son's age. I knew he rode a bike because, in the dream, I struggled with him and bashed his head in with his bike helmet. (I withheld that little detail.)

The woman scanned me up and down and responded, "When my son was 32 years old, he was hit by a tractor-trailer while riding his bike. His head would have been crushed if he hadn't been wearing his helmet. Please, step inside."

Before this tale gets any weirder, here is the dream in question:

About two weeks prior to this encounter, I re-read a dream in my journal from a few years back about meeting a woman at the front door of her hexagon-shaped house. She then led me down a curved descending ramp leading to a giant hexagon-shaped room with one step down into it from all sides.

I was terrified that if I touched the floor of that room, I'd be electrocuted. Her son tried to get me onto the floor. We struggled, fell onto the floor, and I bashed his head in with his bike helmet. The woman started laughing and flipped a switch on the wall. Instead of being electrocuted, I was raised into the air on a giant cornucopia of crystals and gemstones. Then I woke up.

So, here I was, two years later, with the real woman in her real hexagon-shaped house, being led down a curved descending ramp.

I am inside my dream! I thought as I beheld the giant hexagon-shaped room.

"Welcome to my healing room," she said as we stepped down into it. We made our way to the center, where she set up a mattress pad and what looked like a spread of oracle cards next to it.

"I want you to experience my work first. Please draw a card."

I selected one of the 100-plus cards and showed it to her.

"Wow! That is the most powerful card in the deck." She sounded surprised. "It connects you to the central sun of the Universe."

Of course, this meant nothing to me at the time. My mind was racing with the reality that I was right in the middle of a prophetic dream.

She assembled a bunch of tumbled stones I didn't recognize in a line next to the mattress pad to show me the gemstone layout.

She placed them one by one on specific spots along the central axis of my torso and one in each hand.

"I'm going to leave you here for about 30 minutes while I lay on the Biomat." She gave me no explanation, no direction other than to experience the energy.

Okay, whatever. These are just a bunch of tumbled stones.

But then, it started.

After a few minutes, a unified pulsing sensation began to swell in my body, like feeling your pulse everywhere all at once. But this pulsing continued to grow and intensify beyond that. It became stronger and stronger and even stronger still. Eventually, it felt like every cell of my body was pulsing simultaneously. I wasn't being electrocuted. I was being incredibly electrified!

It was one of the most profound experiences of my life. The stones activated something deep within me, something ancient and cosmic.

"Do you feel the stones are done working?" I heard a gentle voice reach through the reverie of awe and bliss I was adrift in.

"Yes." I heard myself respond.

She removed the stones reverently, one by one. When she was through, I sat up and turned to look at her. She was sitting on her legs, knees together with her hands on her thighs like an innocent child eager to please.

"I teach this." She said matter-of-factly.

Without hesitation, I replied, "I have to study with you."

I attended her next class, where my understanding of myself greatly expanded, and life was never the same. I wasn't learning the joy of crystals, I was *remembering*. It was as if a cork had been removed, and all the knowledge came flooding back into my consciousness. I awakened to my greater truth as a master frequency healer.

Turns out, the woman is the head teacher for Universal White Time (UWT) Gemstone Healing for the United States. I went all in. I learned there is a gemstone healing branch and an energy healing branch. Within two years, I became a Level 3 UWT Gemstone Healing teacher and Level 3 UWT energy healing practitioner.

I came to understand my role as an educator and ambassador for White Time. I learned that UWT healing was designed and given to us by benevolent light-being angels, ascended masters, and ETs to heal, unlock the hidden potential within us, evolve spiritually, and help with the transition to the New Earth. It works with all time as one unit and the forces of divine light and universal love.

UWT came to me at a crossroads in my life. I had nothing to lose and everything to gain. I absolutely believe I was divinely guided and encouraged by a prophetic dream to say "Yes" to this incredible modality, philosophy, and way of life. UWT opened access to a wealth of knowledge and information already within me and gave me the tools and the power to heal myself and others on a very deep soul level.

I was fortunate enough to have maintained a strong intuitive sense and inner guidance to say "yes" to the opportunities that led me toward my awakening. By placing confidence and trust in the Universe and myself, I was able to take purposeful action when all hope seemed lost. I took that leap of faith. Dear reader, if I can do it, so can you.

You are not your situation. You are not your diagnosis. There is a greater truth within you yet to be revealed. There is also a greater truth out there beyond Earth's atmosphere. Beyond the solar system, even beyond our galaxy, there are loving, supporting beings who are watching over us. They're reaching out to assist us in remembering who we are and how we can express our greater divine essence as beings of love and light.

THE TOOL

This guided meditation connects you with the Universe's central sun and the Earth's crystalline core for healing, protection, and bringing awareness to your divine essence as a being of love and light.

Find a comfortable, seated position.

Focus on your breathing.

On the next inhale, draw up any tension and stress from your body into your lungs.

Exhale and release it with an audible sigh to transmute energy that no longer serves you.

Breathe this way twice more, inhaling to gather up stress and exhaling with an audible sigh.

Smile.

On the next inhale, draw down pure white light from the central sun of the Universe through your crown chakra to the base of your diaphragm.

Exhale, visualizing it rise up into your heart and spread through your physical body.

Continue breathing, visualizing the pure white light filling your entire body.

Next, allow it to fill your aura until you are completely enveloped by this pure, universal white divine light.

Breathe. Notice how you feel.

Next, send down a column of light from your base chakra to the crystalline core of the Earth.

Ask Mother Earth permission to connect with her rising core frequency.

Send her love and gratitude.

Ask her to send up golden liquid light containing information, knowledge, and activation codes for you specifically.

Visualize this golden light as a double helix spiraling up through your base chakra, through your lower chakras to your heart chakra.

Breathe.

Visualize the golden light spreading into your entire physical body.

Then into your aura.

Call upon love, strength, and courage in the awareness of Earth's healing energy enveloping you.

Breathe.

Focus on your heart chakra.

Gather some white universal energy and some gold Earth energy to create an iridescent sphere of light in the center of your heart chakra.

Allow this sphere to expand until it completely surrounds your body and aura.

This is your sphere of protection and healing that only beings and energies of love, light, truth, and manifestation may enter.

You may begin to sense the presence of angels who are now attracted to your light. Welcome them. Allow them to communicate with you, give you blessings, and perform healings.

Breathe.

Become aware of your energy. This is your divine essence, pure and powerful.

You may stay in this space as long as you wish.

You may return to this space often.

When you are ready, slowly come back to your body and back to the present moment.

You may open your eyes.

Give thanks for this healing.

Visit www.BradfordTilden.com for a free audio of a deeper guided meditation that also connects with your Higher Self to increase your guidance, intuition, and natural healing ability.

Bradford W. Tilden MM, CMT, UWT is an internationally recognized composer, pianist, sound healer, and highest ranking UWT Gemstone and energy healing teacher and practitioner on the east coast of the United States. He graduated *magna cum laude* from Amherst College in 2002, received a master's in music composition from UMASS, Amherst in 2014, and is a graduate of the Globe Institute of Sound and Consciousness in San Francisco, California. He is also an initiate of the puma tribe of the Q'ero shamans of Peru.

Bradford is the founder of the Lemurian School of Intuitive Natural Healing. The mission of LSINH, (pronounced *"listen"*) is to develop one's intuition while opening up to the power of sound and crystals to become an effective healer for oneself and the world. It's derived from the knowledge of the ancient Lemurian civilization, as revealed to him by his UWT master guides and Lemurian priest-healers through his work with Lemurian seed crystals.

Bradford channels angelic and shamanic healing frequencies with his voice. His musical compositions and live sound journeys are divinely orchestrated collaborations with higher beings. He also composes for MediMind, a guided meditation app. Support his music at https://bradfordwtilden.bandcamp.com

Bradford helps people who feel lost, disconnected, and unfulfilled to reconnect with their divine essence and purpose in life. He offers in-person and remote sessions incorporating UWT gemstone and energy healing, spiritual guidance, and vocal toning coaching. He's available for group sound journeys, venue performances, composition commissions, talks, and anything pertaining to his work. He will travel anywhere in the world to teach UWT. Contact him to host a class in your local community.

Visit www.CrystalMusicHealing.com to learn more about Bradford and UWT. Visit https://linktr.ee/bradfordtilden for access to his social media, articles, and more.

CHAPTER 20

IGNITE YOUR INNER HEALER

BREATHING TO RELEASE
BURIED PAIN AND EMOTIONS

Beth Manning, Master Psychic Healer and Medical Intuitive

"I was carjacked on vacation in Costa Rica," Gina explains, as I close the door to the massage room. "The driver lost control and we rolled and rolled." She falls silent, gazing down at the carpet.

"Then we crashed."

Suddenly my neck feels wrung out like a washcloth and I can't breathe.

Just because this is your first client ever doesn't mean you can't help her. Relax. Breathe. You got this!

"Most of the pain is in my neck. . .I have a rod that runs down."

I smile, but my mind is a hailstorm. It's my first day in the student clinic. I know I have 60 minutes for my Swedish massage routine, but everything in my body is telling me to touch her gently and help her remember how to breathe.

None of that was in the curriculum.

When I place my hands on her shoulders, I expect her muscles to melt. Instead, they push back like a steel fortress.

I take a breath and close my eyes.

I see flashes of a little girl being pushed aside by her mom. She's sad and playing on her own. I see her throat and heart closing from carrying all the pain around her. She doesn't feel seen or loved for who she really is.

Gut-wrenching terror follows and I see a large man angrily throw his fist over her mouth. They struggle. Once again, she has lost her voice.

It all feels so real, playing out like a movie in my mind's eye.

I have such a vivid imagination! Always writing stories about the people I meet.

I've always picked up on the emotions of other people - doesn't everyone? But working with Gina causes all of my senses to heighten like I'm Alice lost in Wonderland.

When I give her shoulders pressure, her body recoils and seizes up on me. I see that little girl running to her mom for comfort but coming up empty-handed. She's back in the corner, playing alone again.

"Hold me. Please, just touch me," her body whispers to me.

I forget the routine and help her relax into her body, beginning with her breath.

We breathe together slowly until we find safety.

Gina loves our sessions, though her relief is fleeting. Each week her muscles are still concrete slabs and the pain migrates around her body like an endless game of whack-a-mole.

MY STORY

I haven't taken my massage final yet and I'm questioning the entire thing. When I signed up for the program, it felt so simple: Learn how to work each muscle so clients leave feeling like they're floating in the clouds.

It was never this simple.

My own decade of pain was part of what motivated me to leave my desk job and pursue massage therapy. On paper, I was the picture of health, eating well, exercising daily, sleeping eight hours, and popping fistfuls of vitamins.

In reality, I was frequently injured and woke up most days with a brain-searing tension headache and enough anxiety to convince me to oversleep most mornings.

I was lifting heavy weights and cycling like I was training for the Tour de France, two sports I assumed you couldn't excel in without always taping, icing, or rolling something. No pain, no gain, right?

Growing up, when the tension between my parents was thick like smog, I ran laps around the house. The night my dad passed away, I didn't cry. Instead, I grabbed a ball and obsessively shot baskets in the driveway. When I felt buried under the weight of a family secret, I rode my bike until my body was numb.

Whenever I entered a classroom, I could feel who was angry, depressed, or who would act out that day. At the time, I had no idea I was picking up other people's energy.

When I was ten, shortly after my dad passed, I started experiencing stabbing pain behind my eyes. It hurt to read books, something I loved more than anything, and I often felt nauseous. My jaw was sore from clenching and grinding my teeth. My neck and shoulders were made of wood, something my family joked was genetic.

The headaches were relentless and my mom took me to see a chiropractor, a massage therapist, and then an ear, nose, and throat doctor. He was sure surgery would cure my problem.

Fortunately, my mom, who tried everything she could think of to help me, said no, and off we went to a neurologist who ordered an MRI.

The test came back normal. He was kind and fatherly when he told me my problem was likely stress-related.

My mom was a ball of anxiety and I spent my childhood trying to soothe her. I carried that ball, even when it was too unwieldy for my tiny arms. As an only child, I made it my job to shoulder the weight for both of us, but in the end, it crushed me.

At the time, I didn't realize how easily I took on other people's pain and anxiety. I felt it when I locked eyes with strangers at the mall, when my mom was worried, or even when I watched a scary movie or read a heavy book. That night, I stared at the ceiling, still living with the characters, unable to shake it off for hours.

I never excelled at memorizing things. Instead, everyone came to me for advice. "You're so wise," they'd say, confiding their problems. I craved these friendships because I felt special and needed. I always had a knack for making my friends feel better, even though it often meant taking on their problems. My mom could see my anxiety building. She signed me up for my favorite sports, booked sessions with therapists, and even offered me a support group for kids who had lost a parent.

When I played sports, I felt strong and invincible. It shifted my focus out of my head and into my body, which reminded me that I was strong enough to get through anything. So many people took me under their wing, but I didn't understand how to let them fully support me. I didn't want to burden them with my own problems or have them feel sorry for me.

By the time I started massage school at 29, I had already racked up a list of injuries and diagnoses: tension headaches, gluten intolerance, chronic urinary tract infections, ovarian cyst, torn hamstring, separated shoulder, calf strain, plantar fasciitis and bulging, degenerative discs in my neck and lumbar spine.

Armed with custom orthotics ("You'll never have an arch without these"), a special diet ("Some people just can't eat gluten"), a million corrective exercises ("Your glutes aren't firing"), and a list of things not to do ("Lifting heavy isn't good for your lower back"), I tried to live a normal life. I refused to give up. There was no way I could be this young yet feel so old.

Everything came to a head shortly after I graduated from massage school. I was deadlifting and trying to strengthen all my weak parts when I heard something pop. If my spine was a taut string holding my body up, it felt like a pair of scissors cut me loose. I went limp with pain and spent the rest of the week in the fetal position giving in to my own pity party. For the first time in my life, when I succumbed to total rest and quiet, I heard my body screaming for me to stop.

Against my own intuition, I entrusted a well-known chiropractor to treat my back. It was a Hail Mary last-ditch effort. In the end, it only made my back worse. I realized I was running out of options. She finally referred me to a pain management doctor. "That's really the only thing left," she said with a shrug.

That was when I crossed paths with two holistic healers and the first time I heard the term "medical intuitive."

At first I was resistant because I wasn't into woo-woo. I liked things backed by facts, numbers, and double-blind studies. Later I realized this was my logical mind protecting me because I had yet to fully trust my intuition.

When the first healer placed her hands on me, I felt all my pain rise to the surface, yet I fought hard to push it back down. It felt uncomfortable and larger than me. Like if I let go, it would engulf the room, a monster rising up and swallowing me whole. I could feel all the places in my body where I was barely hanging on, my fingers white-knuckling as I grasped at the ledge.

One day as I was leaving, she handed me a note. "Read this when you feel ready," she said with a warm smile. Later that night, the crumpled paper fell out of my pocket.

Let yourself break.

The letters blurred with my own tears as my lower lip shook uncontrollably. My body's final Jenga piece was removed and I shook to the floor as a surge of emotions earth-quaked out of me. Everything inside me wanted out. For the first time, I let my body take what it needed. It led me through waves of anger, grief, sadness, and shame.

When I finally gave it free rein, the monster inside of me wasn't a *Jurassic Park* villain. It was a scared little girl who was afraid she wouldn't be loved unless she was helpful. Through my healers, I learned how to talk to her, comfort her, and make sure her needs were met. I allowed her to cry, grieve, and realize just how powerful she was. I gave her permission not to have to be strong for everyone else. Together, we found her voice.

Another healer helped me discover that I'm a medical intuitive, healer, and psychic. She helped me understand that feeling everyone else's energy and emotions is a gift, not a curse. I learned how to be aware of, but not take on, everyone's pain and how to check my body for other people's energy.

Everything I saw with Gina was real and she was the first of many clients whose energy I realized I could read. Her body trusted me enough to share what it needed to heal. I just hadn't learned to speak its language yet.

After decades of walking my own health journey, today my body is free of chronic pain. I'm able to recognize the connection between my thoughts and beliefs and how they manifest as physical pain in my body. Now, instead of stuffing down an emotion, I try to acknowledge it and understand that it's often a reminder to check in with myself to ensure I'm not putting the needs of others before my own. Accidents, illness, and injuries are catalysts that force us to stop and pay attention. When we commit to going into the darkness, we recognize how to shine our own light.

My journey is far from over, but as I reach 40, my body feels better than it did two decades ago. Today, my feet have developed their own arches without ever wearing orthotics. My back is strong as I deadlift, despite still having degenerations in my spine, and I can eat gluten without any painful side effects.

Since I learned to process the emotions triggering my headaches, I rarely have pain behind my eyes and no longer reach for Excedrin every day. I still ride my bike and lift weights, but I now opt mainly for joy rides and balance exercise with other things I love. I finally feel present in my body, which is the first step to healing and where I begin with most of my clients. Breathwork and meditation strengthen this connection to my body. The body's natural response is to move away from pain, but this causes a disconnection from your body, making healing more difficult.

Your breath is one of the most powerful tools to bring your focus back, to go within and explore your own landscape. It seems so simple, yet things like trauma and living in our fast-paced, over-caffeinated world have altered how we breathe. Just a few minutes of tuning into your breath each day can drastically change how you feel both mentally and physically. Breath work helps improve your mood, energy levels, and sleep. This one tool can shift your body from stressed to calm in an instant.

Let's explore this tool as the first step in your healing journey.

THE TOOL

Learning about the breath changed my life.

I remember so many times in childhood when it felt like I was living outside my body: When I was called on in class and didn't know the answer, when my dad snapped at me for no apparent reason, and when I was injured.

As humans, we naturally move away from pain. But pain is a useful messenger when we learn to speak its language.

During one of my first bodywork classes, we all laid down on the floor and learned how to breathe.

This is so silly. I know how to breathe!

I quickly realized I had much to learn about this seemingly simple exercise.

As I followed each cue, the jumping beans in my stomach calmed. I felt my body in a whole new way.

I want to teach you a simple breathing exercise called box breathing. It's powerful because it shifts your body away from fight or flight and into calm. It's in this calm state that your body prioritizes healing, digestion, and sleeping deeply. In short, your body feels safe here.

When you're stuck in your stress response, your body lives in survival mode. As humans, we weren't designed to stay here for long, just enough time to escape immediate danger. If you've ever felt impulsive, reactive, like your heart is racing and your body is always on, or like you can't control your emotions, it's likely you're spending too much time in your sympathetic nervous system. Many people live with this gas pedal pressed to the floor.

Your breath is your brake. Use this tool often and you'll feel a shift over time. It's perfect in moments of anxiety or when you can't sleep.

BOX BREATHING

1. Place one hand lightly on your chest, the other on your stomach. Notice where you're breathing. If you can, close your eyes.

2. Slowly take a few breaths in through your nose and out through your mouth. See if you can make these exhales longer than the inhales.

3. Next, close your mouth, resting your tongue gently on the roof. Take a breath in through your nose to a count of four. Try to feel your ribcage, belly, and back expand like you're filling a balloon. It's okay if you focus on one area at a time to start.

4. Now hold your breath for a count of four. Relax.

5. Slowly exhale for a count of four.

6. Hold your breath again as you count to four.

7. Repeat this cycle several times or until a feeling of calm washes over your body. You might yawn or feel your stomach gurgle. Be patient. This takes some practice, but know you're heading in the right direction.

This is such a simple yet powerful exercise for several reasons. Nasal breathing naturally filters the air, signals safety in your body, ensures you don't over-breathe (which creates stress), can improve oral health and jaw development, and allows you to utilize nitric oxide, an important gas produced in the nasal cavity that helps increase blood flow and lower blood pressure.

Ideally, you should breathe through your nose, even during sleep and exercise. You'd be surprised by how much your fitness and sleep quality improves when you do.

The breath hold is a wonderful distraction for the monkey mind. Counting to four shifts your focus away from any current thoughts and brings you out of your mind and into your body.

We've been encouraged to place our focus on the mind memorizing facts and we often repeat the same habits and thoughts year after year, creating the same outcomes because our thoughts are on autopilot. When you breathe with intention and curiosity, you begin to flip the switch from autopilot to conscious awareness, from living with your focus outside your body to bringing awareness back within. When you begin to live more in your body, even if it's for seconds at a time, you become more aware of what your body needs and how it's responding to your life choices.

Pain is a message. Breath work brings you to a space where you can safely meet your body and understand and honor its needs with curiosity, love, and grace.

To bring you closer to a place of understanding, I invite you to download a free meditation that guides you through connecting to your breath and body in order to understand the deeper meaning behind pain, illness, or lack of energy and vitality.

Download this free meditation at
bethmanningintuitive.com/energymedicine

Beth believes everyone has the ability to heal and that no one is broken. She has combined her years of working as a bodyworker and movement therapist with her ability to read the energy of the body. This informs a deeper understanding of the root cause of pain, disease, illness, and injury. It also provides a way of listening to what the body requires for long-lasting healing and pain relief.

As a medical intuitive and master psychic healer, she helps heal and balance the mental, physical, emotional, energetic, and spiritual aspects contributing to pain, ongoing stress, and other physical or emotional challenges. By addressing the whole body, clients experience long-lasting healing and pain relief as well as a level of freedom and peace many have long been searching for.

Beth specializes in seeing clients who have exhausted other avenues of pain relief as well as chronic and autoimmune conditions. She offers remote healing sessions and customized programs.

A former professional journalist and magazine editor, she continues to nurture her love of writing, sharing her experiences and teaching on her blog at http://blog.bethmanningintuitive.com/. Stay up to date with the launch of her own book, download a meditation or sign up to receive updates at https://www.bethmanningintuitive.com/.

A natural teacher, Beth creates courses for healers, therapists, and practitioners interested in integrating energy work into their practice. Her courses focus on teaching practical strategies for managing your own energy when working with clients and using the breath as a healing tool. She also hosts the free Facebook group Empowered Energy Healers. You can join the group at https://www.facebook.com/groups/empoweredenergyhealers.

Beth can also be found teaching on Instagram @bethmanningintuitive and on Facebook at facebook.com/bethmanningintuitive.

CHAPTER 21

THE MAGICAL LANGUAGE OF THE NERVOUS SYSTEM

AND HOW TO ACHIEVE YOUR GOALS USING IT

Dr. Edward L. Frey, DCBA

MY STORY

Imagine my first trip to Europe—I was flown to Italy first class to treat a man known across the globe, perhaps the world's wealthiest in the recent past. He's an older gentleman having significant health challenges, including the inability to get up on his own and walk. Two weeks later, he was able to do just that! What a memory of hearing his wife in her usual gravitas appearance saying, "Bravo, Dr. Frey!" before I left.

How was I able to attract such an amazing event? More importantly, how was I able to improve his clinical picture so quickly? The answer—I figured out the magical language of the nervous system. In knowing this language, I simply did what I've normally done for all my patients over the last 30 years. As you will see later, knowing this language allows you, the reader, to take an active and very significant role in determining how to optimize your health and longevity. It can be used to make vital changes in your health, symptomology, pain, your aging, and your clinical picture. It can even help you achieve your life goals by removing blockages. It allows for more effective healthcare and would be a vital addition to your healthcare regimen. I am positive that not including your nervous system in optimizing your health would be a tragic mistake.

In order to explain this language as used in a doctor-patient setting, I am going to use a typical new patient exam example from the perspective of the new patient:

You come into the treatment room clueless about what I do. You were referred to me by a trusted friend who has trouble describing the work—just that it is very effective. I begin to isolate and test different muscles in your upper and lower body for strength or weakness. Some are familiar to you, like the biceps and triceps muscles. Many are not. Some muscles test strong, and some test weak. I ask you to hold the area that prompted you to seek care. When you do so, I test the strong muscles. They all weaken!

That's just the beginning. I ask you, "Hold your left hip," and suddenly, when I test all your weak muscles, they're all strong. And when I test the strong muscles they act differently also. They test weak, then strong, then weak, then strong over and over again. Finally, when holding your area of pain, which caused all the strong muscles to weaken moments before, they don't, but only if I hold the left hip. After I fixed your left hip mechanics, your chief complaint area was pain-free, and all the weak muscles were now strong. It's like magic!

You say, "What the heck, and how did you know it was my left hip?" My reply: "This is the language of the nervous system, and knowing this language allows me to do precise and effective work."

I have always been very sensitive. An astrologist told me in the past, based on the date, time, and location I was born, that I'm a triple Cancer, and maybe that's the reason. I also think that most—after many years of doing their job, develop a sixth sense in their work. Nevertheless, I've developed the ability to feel things, and it has especially helped my effectiveness as a doctor. Feeling strength and weakness in my patients led me to this magical language.

When I see strangers out in public, I can easily tell which of their muscles are weak, which are strong, and what area is the cause, and I show them that right then and there. It is actually one of my most effective marketing tools. In my practice, I was never able to show what I felt to my patients until I learned about muscle testing—a common tool used by many practitioners over the years. I found myself on ABC's *Good Morning America* demonstrating muscle testing when they did a story on alternative healthcare early in my career. Learning more about the nervous system made me better able to articulate what I was doing to my patients years later. I figured out it was probably our nervous system's mechanoreceptors whose language I was using.

Let's talk about these mechanoreceptors that are so vital to this language. Our nervous system runs our body, and a vital part of it is webs of mechanoreceptors layered throughout our bodies. These affect our aging process, pain, our symptoms, and our muscle function (being on or off), and they require normal body mechanics and tone in order to do these things.

I can feel their own unique language.

It's very accurate and always consistent with what I feel with each patient. Since these mechanoreceptors require normal body mechanics to be active, their language literally guides me to fix your body's mechanics very specifically.

With this guy in the example above, I was able to use his body's language to figure things out, showing him what I do. "There is nothing more specific," I told him, "Than your own body showing me exactly what's going on, including each factor that causes it, and most importantly, exactly how to fix each factor."

For each of you who have had body work and manipulation before, imagine your neck, which has seven vertebrae having a mechanical issue, in this case, a misalignment. Imagine me using a strong muscle first and going down the neck's vertebrae with my hand until your fourth one on the right causes your strong muscle to weaken. We have now found the area to manipulate. In order to see which exact way the vertebrae needs to move to get back in alignment, I can now use any weak muscle in the body, and pushing the vertebrae in only one direction will strengthen that weak muscle. Bodywork is an incredible modality for our nervous system and our health. Specificity is the key determiner of our ability to do effective work.

All of us humans have multiple areas with faulty mechanics. Therefore we all have multiple areas, and even many layers, of inactive mechanoreceptors. This, in neurology, is called deafferentation and leads to injuries, symptoms, disease, accelerated aging, and even poor healing. Having a complete nervous system creates a more powerful, healthier human being. And what's more, our mechanoreceptors stop the effects of deafferentation in its tracks as long as they're active. This is always a big determiner of the present clinical picture. So for each patient who comes in for care, I normalize their mechanics from their head to their toes in order to rid them of symptoms and create optimum function.

Let's add more pieces to this puzzle regarding this type of healthcare.

Do any of you do the following?

1) Sit at a desk for work.

2) Look down or up for a computer or cellphone.

3) Eat sweets.

4) Enjoy processed foods, including packaged foods and fast food.

5) Have a negative opinion of yourself at times.

6) Have a relationship or friendship full of drama or worse.

7) Live in an environment with poor air quality at times.

All of these seem fairly innocuous. But from a nervous system perspective, you'll discover nothing could be further from the truth. You will discover that we are like sponges to our environment, and whatever we expose ourselves to can have a critical effect on our lives. Specifically, all of us humans have stimuli in our lives in the form of mechanical, chemical, and energetic. Above I asked each of you if you do those things. Each creates bad change.

We were made to do things functionally for how our bodies were constructed. For instance, our bodies were not created to sit for long periods of time, and we're supposed to keep our work at eye level. When we sit for long periods of time, or we look down to text or work on our laptops, we're creating bad change. It's called nociception. We have nociceptors that are stimulated by poor posture mechanically, by poor diet or exposure to pollutants chemically, and by disempowering thoughts or people in our lives energetically. Pain and other harmful effects occur due to nociceptive effects.

I thus take a two-pronged approach in the care of my patients. First, I remove mechanical problems to activate the mechanoreceptors so they can do the jobs they normally do. I also talk about lifestyle, so effects from harmful stimuli can be avoided. For a person with elbow pain, for instance, I might treat ten different areas in order to change mechanics and promote healing (as opposed to traditional medicine's treating the elbow directly). I also make sure the patient keeps their work in front of them at eye level as best as they can to avoid this nociceptive change. Diet and other lifestyle changes, including exercise, breathwork, meditation, and creating good boundaries with people, are also included.

Being sensitive has really created a rewarding life. It made me a better doctor as it led to this magical language. I even use it to treat most of my own health issues. Yes, I am able to fix myself and have for over 30 years. I became sort of a guinea pig to test and try new methods of care which I later incorporated into my practice. In addition, it has made me more spiritually inclined.

Energy work becomes possible with this work. Often in the context of treating my patients, energetic issues show themselves. I handle them differently, but muscle testing remains a big part of figuring out what is going on and what to do to clear this energetic issue. When a person puts their hand over their solar plexus (our power center or chakra) but off their body, and weak muscles all suddenly strengthen, that has meaning. We can further clarify what the issue is by challenging different questions and seeing muscle test results change. For a person who is in a disempowering relationship, saying the disempowering person's name can completely change the muscle testing result. Things that have meaning do just that. We can then figure out how to clear that energy by challenging different colors of the spectrum, for instance, or pushing energy in different directions to see what negates the negative energy. I also try to get my patient to establish better boundaries with their negative friend too. In general, I tell all my patients to avoid negative or stressful people and environments.

Removing blockages in order to achieve our goals is also possible. All we need are strong muscles, and we can figure out situations that have meaning or blockages preventing us from achieving our specific goals. It's quite effective. This magical language of our nervous system makes us more powerful human beings able to win in life. With this idea, it's time for you to try out a few tools to give you some experience with the work.

THE TOOL

I am going to have you rub some areas of your body. After treating so many over the years, I see certain common patterns in most of my patients. Rubbing these areas out will activate quite a few inactive mechanoreceptors in most of you. And you will definitely feel a nice change after doing this.

For anyone with lesions or injuries, or those who bruise very easily in some areas particularly, please show caution and even skip some or all of the tools. Have a partner do it instead.

Rub out these areas (or have someone do it for you):

Go to your armpit first and push in a few directions. For the tender areas, push and massage with two fingers together for 30 seconds. Then go lateral to the outer side and keep going till you feel the edge of your shoulder blade. Rub this area out, focusing on the tender areas there for about 30 seconds. You will know if you need more pressure. Do both sides.

Next, go to the front, side, and back of each of your shoulders and rub out for 30 seconds each. Again you will feel some tenderness. That's a good sign. Go along the top and bottom surface of each of your collar bones, rubbing against the bone, especially where most tender.

In your lower body, rub out both of your hamstrings with a flat surface created by putting all your fingers together except your thumbs. Focus again on the tender parts of your hamstrings, which are found on the back of your thighs above the knee and below your buttocks.

Finally, go to the lateral or outer muscle tissue of your calves and rub those out.

I am confident all of you will feel much different in a few ways, including experiencing anxiety reduction as a result of addressing these areas of your body. All of you now have more active nervous systems.

 **Dr. Edward L. Frey,** DC, has been practicing chiropractic in Atlanta, Georgia, for over 30 years. Having treated several internationally known families locally and abroad, he has enjoyed a lot of amazing experiences along the way. Encountering the late Benazir Bhutto, the former prime minister of Pakistan, was one of these extraordinary moments in his life. Never having been social media or technology conscious, he now seeks to spread his work around the world through these outlets, and especially with video in the near future.

Connect with Dr. Frey:

Email: sakdocfrey@icloud.com

Instagram: Nervoussystemthis (under construction)

Facebook: Dr Edward L Frey

CHAPTER 22

THE BIRTH OF TRUTH

THROUGH ENERGETIC ANCESTRAL HEALING

Trudy M. Rouillard Soole-Iyan Duta Wi
(Red Stone Woman), MA, LMHC

MY STORY

Seven months before my 60th birthday, 35 years in sobriety, in and out of therapy, working 12-step programs, working with medicine people, attending ceremonies, and surviving cancer, I have already overcome huge barriers in my life.

I'm half Native American with a mix of German, Irish, and Swedish descent (I think).

From time to time, gnawing, nagging thoughts turned into bouts of blah, depression, bitterness, sarcasm, and loneliness. These thoughts have a voice I recognize as belittling and patronizing, keeping me stuck and frozen in fear, not teaching me what I came here to do next—which is share my story, visions, and gifts that no one talks about, cares to listen to, or seemingly understands.

Thoughts from inception became my biology. It was all I knew. Therapy assisted, yet my spirit yearned to resolve something deeper and find my passion and next step in life.

So, it began. My dear spiritual sister, Leah, gifted me a retreat in the North Carolina mountains, and I said, "Yes!" At the retreat, I won a gift from Jacqueline Kane, a woman I'd never met, to do ancestral energy work.

Several weeks later, Creator spoke, and I listened. "Get ahold of Jacqueline and see what she's all about," I heard with the ears of my heart.

Little did I know what Creator had in store for me. Of course, I had all kinds of excuses not to commit to the gift she was offering. I heard the message from Creator saying, "Wow, really, Trudy, when is it time for you? This is something you continually put out into the universe. Here it is!" So, I said, "Yes!"

Immediately I could feel Jacqueline's energy and that she knew on a deeper level what I needed help with. I thought: *someone finally speaks the words I think. Someone finally knows of the ancestors I see and the energy we carry.* Every part of me knew this was a missing piece for my continued journey of healing.

As soon as our sessions began, my ancestors from the other side came in and witnessed what I was doing and orchestrated a healing releasing ceremony—releasing sadness, anger, disappointments, and heartache. I could see the beginning of where it all started—the thyroid cancer I had. I could see themes and patterns in my life that carried over from generations before me. The work we did unraveled deep-seated memories and emotional pain that I could never put into words. I saw the younger version of me and the start of oppression of the self, holding my tongue, not sharing what I saw or knew. Trying to please others. Taking care of others. There is no blame; it merely happened.

I see it clearly now. We carry emotional pain, spoken and unspoken, and experiences from our ancestors, repeat the cycle and the self-defeating behaviors, and the start of illness and disease begins. The negative thoughts and memories served a purpose of a limiting lifestyle. I was ready to tell a new story, the one where I called my power back, integrating the younger version of me with the woman I am today.

Each session, we used EFT (emotional freedom technique) that supported me to re-align with my spirit. I call this spiritual housekeeping. Things I wanted began to show up in my life so fast, and I got my voice back. I was able to give voice to the memories. Then, one night, I was called (by my inner child) to sit down and write. Stored emotional, painful memories became wounds, and she wanted to share them from her perspective in her own way. She wanted to help me release them and awaken my passion. The more I allowed her to speak her truth and put words to the memories, the more healing and joy came into my life. It was time to let her tell her story. I sat and wrote until I was done.

Memories from in-utero, where I heard on a vibrational level 'there is no room for me,' to about six to seven years old, to the adult I am now, poured out of me. I came to learn and understand that I created a life around memories that are a part of me, my DNA, and the life I lived. That was all I knew. I see it clearly now. I blamed others for my life circumstances, forgetting my spirit came here to learn, move through it, heal it, and pass it on through storytelling and teaching, promoting healing and wellness.

In all my years of therapy and sobriety, I have never been able to get this far in my mental and emotional well-being. The energetic ancestral work I said yes to gives me the freedom to speak my truth from a deeper place of understanding and compassion so I may teach others and offer healing gifts to others.

Here are energetic memories that came and wanted to be heard:

What's wrong with you?

Why are you crying?

Why are you so angry?

Why are you so sensitive?

Others have it much worse!

At least you have a place to live!

At least they kept you in the family!

This family, ugh! Oh, my golly!

What was I thinking?

Why did I stay?

Why did I choose this one?

"Lessons, my Dear," she said, "Lessons." (Voice from ancestors).

"You are a teacher."

"You will be a teacher." (Birth mother's words).

I don't want to be a teacher!

They are mean.

It hurts to be small.

It hurts to be big.

Where do I go?

Where is there room for me? (In utero memory).

Who will listen?

Why don't they speak the truth?

I'm this; I'm that. Where do I fit in?

I'm not full-blood anything!

Why do they discriminate?

Why do they mistreat their own people?

What happened to them?

Why do they take it out on me?

I AM THE VOICE FOR THE PEOPLE!

Oh! This is what my birthmother meant when she said, "You will be a teacher, my girl." "My girl" was a term of endearment. *No one calls me that. No one but her. I file this away and will always remember.*

No wonder I love horses! No wonder I love eagles. They represent freedom—freedom to be who they are! Tall and proud! Small and proud, big and proud. Proud, proud, proud, proud, proud.

I'm here now! This is me. This is all of me. I get to be me. All I've ever wanted to be! I am the voice of the people for the people. I represent truth. I am a truth-teller. I am a storyteller; I am wise beyond wise; I am brilliant. I am kind; I am thoughtful.

As I recall and read Joy Harjo's poem about fear, this poem came through me:

Come here fear.
You don't get to hold me.
You don't get to keep me.

This shame is not mine.
This guilt is not mine.
It does not belong to me.
I came to stand in the light, not the darkness.
I came to speak the truth, not withhold it.

I realized the younger version of me had become the voice of despair and doubt. I realized I carried ancestral energy and trauma that generations before me experienced. I was the voice of, 'this is all I know.' I was the voice of, 'this is what I was dealt.' I was the voice of betrayal, mistrust, abuse, neglect—cut-like-a-knife voice. I was to take what they dished out. Stand there and take it! I was to take what I saw, take what I experienced, take what I heard, and make no mention of it.

I see how our woundedness plays out in our lives, creating divisions and dysfunction separating us from our inner self-perpetuating pain, heartache, and despair. My wounded inner child carried this. She didn't have the words to communicate her pain. At the age of two, I was separated from my twin sister and mother and sent to live with an older sister because Mother was poverty-stricken, diabetic, and had heart problems. My dad was out of the picture and denied my existence.

My inner child continues to write her memories of watching her sister/ mom, husband, and their family all screaming over one another, fighting to be heard.

Fighting, looking like fools! Fighting for what? *Do they not know how silly they look? Do they not know how silly they sound?* So harmful, all of that... how do you manage that? It spins and spirals and takes on a life of its own, and then one day, you become it - it becomes you. It is all you know.

Who made up this stupid saying: "Sticks and stones may break my bones, but words will never hurt me?" Oh, my golly! *How insane. How inhumane.* I remember my sister/mom saying that.

Words! Words become us! Words are us! Our thoughts become us. We become them. What the hay were they talking about? That could not be farther from the truth. Ah, the truth - there it is. Yes - the Truth.

These were the questions I heard my inner child say. I started asking how my people became known and took on this energy of fighting and battle.

I started hearing questions in my head. *Where have these people gone?* So far away from themselves I see. This I know. This I see. This I live. I file this away for later use.

My inner child was told: "She has a bad temper. She daydreams too much." Just like it was yesterday, I recall those words. She was worried about her survival. No one asked her what she was feeling. They just made assumptions.

Let's tell the world. Let's not tell them how resilient she is, how beautiful she is, and how she will be a teacher someday.

Another stored memory:

Who will be home when I get there? Will there be food? That little girl had to become an adult at an early age because there were times when she came home and bags of clothes were outside on the lawn. The fear of who was going to take care of her was birthed, alive, and growing rapidly.

Sister/Mom says, "When the food is gone, you have to wait until the next grocery store run." So, I savor. I eat little and share the rest because they are her children. I am not. I'm the sister. The little sister. The one who is to be quiet. The one who is to remain small. The one who is to raise the children. Her children. All four of them. The one who is to represent this family. She did her best to make me feel like I was her own, but I always felt different.

The young adult in me operated from the place the younger version of me and the system of beliefs witnessed and carried. Beliefs that said: *What do I know about being a parent? An adult? They are mean. They do not speak the truth! They have sharp tongues. They throw things at one another. They make fun of one another's heritages. Hey, wait a minute! That is my heritage they are screaming at and making fun of! What is going on here? Violence! Noise! All this loudness! When will they be quiet? When will they stop? Oh, that's right, when they leave the house. Or better yet, when I do.*

I became good at suppressing emotions and learned quickly that the only emotion allowed was anger. One of my scariest moments as a child was when my sister/mom, and brother-in-law were violently fighting. She shouts to me, "Get my wallet, get the kids, put them in the closet upstairs, then, come back downstairs, pull the kitchen chair up to the wall phone, stand on your toes and call the police on him—yes, him—your dad." *He's not my dad! He's your husband! Why don't you do it? Why do I have to? Why not your kids? Why me? I am the smallest one! They are all taller than me. Who will protect me?* I'm scared. I'm frozen in fear. I do as I am told—angry, bitter - and mighty! That is me. I fight, and I fight, and I fight. *Of course, I fight because no one sees me! No one listens to me! I have an inner knowing of the truth. No one wants to hear it, and no one is talking about it.*

From those horrifying events, a blessing came. One that is treasured. I appreciate being alone, especially outside where there is peace and solace. I learned how to listen on a different level to the vibration of life and all of its inhabitants. I recall vividly, through the eyes of the younger me, the story and the feeling of being outside under the stars—the star nation in our culture. *This is my family! Them up there! They listen. They know.* It feels like home. Being outside is magical. It was then that I embraced spirit guides, star nation, and the unseen.

This was the moment I thought to myself: *it's me now.* I put the stories all into perspective. They all make sense now. I know now that I don't have a bad temper - I have a passion for the truth, our natural birthright. This sacred Earth, our Mother, is here for us–for healing as a people if we so choose. Something inside of me shifted. The messiness I was born into does not have the emotional charge it used to.

The work I've done allows me to expand my life, passions, and dreams, speak the truth and stand in the light. It helped shape me into who I've become—a storyteller promoting healing and wellness through counseling, coaching, and consulting. It's an honor and a privilege to hold sacred space, assisting people in healing their woundedness.

THE TOOL

Close your eyes, take three slow deep breaths, relax your body. Invite your wisdom from your higher self and Spirit to assist you. Honor the four directions, up above, down below, and the center of the Universe by acknowledging them.

Recall a memory you want to heal.

See in your mind's eye yourself at the age that is attached to the memory.

Invite your parents to come into the vision whether they are alive or deceased.

Bring your awareness to the memory of where you feel its energy is stored in your body. With both hands, start pulling energy from the area of the body as though you are weeding a garden. Take all of that energy and put it into a ball.

See your parents standing across from you with their hands out eager to assist and heal. Give the ball of energy to them.

Notice behind your parents are their ancestors from generations back standing in line behind your parents single file as far back as you can see. One by one they turn around and give the ball of energy to the person standing behind them. Do this until you see it complete.

The people in line form a big circle with you connecting it. One by one they all come by and shake your hand thanking you for putting words to the energy stored in your body-the memories. They tell you they are happy that you're here and that you have the courage to do the healing work for yourself and all of them.

After they have all shaken your hand, they move back to their respective place in the circle.

See them all sparkling and shining brightly.

Take three slow deep breaths, wiggle your fingers and your toes and say:

For those who have gone before me, for those who walk with me, and for those who are coming, I honor you!

Mitakuye Oyasin! (We are all related!)

I am a proud mother of two sons from my first marriage and a mom and grandmother from my second. In my Native American culture, "I am an ordinary woman." My greatest gift is being in alignment with Creator. I have learned so much from life, the life I chose, my family of origin, my own family, those I have worked with around the globe professionally and personally, and the medicine people who have helped me in ways that I am much stronger for.

Enrolled descendant of Mdewakanton (Dwellers of the Spirit Lake) of the Dakotah Santee Sioux Nation of Nebraska my Indian name is **Iyan Duta Wi** (Red Stone Woman) the sacred pipestone of Pipestone, Minnesota.

I have been in the field of helping others for decades, dedicating my life to learning and healing so that I may teach others, inspiring and planting seeds of wellness where ever I go.

In my 25+ years as a psychotherapist I developed out-patient treatment programming specifically designed to meet the needs of the Native American population, facilitated counseling in school systems and domestic violence programs, and was a director of a federal in-patient treatment program and Director of State of Operations for Premier Care managing an ATR (Access to Recovery) grant for the State of New Mexico.

Currently in private practice as a Licensed Mental Health Clinician (LMHC) I enthusiastically, optimistically combine psychological counseling with spiritual practices assisting clients in their search for meaning, purpose, and direction in their lives.

I love to sit with nature to listen and learn, ride horses, sew, hug trees, laugh at myself, and spend time with my husband and family.

You may follow me on my website:
https://www.soolesolutions.com/
Facebook business profile – Soolesolutions.com
LinkedIn and Psychology Today

CHAPTER 23

JOURNALING

HEALING YOUR INNER CRITIC WITH COMPASSION AND KINDNESS

Mandy Pullen Barr,
Reiki Master Trainer, Sound Healer, Clarity Catalyst Coach

MY STORY

I can't remember my first negative thought or the first time I wished I had a different life, a better body, or a prettier face. But I do remember, as if it was yesterday, the first time someone called me fat: "Here she comes, folks, wide load. Watch it; she will take all the water out of the pool." I was just an awkward kid flirting with puberty, maybe ten or eleven, when my friend's older brother said that to me.

God, I was horrified, and I remember this tiny voice inside me saying—*well, you are kind of fat. I mean, he does have a point. Maybe we should have skipped breakfast today?* At that moment, my inner critic was born.

From that second on, this critic has been with me, presenting itself in the form of self-sabotaging behavior: eating disorder, alcoholism, and, my favorite—blowing up relationships with friends, lovers, and colleagues. It didn't matter that I had a family who loved me, believed in me, and thought I was special. All I could hear was: *you're not good enough.*

Now, you might say, "Okay, Mandy, someone called you fat once in your life, and you came undone?" And the answer is no, of course not; I've been teased and criticized about my weight throughout my life. Next to the pool incident, damaging comments made by the women in my family were equally hurtful. My mom and both grandmothers were obsessed with my weight and my looks.

At almost every family gathering, there were comments made: "You're too heavy," and "Perhaps, you shouldn't eat so much." For some reason, my weight and looks were tied to my self-worth. Maybe they were trying to prepare me for the realities of the world that judges women on how they look rather than their inner beauty. But unfortunately, it only left me with a lifetime of thinking my worth was based on my weight and looks.

And, of course, there were the comments made throughout my awkward periods of dating throughout my life. Guys would say, "I think you have a great personality, but I am not attracted to you." Jab, another dagger straight to my heart and ego. Further proof to my critic that I'm not enough.

Sadly, my inner critic feeds off these disparaging comments, validating its need for existence: *Mandy, you are lucky you have us, keeping you protected from everyone's opinion.* A vicious cycle started each time I felt judged by others and myself beginning with feeling embarrassed, followed by punishing myself by overeating or drinking, to the final phase of further self-loathing.

Now, there have been times in my life where I said *enough is enough, I don't want to look like this anymore,* and I started some sort of weight loss program, usually trailed by intense physical activity like running, cross-fit, spin classes, private trainers, you name it. For a while, it worked, I'd feel great, and I looked good, too. I looked in the mirror and said, "Looking good, kid, let's keep it up."

However, inevitably, something would happen, and my untreated critic would swoop in, saying, *see, I told you it wasn't safe out there. Let's get some ice cream and consider if this healthy lifestyle is really for us.*

Exhausted from decades of trying to dull the non-stop chatter in my head and the cycle of disrupting behavior, I began to understand the origin of my inner critic. Today, I refer to it as my voice of judgment, a sub-persona created to protect me from the big bad wolf.

Realizing this, I began to reflect on my life, looking at my past relationships with colleagues and friends. Still, the relationships I was the master at destroying were my romantic ones. I began to see that I sabotaged them to protect myself from being hurt. It was the old adage: *I am going to hurt you before you hurt me.*

And that is what I did with dramatic flair to my first husband; I destroyed our marriage because I was terrified of letting him in and showing him that my inner critic was running the show. Sabotage Sally, it's how I lovingly refer to her today, and she would remind me daily: *You know, he doesn't love you. I mean, look at you. Your marriage is going to end just like your parents'.*

Day after day, I heard some sort of variation of how I wasn't good enough and how he would be better off with someone else, someone normal. And I believed these voices. Sally got so loud and persuasive that I could barely hear the real me; I was trapped so far down the trail of self-hatred, I wondered, *could I ever be rescued?*

So, I drank a lot to quiet the voices that blamed me and told me that my husband was going to leave me. I was so far down the road of depression and alcoholism I couldn't tell reality from the fiction in my mind. I convinced myself that he and my son would be better off without me. They could start over and build a new and better life filled with less drama.

Some of these feelings came from my postpartum depression, some from being wrongly medicated, and the rest resulted from years of self-hatred. But unfortunately, I knew my husband didn't sign up to play the role of therapist. And honestly, at the time, I didn't have the words or the bravery to tell him I felt like dying.

It didn't make sense. Our life together had everything I wished for: a dream car, a brownstone in Boston, a great career, and our beautiful baby boy. So why wasn't it enough? Why wasn't I happy? What was wrong with me?

Unable to bear it any longer, I mustered enough courage to set him free, "I want a divorce." And as soon as those words came out of my mouth, this soft voice inside me cried: *What are you doing? Don't do this!* But it was too late; it was out there as clear as day—divorce.

And wouldn't you know it? He looked me square in the eyes and said, "Mandy, you better be sure that's what you want because you can't take this back." It wasn't really what I wanted. I yearned for him to be my knight in shining armor, the hero that saved our twisted and broken love story, the one that rescues the damsel in distress.

But that's not what happened; he didn't fix our marriage or me. And how could I expect that of him, of anyone? And I'm sure he didn't want that heavy burden of responsibility.

Shortly after we separated, I spent close to a year dedicating my time to recovery, therapy, and rebuilding a new life centered on caring for my son and myself. But, you see, I became a slave, and my inner critic was my master, and it almost took away the one person I loved with every fiber of my being: my son.

During this time, I healed and promised to be the best mom for him. I didn't know what I was doing most of the time, but I remembered the little things my parents did for me that made me feel loved and cared for, like going to my games, concerts and plays while giving me ground rules and consequences for undesired behavior.

Of course, I encountered setbacks and frustration, and whenever I thought about quitting, I remembered my promise to my son. So I pushed forward, always looking for ways to become emotionally stronger. In many ways, I think my son saved me, giving me the nerve to get off the hamster wheel and try like hell to be the mom he deserved. So that's what I did for both my son and my ex-husband.

I worked tirelessly to find peace and harmony to heal these broken pieces of myself. And along the way, there have been teachers and healers who have helped me along my path. But, possibly the most influential teacher has been my dad—always my biggest fan and the person who told me the truth, even when I didn't want to hear it. Like the first time he told me I needed to love myself. *Love myself? That seems rather self-absorbed.*

"Mandy, you aren't going to be able to love anyone until you love yourself." And I would smartly respond with, "Gee, thanks, Dad, so I am destined to be alone until then? And how do you know that I don't love myself? Look at everything I'm doing to recover from my divorce—therapy, sobriety, exercising, and trying to be a good mom."

"Yes, you are doing good work, and there's more. It's the way you talk to yourself. But unfortunately, it's not from a place of kindness and compassion. And if anyone knows about that, it's me. It took more than 60 years to find peace with myself. But, today, I can say that I truly love who I have become."

I guess I should feel lucky that it only took me 50 years to understand what my dad was saying. Well, 50 years, several failed relationships, a ton of therapy, a 12-step program, Reiki, sound healing, and finally being introduced to the Creative Insight Journey.

Today, I have a healthy relationship with my ex-husband, and we do a beautiful job co-parenting our son. He is a senior in high school, captain of the basketball team, and the kindest, most compassionate kid I could ever imagine. My heart is filled with joy for his future, feeling blessed beyond measure for our relationship.

I have also gotten another shot at marriage. I married a terrific man, and we celebrate all that life has to offer, including our blended family of three adult children, three dogs, and my mom. We are both committed to our self-discovery and nurturing our marriage daily. It's not easy, but it is so worth it.

THE TOOL

A FIVE-DAY JOURNALING PRACTICE

The truth is, I have never been one of those girls who kept a diary or a journal. It always felt so personal writing down my thoughts and feelings, making them real, and giving these words a life of their own. But that's the point, right? Writing down what's inside of you, getting it all out on paper, frees your mind of the chatter. Yes, it can be scary, and it's also where significant breakthroughs can happen. So, let's get at it!

I learned early on in my journey that taking time to settle down before beginning any inner work yielded the best results. So I'm offering that to you now. Please know I'm here, holding this sacred space for you filled with heart-based Reiki energy each day you sit down to journal. I have also created a ten-minute crystal bowl mediation for your practice. I encourage you to listen to this while journaling - https://bit.ly/YouTubeMindfulBarr

Each day, before you begin your journaling practice, I invite you to sit in a comfortable position, with both feet on the floor. Place one hand on your heart and the other slightly below your belly button.

Now, close your eyes and take five full breaths—you should feel your hands rise and lower. On the in-breath, say to yourself, "Here," and on the out-breath, "Now." Then, settling deeper into this posture, feel these breaths and the energy from your hands.

Notice how your attention shifts as you continue breathing, bringing you into the present moment. After you have completed your breathing and feel centered and grounded, I invite you to begin your journaling.

DAY ONE: LET'S MEET YOUR VOICE OF JUDGMENT

Before you begin, remember that your voice of judgment, VOJ, is a sub persona you created to protect you at some point in your life's journey. So let's enter this conversation from a place of curiosity and wonder.

1. Do you have a name, something I should call you?
2. What do you enjoy doing? Do you have any favorite hobbies or favorite pastimes?
3. What time do you get up in the morning? When do you go to bed?
4. Do you have favorite foods? Shows? Music? Sports teams?
5. Ask any other questions, thank them for their time, and let them know you will be back tomorrow to get to know them better.

DAY TWO: LET'S DIG A LITTLE DEEPER

Before starting your journaling practice, remember to take a few minutes to center yourself with your feet planted on the ground, one hand on your heart and one below your belly button. Now, begin breathing, feeling into the here and now. Then, once you feel centered and grounded, you may start.

The goal today is to get to know your voice of judgment better, digging a little deeper to understand when they became a part of you and how you will learn how they are feeling.

1. Is there a reason or myriad of reasons why I manifested you? Or a defining moment from childhood or adolescence that brought you to life?

2. How can I know how you're feeling—lonely, sad, angry, fearful, stressed, etc.—and when you think this way, what do you need? And how can I help before acting out?

3. What else would you like to share with me to get to know you better?

DAY THREE: LET'S HEAL WITH LOVE AND COMPASSION

Before you start, ground and center yourself; enjoy those five deep breaths. Today, we will reread what your VOJ had to say regarding the defining moments from your past and the reason for existing.

Now, from a place of compassion, write your voice of judgment a gratitude letter, thanking them for their time and service. Let them know you will work harder at acknowledging their feelings and work with them to help overcome any negative emotions. Let them know that you will be living your life for your highest good. Check out my letter to Sabotage Sally.

Dearest Sabotage Sally,

Thank you for spending time with me the last two days and sharing your thoughts and feelings. I appreciate you telling me the story of your childhood with your neighbor, who was a bully. I am sorry to hear about the names he called you, especially regarding the time in their pool—calling us a "wide load." Gosh, that must have been painful to hear, and I can certainly understand your desire to protect me from other disparaging comments.

I understand now that you came to me as a way to protect me from people that might judge or call me names. However, I was hoping that we could work together so that you feel heard and supported while we use some newer and more nurturing tools for managing painful situations. For example, taking a meditative walk in nature always helps to calm the mind, and we always leave feeling refreshed while giving our body the gift of movement.

Another excellent tool to share how you feel before we "sabotage" the situation, the relationship, or health goals is journaling. Journaling allows us the opportunity to identify potential triggers or traps. In addition, writing is cathartic, freeing ourselves by releasing how we feel to the paper. From there, we can look at a positive way to express ourselves.

Finally, the third tool we can use is mindfulness. Mindfulness gives us the freedom to live in the present moment, not regretting the past or worrying about the future—where peace lives.

I look forward to talking more tomorrow.

Love, Mandy

DAY FOUR: LET'S MEET YOUR VOICE OF WISDOM

Your voice of wisdom (VOW), higher self, or witness is your true authentic self, who you are at your core. As you get to know this part of yourself more intimately, your voice of judgment becomes quieter and quieter, allowing you to be your true essence.

So, let's meet this warrior god or goddess who always watches from a place of love. They are confident, clear, and peaceful.

1. Do you have a name, something I should call you?
2. What do you enjoy doing? Do you have any favorite hobbies or favorite pastimes?
3. What time do you get up in the morning? When do you go to bed?
4. Do you have favorite foods? Shows? Music? Sports teams?
5. Is there anything else I should know about you?

DAY FIVE: LET'S CHAT - A HEARTFELT CONVERSATION BETWEEN YOUR VOJ AND VOW

For today's journaling, let's have an open, heart-centered conversation with your higher self and inner critic. As we have learned from our earlier journaling, our critic was born out of necessity for protection. So, let's connect to see what we can learn and how our voice of wisdom offers solace to our voice of judgment.

1. What is the best way to offer you love and compassion?

2. Is there a way to know when you might need something?

3. How will I know when you feel overwhelmed, sad, angry, frustrated, etc.?

4. How can I make you feel safe, secure, and heard?

5. Anything else you would like to share?

EXTRA CREDIT

A day will come when a person, place, or situation triggers your voice of judgment, and you will want to act out. It still happens to me. But, at the moment you realize what's happening, immediately pause and, ask yourself what is happening that is triggering your VOJ. Then, acknowledge what you hear and hold space for your VOJ while trying to diffuse the situation using meditation and journaling.

For me, being part of this collaborative book and writing this chapter has triggered my VOJ during various points: "Hey kid, it's not safe out here. How about we dim your light and keep quiet until this desire to write a chapter passes." Instead, I allowed myself the space to acknowledge this fear, gave my inner critic the time to share, and then assured her that our brave words will help others heal. After all, it's what the world needs—love, compassion, and kindness.

Mandy began her holistic journey 11 years ago, shortly after her divorce. She stumbled upon Reiki after becoming ill with mononucleosis. Reluctant and desperate, she went to see a Reiki practitioner that would change her life. Not only did receiving Reiki aid in healing her illness, but it also lit a spark inside her – this began her journey to become a Reiki Master trainer.

During this time, she met a holistic practitioner specializing in sound healing. After attending several sound baths, Mandy found her second teacher and mentor. Loving the effect of incorporating Reiki and sound healing, Mandy began her practice offering these together in both private and group settings. Being an extrovert, she loved the group classes the most and felt it was a way to impact the collective positively.

In 2020 with the rest of the world, Mandy's blossoming practice abruptly stopped, triggering a time of inward reflection. During this time, Mandy worked part-time with her best friend's company, Vesta: A New Vision for Divorce. During her time with Vesta, she became fascinated with their work, particularly the coaches. She loved learning about how these professionals helped to transform families impacted by divorce.

She began to wonder—is there a space to incorporate coaching with her holistic practice of Reiki and sound healing? Then, as luck would have it, she learned about the Creative Insight Journey course her friend offered. Entirely moved by the program, Mandy interviewed to become a coach, and the rest is history.

Today, Mandy works with groups and individuals helping them get clear on their dreams so they can manifest them—allowing them to live their best lives.

Connect with Mandy

Website: https://mindfulbarr.com

Facebook: https://www.facebook.com/mindfulbarr

Instagram: https://www.instagram.com/mindful_barr/

TikTok: https://www.tiktok.com/@mindfulbarr2022

LinkedIn: https://www.linkedin.com/in/mandy-pullen-
    barr-cdm-cfpp-16870530/

YouTube: https://bit.ly/YouTubeMindfulBarr

CHAPTER 24

DIVINE BUBBLE OF PROTECTION

GRATITUDE AND GRIEVING

Sunshine Layne

MY STORY

I feel vulnerable, raw, exposed, and shocked as I share this story. At the same time, I'm aware of renewed connection to healing, the process of accepting what occurred, and the birth of a "New Me."

This latest life experience forced me out of my comfort zone. Now, I know for my soul's growth. All prior beliefs, knowledge, and behaviors were questioned; I was shaken to my core. In the end, I emerged with new lessons, teachings, gifts, and healing to share with others.

It's Saturday, May 21, 2022. Overhead, there is a bright, crystal-blue sky on a hot, long weekend! My partner Jordan stays in the city all week and comes home only on weekends. So, on that warm May morning, we loaded up the car with our dog Brutis. We drove into our small village together, ran errands, and visited friends.

Once home, we focused on various chores. Jordan stacked wood for the winter, and I tended to my veggie plants grown from seed. I placed them at the end of our driveway, a five-minute walk to the road, to share with the community. We kept some to plant on our next full moon. They patiently waited on the deck, receiving my TLC. Next up, I planned to paint the new front door a vibrant orange. I checked the weather online, which stated a thirty percent chance of rain from 2:00-3:30. I thought I had time for a quick nap.

So, I turned on the ceiling fan and cozied up. As soon as I dozed off, the fan stopped. *That's strange.* I got up and ventured outside.

"Jordan, the hydro has gone out," I said.

"Yes, the radio stopped," he stated.

Brutis and I went to sit by the fire pit. I closed my eyes, feeling the sun. Then, I heard this unearthly noise and opened my eyes to see near-total blackness from the western sky.

"Jordan, what is that noise?' I asked.

He froze and listened. "I have no idea, but we should bring the plants in," he said.

I tried to identify the noise—*a tornado? No, we rarely get those here.*

As Jordan started putting the trays of plants into the house, I thought I'd get the plants at the end of the driveway, but my intuition kicked in: *Help Jordan with the plants close to the house!*

As I bent down to pick up a plant tray, there were raindrops the size of my head. With the last tray of plants inside, Jordan went to close the shed. I yelled, "Jordan, get in here now!" I closed the door as he ran by me and a big window in the house he must have opened earlier.

With every passing second, Mother Earth unleashed. We were fully caught up in that otherworldly noise, along with the sound of wind, rain, crashing, banging, cracking, and thuds. There was wind like we've never encountered; a whitened rain like a lake had descended upon us. Treetops, furniture, plants, and items took flight! Trees fell to their deaths on our house, Jordan's car, and as far as the eyes could see. I paced, exclaiming to Jordan, Brutis, and our three cats: "There is something happening; this isn't good; we should go to the basement."

"But we can't make it," Jordan said.

I paced and thought. *If those trees break the windows or the bolts on the BBQ give way, all will fly into the house, and our journey in this physical lifetime will end.*

I remembered the friends I'd just hugged, love for our three children, parents, pets, and friends, along with their abiding love for us. We were expecting a grand-baby boy we might never meet in person. Throughout this time, I felt the presence of my beloved ones, people that have passed: Greg, Glenn, Adam, Al, Roger, and Jason. And other beloved ones too, as well as angels. On a spiritual level, our beloved ones, angels, and guides fully protected us. This was our Divine Bubble of Protection, that's unseen physically. This protection is not seen by our physical bodies. It's Divine energy that each one of us has.

As quick as this event came, it left. We stood in disbelief.

The kids! We need to make sure they are safe, stat. Raeannalyn, age 20, was home from college and working ten minutes away. Nate, 19, was a bit further, while Brayton, 27 and pregnant, lived in another Canadian province. *What about my parents and our friends? Did this happen everywhere?* We live in the woods, and everything is out when hydro is out, including cell service.

Slowly, we opened the door, but nothing looked familiar. There was total devastation, loss, and complete disorientation. Piles of trees covered our heads; the driveway was gone, along with the yard and all we owned outside. Neighbors who lived off-grid weren't home. Still, we had to get to their property for cell service and to contact our loved ones.

In shock, we headed out to make contact. It was still raining. We were wet to the bone, trees still falling, slipping and sliding in Mother Earth's rich soil, feeling blindfolded, not recognizing any terrain we climbed over or under. The smell of Mother Earth's soil, her trees, wet slippery bark, exposed roots, and wet leaves were all on us with each step.

We made it, assessing damage to our friends' property, and beginning the long check-in process. It took twenty minutes to connect a single call. Watching my cell battery's bars, I called my parents. "Please call the kids to make sure they're safe. Tell them not to come home; it's not safe. The roads are blocked by downed trees, and hydro lines are covering the ground. There are wires dangling."

Then, we began the hike home with our senses in overdrive.

Once home, I noticed a clearing of trees where Brutis and I sat at the firepit, and Jordan was stacking wood. *Miracle?* There was a clear spot without the pillage of trees. His car had piles of white birch trees on it but looked unharmed. Our Divine bubble of protection was clearly with us— beloved ones, angels, and the God of our understanding. *We are so grateful!*

Breathing in, our eyes reopened to the physical world and its natural state of reality. We heard hummingbirds cry, looking for their families; wildlife seemed stunned, disoriented, traumatized, and shocked, just like us. That night passed in a daze. *How do we transcend this experience? How do we even start to recover?*

That evening Spirit came to me with two statements: *What is now is what is becoming or what one can be stuck in. The question is, what do you need to change?*

I was curious. Why in life, when we need our soul connection most, do we abandon the connection? I listened and felt it but needed time to process it. Instantly, I thought: *I will not get stuck.*

It was instantly clear to me what I needed to change. Because of this physical experience, I chose to trust myself, to live in each moment, change my work schedule, live completely off the grid, grow veggie gardens deeper in the woods, do more for Mother Earth, have Jordan at home full time by my side, and spend more time with family.

Exhausted, raw, and numb, sleep came for a little bit but was disturbed by untruths, nightmares of the subconscious mind, in fear, trying to compute the experience. This played out for weeks.

Moving forward, each day was spent working in alignment with Mother Earth and sending her healing, loving energy. I was grieving. Without Mother Earth having us as guests in the physical realm, we wouldn't be here as souls having a human experience—to love and heal our souls.

All my spiritual work begins with connecting with Mother Earth; replenishing, restoring, and making her anew. To illustrate, one old tree communicated with forty trees. Old, sturdy trees, three generations old, died. During this tornado, they lost their main communicators, and all known communication was in chaos. It will take one hundred years or more for the three generations of trees to be restored.

Of course, I'm grateful we survived with minimal damage to our home and family. But there are so many dimensions, layers, and feelings beyond that. Every animal, tree, plant, leaf, and root is alive and has a soul; we are all equal. So much death surrounded us. So many animals died, trapped without food, water, or homes. For weeks, we spent our days cutting trees and clearing brush, which is an ongoing process. Their sweet earthy smells, bark, leaves, and beauty, are all over us—our hair, clothing, skin, face, fingers, and nails. The clearing process destroyed them even more. It was like moving body parts and dragging them deeper into the woods, but at the same time, becoming one.

The once quiet home, our retreat and quiet oasis and community, is now noisy with chainsaws, heavy trucks, and machinery daily. As the chainsaws ran nonstop, I sent energy to everyone's Divine Bubble of Protection. I have no idea where our physical strength, courage, stamina, focus, and adrenaline came from, but they arrived.

Still, my feelings remained in inner turmoil. I was numb, vacant, and unable to cry or relay what I felt - unlike myself. I found the question "How are you?" triggering and annoying. It allowed me to check in with myself, though.

I finally understood that I was feeling gratitude and grief at the same vibration, frequency, and consciousness. There are other layers of feelings underneath, but they needed more processing, time, and perception. When feelings came up, like frustration or anger, I'd layer them with guilt, thinking things like, *but people are going through much, much more than this.* I found resolve by tapping into Mother Earth and her words to me: "You have given so much for our collective healing; now this is your healing time, your experience, your soul transformation. Allow, accept, acknowledge your feelings and pain, and then move them out!"

I teach this healing process, but in this experience, I was truly challenged to survive in the earthly realm. We had no hydro, running water, or ability to bathe. We used pails of water from the pond to flush the toilet. There were no lights or services of any kind, and a lot of clean-up that took a long time.

To this present day, hydro is not stable. It's a feeling of everything falling on you, closing you in. All our hiking trails and crown land is gone. These are places I found solitude, peace, love, and understanding. I enjoyed visits with my beloved ones. I experienced trees supporting me and listening to me on my journey. I engaged in daily tree hugging and took people there for meditation.

One weekend, as friends helped once again with cleaning up, Val said, "It's like a big white wave has come hit everyone in the world, and everyone's lives were tossed and thrown. Everyone had to find their way in the last few years."

Jordan shared, "It was like we were in a snow globe thrown and shattered with all its insides left astray." I asked, "Do you look for all the old pieces or start anew?"

It has been weeks since this life-changing event; we're still stepping into our new selves, adjusting, and finding our way, just like the wildlife. They're still confused and side-stepping back to life too. As I open our front door, there is a snake coiled on top of the door frame or a turtle planning its entry through our front door.

I have finally painted our front door that vibrant orange. It represents our becoming, our anew, our healing. The doorway is now an even greater threshold to love, joy, peace, ease, grace, and to move forward. *Your soul has more to do.*

Spirit shared with me that Mother Earth inhaled and exhaled a breath, clearing out the overcrowding and making room for the new, fresh air and growth. There are now beautiful surreal baby plants and trees growing everywhere. We have the honor of witnessing this; it reminds me of how our bodies heal. We're supported and divinely protected all the time. This is true from our first breath to our last exhale. All things born on Mother Earth in this physical realm will end their physical lifetime here once the soul has completed its cycle.

Sometimes, as I did, we need to empty and leave our comfort zone for rebirthing. This allows the entry of expanded, new vibrations and frequencies. We can have gratitude and grief for our experiences, turning them into new healthy perceptions to expand, grow, and share with others as we illuminate love and heal each other. There can be resolve, love, healing, and empowerment through chaos, destruction, trauma, and pain. We can surrender, allow, accept, feel, align, and gain courage and strength.

We're so blessed, honored, and forever grateful to all our loved ones who gathered to help us through this dark time and those that followed. You dedicated yourselves to us daily—physically, mentally, emotionally, and spiritually. Thank you for your love, time, understanding, patience, and support!

Please take a moment with me to honor Dwayne Nicholson, age 54, a gentle, wise, loving, and inspirational soul who transitioned to heaven weeks after the tornado. Dwayne was a devoted husband, father, brother, son, and friend—the heart and heartbeat of our community. Dwayne: you were taken way too soon; we love you!

THE TOOL

For the last few years, others have asked, "Sunshine, what is happening in the world?" We're shifting into new vibrations and frequencies on Mother Earth. The time is now to live connected to your soul, rooted in intuition more strongly than ever before. Can you imagine if we turned on the TV, radio, or internet and heard of all the miracles that occur every moment of the day? We would all transform and heal Mother Earth, bringing the frequency and vibration to love and heal our souls while we're here—a flavor of Heaven on Earth!

Ever since I was a little girl, I have always felt that today is a present and tomorrow a gift, if given. I wake up in gratitude to be alive for breath and movement. What miracles will manifest? What magic will I experience? Who will I become with my new experiences today? Who will I hug and connect with? I believe all our bodies and systems are energy—physical, emotional, mental, spiritual, and ether. Energy is always flowing and constantly changing. I am, and so are you.

We all have experiences that are transitions for our soul's growth to love and heal to evolve. A transition has three distinct stages: The first stage of a transition is an ending (usually a surprise or shock) of something we know. This could be the death of a loved one, adult child, or animal. It may also involve a change in life or job, residential move, retirement, illness, divorce or marriage, a child moving out or going to college, or a natural disaster.

The second stage of a transition is known as the Limbo stage. It represents all we desire, want, and need as of now (our creation). Unfortunately, many skip this stage or delay its coming.

The third stage of a transition is the new beginning!

Society has conditioned us to know our physical body, to just focus on that, because it is known, seen, and scientifically proven. This takes away from our empowerment. We have other bodies. There are the physical, mental, emotional, spiritual, and ether bodies. All bodies are energy, which moves, changes continuously, and flows. We shall not let our physical body overrule other bodies and systems. This is what causes blockages in our flow of energy and dis-ease. Our other bodies may feel unknown and invisible. They're the source of all healing and should balance each other. They're all connected to the Divine and the God of your understanding. Each of us is a unique, Divine soul having a human experience to love and heal in this physical lifetime.

We all have angels, guides, guardian angels, and beloved ones in the Divine. They are there to love, support, teach, guide, and protect us. This is the Divine Bubble of Protection!

To start bringing The Divine Bubble of Protection into your daily life, there are practices and techniques you can use:

Close your eyes and envision a pale pink color surrounding your body—the color of pure love and acceptance. Breathe this in now; take that pale pink and make it a bubble radiating about a foot and a half around your physical body. Now turn it into an iridescent color, like a ring around the moon. Feel your feet growing roots deep into Mother Earth. Call in your guardian angels, angels, and beloved ones, allowing them to direct and protect you. Breathe! You can use this daily or send it to your loved ones. Example: If you're concerned about them driving in bad weather, send them their Divine Bubble of Protection.

To experience the Divine Bubble of Protection in Meditation, visit this link: https://bit.ly/DivineMeditation8

Sunshine has been open to Spirit and her Soul Connection since birth. She believes we are all Divine Souls here for a human experience to evolve our souls. Sunshine works with a knowing that we are all unique individuals possessing unique gifts. However, our human experiences may lead to the loss of them. It is about connecting once again with oneself and remembering. She works with a pure heart and pure love and asks for the highest form of healing for each person. At the same time, Sunshine provides a safe space allowing healing to flow, as the conduit and tuning dial for transformation. Sunshine supports all Souls—adults, children, animals, beloved ones, and spirits here and above. She involves Mother Earth in all her work and teachings to help us to connect with Mother Earth, to replenish, restore, and make her anew. She believes there is more love, healing, peace, joy, happiness, and a deeper understanding and knowledge when we are in our continuous Soul connection. This connection moves us from survival mode to loving life—thriving, peaceful, happy, and fulfilled. Sunshine is a medium, energy healer, and holistic Spiritual/Soul Life Coach. She has an Infinity Soul Connection Program channeled from Spirit. Please check out the following links for more information:

Website: www.infinitysoulconnection.com

Free Facebook Group: www.facebook.com/groups/soulconnectionseekers

Link for Meditation: https://bit.ly/DivineMeditation8

Email Sunshine at: infinitysoulconnection@gmail.com

CHAPTER 25

YOGA THERAPY

PARTNER WITH YOUR BODY TO MANAGE ANXIETY AND MORE

Christine Badalamenti Smith, MS

MY STORY

One hand tightly gripped the hot water handle of the faucet, and my gaze was penetrating down at my cream porcelain sink. "Don't look up. Don't look up!" What would happen if I lifted my head? I couldn't bear the possibilities; I was *terrified*.

For over a year, my eyes diligently followed the water as it ran down the drain of my sink when I brushed my teeth, because something horrifying would reveal itself if I lifted my gaze toward my reflection in the mirror. It was just one of the countless ways I modified my behavior and how I lived life because of my anxiety.

This intense manifestation of anxiety showed up in my early 30s after several big, personal transitions. Some of them were wonderful: completing my master's degree, marrying my best friend of eight years, and moving to a sweet little place in Vermont. However, others reached down and dredged up some of the trauma I experienced as a child. Collectively they meant my foundation and safety net were shifting and changing, culminating in a perfect storm of instability. I gradually started to do everything differently. I stopped listening to music, I was afraid to be intimate with my husband, I had to leave events and buildings, I wouldn't eat new things, only *I* could turn on the TV, and airplanes were not an option. As I write this, I can still feel the echoes of that anxiety in my body—a tingle on the periphery of my skin, and then it disappears as I breathe.

One spring morning, I sat in the dentist's chair. The technician seemed rushed; her answers to my questions felt pointed and cold and had that bite of "you're wasting my time, this is obvious, no one else asks me these questions." I've had over a dozen fillings but never a crown, and I couldn't bear the idea that they were going to shave my tooth. The only reason I was there that day, was because I'd already canceled and rescheduled this appointment too many times. Obligation and shame turned the key in my car ignition that morning. When the technician abruptly shoved a stick with numbing jelly into my mouth, I thought, *I'm not ready for this! No one explained anything about this procedure to me. I'm in danger.* I burst into tears, and the words I'm so sorry tumbled out of my mouth as I ran to my car. I never returned to that dentist. I promptly started researching a therapist.

I had one swing and a miss before I met Holly. Holly helped me see how anxiety was always a part of my life. But I never had a name for the periods of my youth when I couldn't fall asleep until sunrise or without the aid of a Disney movie. Surprisingly, learning I had a tendency toward this condition made it less intimidating and more manageable. I made it through those episodes, and that was reason to believe I could make it through this.

Holly was an outstanding therapist. She was down-to-earth, casual, and friendly, and we talked like equals. She truly listened, and I felt she saw me as a whole person and not something broken. She remembered, "You used to do yoga, right? I think you should find a studio where you feel comfortable trying it again; it could help." That was a turning point when my therapy went beyond talking and thinking into action, into my body and my breath, and involved other ways of seeing and coping with my experiences.

While it took me months to be able to close my eyes during savasana, it didn't take me that long to get to a place where I was living my life nearly entirely as if I *didn't* have anxiety. Of course, I'll always have the tendency toward that condition, and there will be triggers in my environment or relationships that surprise me and require mindful maneuvering to mitigate, but most people who meet me now couldn't conceive of what I went through those years ago.

How did I get there? Therapy and yoga. The combination of a cognitive process and an embodied process. Curious by nature, I started Googling "yoga" and "therapy" and found "Yoga Therapy." I researched the many kinds of yoga therapy and resonated with one school's approach. They offered a friendly, low-risk, affordable weekend workshop. I was off to Massachusetts to learn about Phoenix Rising Yoga Therapy, a practice for healing and transformation.

I began the weekend with an above-average amount of skepticism and left on Sunday knowing I'd sign up for the next week-long Level One course. The weekend wasn't without triggers, anxiety, frustration, and fear (certain smells in the studio, the small population of the town, imagining classmates staying in strangers' homes). There was plenty to make me uncomfortable, but it was also full of life-changing, mind-blowing, exciting, and fun information, experiences, moments, and people.

Level one, then level two, then level three plus all the supplemental courses I just *had* to take began to amount to a second master's degree! Suddenly I discovered I was on a new career path, completely out of nowhere, utterly out of character, yet wholly committed to bringing the tools and knowledge I was learning to other people.

The kind of yoga therapy I practice has roots in yoga, Ayurveda, Buddhism, psychology, and neuroscience. Yoga itself is an embodied method of working with the mind. What I love about yoga therapy is anyone can do it, including - and especially - people who aren't interested in yoga. It's a powerful stand-alone therapy and a great complement to talk therapy. Talk therapy centers on change in the mind and requires the body to acquiesce; yoga therapy centers on the body.

Many of us live with internal conflicts—our mind, emotions, body, energy, and spirit can be at odds and inhibit wellness and happiness. An absence of conflict might be because we're disconnected from our internal world. We might not be checking in with our heart, gut, or our body, and we may be living isolated from essential parts of our human experience.

Yoga therapy helps people identify other ways of knowing and experiencing life, and provides skills for awareness and discernment that help them find alignment, and feel complete, content, and capable.

Now and then, I still get anxious feelings. I notice them in my body first: tightness in my chest, increased heart rate, shallow breath, small beads of sweat at my temples, that familiar sharp pain in my skull above my right ear, acid reflux. I see them as they arise. I watch my energy shift as I get more agitated, and then my emotions kick in—fear, frustration, dread. Nowadays, my mind joins the fray last, with that scary thought reel that keeps me from wanting to see my own face in the mirror or imagine a happy future for myself. When I sense the earliest of these symptoms arising, I step in with tools and practices to manage them, and the scary thought reel never appears. Instead, I think: *Wow, by now, I would've been in a ball on the couch, trying to breathe, fumbling for the remote to put on HGTV, reaching for the phone to call my mother, and fearing for my life. How far I've come!* I celebrate my successes and never judge myself for my first reactions because they're an opportunity to practice what I know and embody my healing and wellness.

Throughout this process, my husband changed a lot of how he lived *his* life to help me feel safe in mine. I'm still in awe of who he became for me and grateful for his sacrifices and growth. When we were young, we anticipated we'd travel the world and learn new things together. My anxiety prohibited me from flying. When we could drive somewhere, I strategically avoided anything new. I was relieved when nearly every time we had big travel plans, we miraculously had to cancel.

Last summer, my husband and I took our first big trip on an airplane across the country to the west coast! We'd been together 18 years at the time. It felt like our honeymoon. I ate hot dogs from a less-than-clean roadside market; I slept in different places every night; I brushed my teeth in two dozen bathrooms and never thought about the mirror once! I flew! I felt like me.

I came home, and social media was advertising fancy luggage to me. Instagram knew I was getting over my anxiety! I picked out a new white suitcase and carry-on with this earthy, faux-marble pattern, excellent spinny wheels, sturdy handles, and the carry-on had a laptop sleeve! They smelled new. They felt new. They appeared empty, but they contained promises and possibilities I wouldn't have dared to dream of in my early 30s for fear of retribution from the universe.

Today, my hand lights gingerly on the handle of my carry-on as I gaze lovingly at the established yoga therapist in the mirror, preparing to travel alone to Colorado for ten days of continuing education. I'm overjoyed because I get to help others become the people they want to be. I know that nothing is impossible when you partner with the body and the whole human being in healing, change, and living.

THE TOOL

The yoga tools I love are effective in more applications than just anxiety. They help me observe my reactivity to any situation or stimulus and give me opportunities to intervene. They're effective during an argument with my husband, a stressful situation at work, when receiving sad or overwhelming news, and (insert unpleasant experience here).

The practice described below is useful when anxiety is starting to percolate, as well as anytime you want to engage with your emotions, reactivity, counterproductive habits, interpersonal conflicts, and more, including when you just want to connect to yourself and ground. I use portions or all of this practice all the time, even when driving, flying, or sitting awake at 3:00 a.m. with no sleep in sight.

It's best to read the instructions below completely first and just remember what you can rather than reading while doing it, or you can visit my website to listen to a recorded version. Here's the link: https://www.oggibe.com/tems

You may want to put yourself in an environment that's not disturbing or distracting. If you don't have that luxury, this can be done in the middle of a party or Times Square.

Consider what you can control in your environment and make changes to better suit your needs. You might soften lights, close windows to keep out traffic noise, or open windows to bring in the fresh air. You might shoo your pets into the next room to remove distractions or keep them nearby if they bring you comfort and safety. The first part of this practice is asking yourself what you need right now and meeting those needs.

COLLECTING AWARENESS WITH CALMING BREATH

The following instructions assume you're at home or in an indoor space with little distraction. Please read through them before undertaking the activity and if you're driving or are otherwise engaged, modify them where appropriate and necessary.

Find a comfortable seat. Sit so your body is supported and not a distraction. There's no need to force yourself into a meditation seat. Feel free to sit on a chair, lay a blanket over your lap, etc.

While it's important you're comfortable; you still want to pay attention to your posture. If you're most comfortable rounding the shoulders forward and tilting the head down, that's not conducive to this practice. You're making the area where you breathe small and compact. So, as comfortably as you can, find some length in your spine, roll your shoulders up and down onto your back, and create space in the front of your body for your breath to grow unencumbered.

You can change how you're sitting to make yourself more comfortable at any time. Also, if you need to fidget or squirm, let that happen. There's no need to fight the body; just be with it as it is.

Once you're situated, supported, and ready, close your eyes. If closing your eyes isn't okay, just let your gaze soften down toward the ground or out a window toward nature. Softening the gaze is not focusing on anything in your view, letting the eyes be restful.

BEGIN CALMING BREATH

To perform Calming Breath, inhale to a count of eight, hold the breath in for a count of two, exhale for a count of eight, and hold the breath out for a count of two. Notice when you begin how quickly you're counting from one to eight. Over time, try to slow down the pace of your counting. Count in your mind and not aloud. If it's difficult to count in the mind, you can aid yourself by tapping out the numbers with your fingers on your body.

It's normal to struggle with this breath at first, even in the best of circumstances, especially if you're experiencing anxiety and the breath is already short and shallow. Give yourself plenty of time to ease into it. Remember, other people struggle with this breath too. You can begin by counting to eight more quickly or by counting to six instead; just ensure your inhale and exhale are even and at least double the length of your held breath.

If the mind is busy, focus intently on counting. Counting and breathing may be all you do when you first start practicing. Once you're comfortable with the rhythm and no longer need to count to maintain it, you can move on to the next phase of this tool.

START COLLECTING AWARENESSES

What's in your immediate environment? What are the sounds, the smells, and the textures of the items you're leaning on or nestled under? Take it all in. What's beyond your immediate environment?

Keep breathing.

What are you noticing in your physical body? What are the sensations? What's your heart rate? What's happening in your intestinal tract? What's your body temperature? Is your neck tight, are your shoulders tense, are they raised toward the ears or forward toward the heart? Start to collect this data. You can imagine plucking information like fruit and putting it in a basket. If that visualization doesn't resonate with you, pick another or disregard it. Notice what works for you.

Keep breathing.

Once you've got a handle on your physical experience, you can move on to the other ways you experience the world. What emotions are present? What do you notice about your energy? Is it buzzing with anticipation, is it calming down as you breathe, or is it reaching out or turning inward? What's happening in your mental state? Is your mind busy or calm? Do you hear the same thought reel over and over, or are you just counting your breath and collecting awareness? Is your mind pointed toward the future, the past, or right here? There's no need to judge what you're observing and collecting. This is a neutral exercise.

Keep breathing.

It's natural to have moments or breaths when you're fully present, and you're going through the practice as written or spoken, and then moments when the mind is racing, the heart's pounding, and the doubt starts to creep in around the edges of your experience. Notice when you start to shift from one way of being to another. Just watch the shift happen and report to yourself what you're observing without being attached to it. You're just watching and noticing—plucking fruit to gently place into your basket.

You don't need to do anything with the basket until you eventually put it down. How do you know when you're ready? Well, you can put it down any time you want! However, when you start to see and feel that you're the *observer* of these awarenesses and *not* the anxiety, depression, anger, etc. itself, that's a good indicator you might be ready to put the basket down and move on. Or when you feel a shift in your energetic or emotional state and notice the mind has quieted and slowed down. If the basket gets too heavy, put it down.

Once you're no longer holding all the awarenesses, return to your breath for a few more rounds. If you need to return to counting, then count! When you feel you're nearing the end, bring your hands up to your body. If it feels good, rest both hands, one on top of the other over your heart, or maybe one hand on your belly or your forehead. You can let the body tell you where it could use the presence of your hands. Stay there for a few more breaths, and then share a few kind words with yourself, anything that feels right at the moment. It could be as simple as, "Thank you, body, thank you, breath." It can be anything.

To close the practice, take a deep breath in through your nose and let it fall out of your mouth in a sigh. Repeat one or two more times if it feels right.

When you're done, take stock of your state of being. Note if this was helpful or if this was tough to do. What changed, and what stayed the same? Why do you think that is? Remind yourself you've tried something new that can be difficult for most people at first. Try to be grateful you've given yourself the time and space to do this.

If you have questions about this experience or you need assistance with this, you can connect with me directly through my website, https://www.oggibe.com/. There you can also sign up to join my community, set up a free session, and learn what happens next and where this practice can lead you. This is just one step in the yoga therapy journey, and so many more experiences, opportunities, and possibilities await you!

Christine Badalamenti Smith is a yoga therapist, rewilding guide, environmental advocate, and writer. Christine's mission is to help people feel at home, alive, and powerful in their bodies and the natural world. She believes people who feel whole, safe, and empowered will be better stewards of their lives and the planet. Christine founded OGGI BE to offer services and resources and convene a collective of people who want to be present, authentic, and intentional. Clients come to her for healing, change, alignment, and deep connection.

Christine is certified in Phoenix Rising Yoga Therapy, a trauma informed practice which utilizes the teachings, research, and practice of yoga, Ayurveda, Buddhism, neuroscience, and psychology to offer a therapeutic experience addressing mental and emotional wellbeing. She sees individual clients, couples, and groups at her office in Vermont and online.

Christine is a certified mindful outdoor guide through Kripalu School of Mindful Outdoor Leadership. She curates rewilding experiences in nature that connect participants to their inner wild and vital relationship with Earth.

Christine has over 2000 hours of specialized training in diverse yoga modalities and is registered with Yoga Alliance.

Christine has a Bachelor's in English and Philosophy from the University of Delaware and a Master's in Environmental Studies from Antioch University New England. These foundational studies inform her curiosity, critical mind, and passion for understanding.

CONNECT WITH CHRISTINE

Website: https://www.oggibe.com

Facebook: https://www.facebook.com/OGGIBE

Instagram: https://www.instagram.com/oggibealiveandwild

LinkedIn: https://www.linkedin.com/company/oggibe

Email: christine@oggibe.com

Schedule a free consultation with
Christine: https://www.oggibe.com/consultation

BELONG

Root to Reach—a safe place for people seeking a balanced, grounded approach to personal discovery using yoga therapy, rewilding, meditation, mindfulness, Ayurveda, and more: https://www.facebook.com/groups/roottoreach/

Transformation Gathering—a supportive place for those who seek and work to manifest positive change: https://www.facebook.com/groups/transformationgathering/

CLOSING CHAPTER

As you come to the end of this book, which chapters did you resonate with? Which stories are also your stories?

Make sure to connect with the authors and get on their email list. Reach out to them and let them know what you thought of their story and tool.

And if you know it's time for you to heal on a deeper level, do yourself a favor and have a conversation with them. Each one has learned their own dynamic healing process and is helping their clients live happier, healthier lives each and every day.

Healing happens faster and easier when you tune into your energy and discover which tools are best for your body.

Whether you're looking to improve your physical, emotional, or financial health, you'll find relief with these authors. I've personally experienced the work of many of these authors and have had amazing shifts in my life.

Using Feng Shui to align your personal energy to the energy of your home will help you to attract all the right people, places, and events so that you can achieve your intentions and desires.

Make sure to connect with the sound healers. If you've never experienced a sound healing event, you're in for a treat! It's a wonderfully relaxing experience for your mind, body, and soul. You'll find yourself drifting out of your body, letting go of all your daily stressors, and allowing your body to feel a new level of comfort.

Make sure to connect with the healers. Each one has mastered their own unique healing techniques. These practitioners have experienced challenges that caused them to take a deep dive into their own wounded selves, only to come through as better, stronger individuals. And that's what's possible for you.

Stay tuned for future Energy Medicine Solution Workshops and in-person retreats. It's your time to step into your full potential and experience all that is possible for you.

WITH LOVING GRATITUDE

To all the clients who trusted me to help them heal and feel better. So many came in feeling skeptical that anything would change in regards to their health. Each one remained open to learning something new and was able to embrace a whole new level of optimism and hope. Every one of you continues to show me what's possible when we open ourselves up to healing the trauma stored in your bodies. You have all shown me how powerful you are. I'm so grateful for each and every one of you.

To the amazing authors who said YES!

I must have had a hundred conversations with some awesome healers before finding my perfect 24 YES authors. This book came to life because you said yes. Some of you I met for the very first time, and it was love at first connection. I knew you were meant for this book because of your energy and how we connected. I'm forever grateful that you said yes to this so that we can share our love of energy with the world. In doing so, we can help more people heal and feel better and then heal the planet. You are all so gifted, and it's a pleasure to share your gifts in a bigger way.

To Laura DiFranco:

My friend Carolyn McGee said, "I think you should take this class. It'll be great; we can take it together!" Ugh, I thought, another class. I'd taken so many classes and programs and really didn't want to take one more. Well, of course, she was right. I took Laura's Intuitive Writing class, and the rest is history. Your class gave me the confidence to share my thoughts and stories. Thank you for teaching me to become a better writer. Because of you, I can now call myself an author with five collaborative books. I'm grateful for all the love, support, and time you gave for this project and for all you give to so many people.

To the readers:

To you, the reader, this book is for you. If you were not here, this book would not have come to be. We are forever grateful to you for purchasing and reading this book. We hope you find the healing you are looking for in these chapters.

To the launch team:

Thank you from the bottom of my heart for your time and effort in reading the book and leaving a review. You have been an enormous support to this project, and we so appreciate you!

THIS IS YOUR CALL TO ACTION, READER!

When you want to change your current negative emotional and physical experiences, you could get additional help from:

- Reading a book. You can even read my book.
- Watching YouTube videos. You can even watch my videos.
- And you can even try to do it on your own.

Reading books, watching videos, and so on—all of that takes a lot of time, and it doesn't allow for quick results.

Let me ask you this: Would you like to fast-track your results?

If you would, let me share with you a special opportunity so I can help you experience a breakthrough that'll change your life and finances forever.

You're invited to apply for a complimentary Real Pain Relief Breakthrough session. This is an incredible opportunity and absolutely free—a 30-minute Real Pain Relief Breakthrough session with me.

During that time, we will get a clear picture of exactly where you are with your health, relationships, and wealth and what is stopping you from achieving the fullest potential in your health, relationships, and wealth. We'll also create a plan for how you can start changing this now.

All you need to do is click on the link: https://jacquelinemkane.as.me/RealPainRelief and answer the questions.

It's that simple.

Now is the time for you to achieve all of your dreams and remove the obstacles getting in your way. With all my heart, I know it is absolutely possible and achievable with the right help.

If what I'm saying resonates with you or you've been seeking help for some time, I am passionate about helping you finally get the results you want.

Connect with Jacqueline:

Learn more about Jacqueline and her coaching programs at https://jacquelinemkane.com/

Click here for resources and bonus gifts from Jacqueline, including an invite to the free Facebook group Healing Circle by Jacqueline Kane: https://www.facebook.com/groups/1239739566211490

Hire Jacqueline to speak to your women's group on soul-aligned success secrets: How to live your healthy, wealthy, extraordinary life today.

Topics:

1. Soul Alignment Success Secrets: 3 expert steps to experience a happy, healthy and wealthy life now.

   Description: Discover the key areas that are energetically keeping you from your ultimate desires and unlock the secrets of what you can do to change that now. Explore how you can increase your intuitive abilities and remove what hinders your ability to connect with your inner wisdom, ready to guide you every step. Turn up your attraction factor and be a manifestation magnet for what you desire most, including healing, relationships, and prosperity.

2. Moms in Pain:

   There are three myths keeping moms in the never-ending cycle of pain, and it's time to bust them now and change your beliefs. In this workshop, Jacqueline takes you through her Hidden Pain Cycle Awareness process, where you gain clarity and understanding of why it's been so hard for you to get out of pain and stay out of it for good. Learn the most effective tools and techniques that will lead you to pain-free and more energized days instantly.

3. Trauma and Pain:

   Everyone has their own trauma and story of pain. No matter how big or small it is, the truth remains that it is impacting every area of your life, and you may not even be aware of it! During this workshop, you will take that empowered step to uncover, understand, and transform your trauma so you can finally live your life with ease, flow, and abundance.

GET YOUR SIGNED BOOKS

Other books by the author can be found at:
https://jacquelinemkane.com/books/

Amazon Author Page:
https://www.amazon.com/Jacqueline-M-Kane/e/B087QMDM63

The Ultimate Guide to Self Healing Techniques
Chapter 24
Energy Healing
Clearing Ancestral Energy for Pain Free Living

The Ancestors Within
Chapter 8
Unlock Your Ancestral Story,
Take charge of YOUR life

Strong Mothers
Chapter 5
Becoming a Strong Mom
The Birth of Self Advocacy

Find Your Voice Save Your Life
Chapter 19
My Path To Freeing My Voice

Inspired Living
Chapter 16
Heal Your Inner Saboteur
Ignite Your Ability to Attract Greater Abundance

WHAT PEOPLE ARE SAYING ABOUT WORKING WITH JACQUELINE M. KANE

"I highly recommend Jackie Kane's VIP experience! I came to Jackie thinking I would have a one-hour massage, but after speaking to her to set up the appointment, I realized that the VIP experience was for me. The lasting benefits have been incredible! I continue to clear old ancestral energy and feel newer and fresher every day. The abundance is flowing into my life, and the pain in my body is slowly receding. Thank you, Jackie."

~ Naomi R, Connecticut

"What I've gotten out of this seven-week course and our small but mighty group is a gentle yet profound clearing of stuck energy I didn't even know I was carrying, as well as a long overdue reinvigoration of desire to energize my living and workspace. I now have tools to bring myself into my body and out of my head—a delicious and serene feeling—as well as mindfulness. Perhaps my most significant takeaway from the class is the miraculous dissolving of the critical inner voice that has haunted me for as long as I can remember. My often heart-pounding anxiety levels are now almost gone, and the negative running commentary that would often make me feel depressed and most unworthy, my "the-glass-is-half-empty-and-it's-your-fault"

inner critical voice, has now shifted to a voice of possibility and
excitement to re-pattern my old destructive patterns of self-
shaming into a state of worthiness. I'm FINALLY feeling ready to
open my arms wide to receive my highest good."

~ Aimee Miles, California

"I have been dealing with fibromyalgia, chronic fatigue, and
arthritis most of my adult life. I also have compressed vertebrae
in my spine and three discs that bulge from time to time,
depending upon my activity. I have used many different kinds of
therapy over the years, which have helped to some degree. But I
was amazed at how well my body responded to the therapy and
different techniques that Jacqueline uses. I have more pain-free
days than not. I could never say I was "pain-free" before meeting
Jacqueline. She has changed my life. Because of you, I'm on the
beach running and picking up my grandkids. All pain free. I
don't even have to wear my magnetic belt! Thank you, I'm so
happy!"

~ Terry L., Connecticut

"My experience working with Jackie was life-changing! I never knew we could carry around generations of energy that hold us back. Her work has helped me in so many ways but most dramatically when I was going through four months of chemo. My path to healing was the path through emotional freedom with Jackie. I will be forever grateful!"

~ Pat McGrath, Connecticut

"Jacqueline is a master at uncovering hidden energetic and karmic blocks. She uses a consistent process to unravel a thought construct and clear the limitation by exploring the inner child, ancestral karma, and tapping. I was able to achieve major shifts working with her!"

~ Holly Segur, New York

"Jacqueline Kane finally relieved my neck pain which I thought was coming from my neck. But it wasn't! It was coming from my psoas muscle. Jackie is so knowledgeable and truly understands how to heal. I am so fortunate to have found her. If you have chronic pain, give yourself a gift and contact her. Life is too short to be uncomfortable or to just live with the pain. Instead, live your best life!"

~ Mary Carangelo, Connecticut

"Working with Jacqueline Kane has helped me on several levels. I was experiencing some pain related to heartburn, and after the session felt relief, and it has continued to be minimal, if at all. I also reached out to her when my dad was in severe pain, and she gave me a short tapping to do, which helped me relax so I could help him better. Then during my next session, she helped me uncover some anger I was holding in my body that I did not know was connected to my dad. After releasing that, my dad felt relief in his symptoms. That was amazing. Jacqueline is also helping with my blocks related to attracting clients, and after working with her, I had a number of clients show up out of the blue."

~ LSR, Maryland

"I drove home in the rain yesterday because I felt so good. I had a good night's sleep. Lower back and hips feel good. I went to exercise this morning. Thank you for helping me. May God bless your hands."

~ Love, Mom, Connecticut

"In the last 90 minutes, since going through your saboteur process, I've received seven solutions for problems I've had. My business is booming, and money is showing up everywhere."

~ Helen Terry, Texas

"*I worked with Jacqueline Kane for a few years uncovering barriers to my success. Discovering the keys to a physically healthier body, mind, and soul. Working with Jackie has been life-changing. When I started working with her, I was looking to dig into the barriers to my financial success. As time went on, my chronic lower back pain disappeared. I was not needing all of the supplements that I thought were giving me joint relief. The pain was diminishing. . . I was not even aware of the emotional barriers I had, and as I became more aware and cleared and healed them, all aspects of my life began to change. The physical pain disappeared. I am a far more active person. More energy and a renewed zest for life. Thank you, Jackie, for all you have meant to my successful life. Your fingerprints are all over it!*"

~ Susan Powers, Connecticut

"*I used to wake up and do what I called a pain inventory to determine the level of my pain, which would dictate what I could get done that day. Over a period of time after working with Jacqueline, I woke up thinking, what is going to hurt today? Then I realized. . .nothing was hurting!*"

~ Robin Crampton, Connecticut

"*I'm a mom living with intense pain four to five days a week, wondering just how long I could make it. I missed out on activities with my daughters, causing guilt that I wasn't as good a mother as I wanted to be. Now I'm walking better, doing more activities, and feeling less guilt spending time with friends because I'm doing more when I'm with my daughters. I'm taking better care of myself, and now my whole family is happy because 'mom is happy.'"*

~ Kerry Kane, Connecticut

"After tapping with Jacqueline, I walked through this whole conference, and I went down to the workshops, and I could walk everywhere, and I was fine - the whole time I was here. I have severe osteoarthritis pain in my right knee, and I have a muscle problem in my back due to my knee because I don't walk normally. . . I thought tapping was very, very interesting. It was like magic! I'm always very doubtful of everything, but it was Wow! Jacqueline, you've won me over!"

~ Pat C., Massachusetts

Healing miracles don't just happen to others. And they can happen in any area of your life—health, relationships, and/or wealth.

Healing miracles happen when you're open to them. Healing miracles happen to people who ask for help when others give up.

You can be a healing miracle even if your doctors, family, and friends tell you nothing will ever change.

Made in the USA
Columbia, SC
17 November 2022

71351432R00157